A Strategic and Tactical Approach to Global Business Ethics

Second Edition

A Strategic and Tactical Approach to Global Business Ethics

Second Edition

Lawrence A. Beer

BEP BUSINESS EXPERT PRESS

First published in 2010 by
Business Expert Press, LLC
222 East 46th Street, New York, NY 10017
www.businessexpertpress.com

ISBN-13: 978-1-63157-071-1 (paperback)
ISBN-13: 978-1-63157-072-8 (e-book)

Business Expert Press International Business Collection

Collection ISSN: 1948-2752 (print)
Collection ISSN: 1948-2760 (electronic)

Cover and interior design by Exeter Premedia Services Private Ltd.,
Chennai, India

First edition: 2010
Second edition: 2015

10 9 8 7 6 5 4 3 2 1

Printed in the United States of America.

Abstract

The inclusion of ethically driven elements into the strategic planning process of multinational corporations (MNCs) is an emerging consideration in the modern era of globalization. Firms pursuing cross-border activities in any capacity and to whatever degree or scale are increasingly coming into contact with differences in morally applied decision making that affects their operational success and sustainability. The choices made require the use of clear and unambiguous codes of conduct for embedded managers abroad. The implementation of a properly administered code, coupled with a program of corporate social responsibility (CSR), can add value to a company, while its misapplication or exclusion can diminish value.

Keywords

code of conduct, corporate social responsibility (CSR), ethical dilemma, ethics, global labor, globalization, multinational corporation (MNC), repressive governments, strategy

Contents

Preface

The work presented in this guidebook is intended to acquaint managers with the tools to handle their ethical encounters on a global operational platform. It is *not* intended to address ethics per se and its presentation and discussion are best left to the vast libraries of thought penned by learned men throughout the annals of history. The subject matter, the ethical conduct of global commercial entities and their managers, cannot be placed in a logical mathematical equation and analyzed with precision to apply to every circumstance. There is no cookie-cutter system or one-size-fits-all formula. Therefore, ethics is about *relative positioning within the context of a directed course, a process called ordered flexibility*. The subject should be viewed as water, a basic element that changes but always reverts to and sustains its prime character. Water in a stream seeks the sea, but it flows through varying paths, in, around, and over obstacles, sometimes at a quick rate and at other times at a mere trickle. Water when heated changes into gas and when frozen becomes a solid substance, but when subject to cooling or left to melt it, returns again to its natural state. Universally applied ethical conduct is all about relative positioning but always retains its key objective. Its application is ordered flexibility, *exemplified by a series of choices*, when applied to the selection of operational tactics and terms of engagement in the face of an ethical dilemma.

The examples in the text are meant to stimulate rather than dictate the development of an ethical consideration in the global managerial decision-making process. Moral judgment involves mankind's treatment of fellow human beings applied within the context of differences among them. Whether such divergence is cultural or sociological, based on theological teachings or philosophical references, or with a commercial environment subject to variances in economic development, global firms are encouraged to set a uniform policy. Integrating a universally acceptable code of conduct across a firm's operations and activities around the world is not an easy task. At times, the ethical opportunities offered may require a leap of faith that not all are willing to take. But in the end, such strategic decisions will need to be faced in the real world. To paraphrase a quote attributed to Ludwig Wittgenstein, an Oxford philosopher, a business executive who is not taking part in discussions of ethics is like a boxer who never goes into the ring.

A code of conduct is merely a set of thoughts, a statement by a commercial entity of the guiding principles that its actions are founded upon. But "with our thoughts we make the world."* As philosopher James Allen tells us, "Act is the blossom of thought," so until one marries thought with action "there is no intelligent accomplishment."[1] Therefore, global companies are encouraged throughout the book not only to develop a code of conduct but also to see that it is enforced and to create a cadre to oversee its implementation.

The lyrics of an old country song recount the point that "if we don't stand for something we'll fall for anything." Global firms are therefore prodded to at least construct a way of doing business around the world with some form of equitable vision. The author knowingly takes a proactive position throughout the book, gently urging commercial firms to get more involved in the understanding and appreciation of ethical and social responsibility considerations in the global business environment. The intent is not to push firms into a rush to judgment, but to ask them to engage their executive managerial staff and bring ethical issues to the forefront for discussion and comment.

The main thrust of this guidebook is to admonish global firms to focus at the strategic planning level on their anticipated external dealings with their worldwide labor force while considering the results of their actions on the environment around them. The issues presented are not directed at internal managerial decisions with respect to financial reporting such as the Enron matter, even though such matters certainly have an ethical component to them. The book does not target specific, individual executive moral actions that always impact the process but engages the entire corporate managerial staff, assuming such personal actions in the end reflect on the company as a whole. To indoctrinate the ever widening

---

* From *Dhammapada* a compilation of the sayings of Buddha, attributed to the followers of Siddhartha Gautama over his lifetime, 563 BCE to 483 BCE. Numerous translations of this work have been published.

strategic planning process involving all levels of management requires an ethical imperative be instituted as guided by the establishment of a universal code of conduct for all global enterprises and their constituents. One doesn't separate core human values from the strategic goals one seeks to achieve. They may be pursued side by side, both complementing and yet entwined with each other.

Within the context of educating future business managers and indoctrinating executives, a mandate to act with ethical judgment is therefore an inherent asset in all people and the commercial endeavors they favor. No man is an island unto himself as his actions always affect others. With decision making comes responsibility, and with responsibility a duty. That responsibility begins with the education of business students in an academic setting.

Professor Todd Henshaw of Columbia University argues that the issue of failed ethical leadership starts not when a chief executive officer takes control but when future executives are educated. He feels that business schools should orient their curriculums to produce strategically oriented leaders, as opposed to functional technicians who respond to problems instead of taking a proactive position by instituting critical ethical thinking into the planning matrix of companies. Henshaw further comments that shaping values is at the core of master of business administration (MBA) programs, but many institutions either integrate the subject into other courses or offer it as a meaningless elective or worse, a noncredit lecture or workshop and thereby signal the peripheral nature of ethical leadership to their students. His message is the following: business schools need to treat the subject as a dedicated matter worthy of singular directed instruction and approach on par with other business skills and disciplines of management.

Henshaw's remarks have generated a number of comments. Most respondents tended to exhibit a biased, pessimistic attitude best summarized this way: "Why should they care, since 'business' and 'ethics' are an oxymoron when combined in a sentence?" Such sentiments seem to permeate general public opinion, thereby placing commercial institutional leaders, as they begin their stewardship, behind the proverbial eight ball on the issue. It is time to change that perception and allow for managerial education to get out front on the matter.

A similar theme is noted by N. Craig Smith, the chair of ethics and social responsibility at INSEAD in France. He admonishes B-schools (business schools) to move dual topics of ethics and corporate responsibility (CR) up the agenda in the scholastic curriculum hierarchy. He first argues that due to globalization and the Internet, multinational corporations (MNCs) are living and operating in a more condensed, interconnected world, where businesses are constantly exposed to scrutiny and their ethical-CR lapses are quickly made public by mass media. Firms need to be more transparent as their veils of secrecy are easily pierced. Given the hyperspeed echo chamber of global mass media outlets, the dissemination of public disapproval is rapidly achieved. On the other hand, Smith notes that there is mounting evidence suggesting good corporate citizenship pays dividends in terms of increased profitability while contributing to the enhancement of a firm's global reputation, thereby adding value to the company.

To combat the negative and accent the positive, Smith proposes a three-tier ethics and CR approach in B-school curriculums. First, the subject should be taught as a stand-alone course, then embedded in core courses, and finally, offered in a comprehensive slate of electives addressing specific issues. Such full-blown indoctrination would be most beneficial to the business leadership of tomorrow.

Many MBA students and managers who read this book may decide that the discussion on ethical matters is within the purview of philosophy and therefore neither a practical nor functional subject. Some would suggest that is best left on the proverbial back burner and therefore it is neither an appropriate, burning issue nor part of the strategic platform in business. However, philosophy is a soft science that explores the relationships of man and the institutions he creates to the surrounding society and environment. As such, ethics is an appropriate field for managers to consider, as they need to appreciate a broader horizon when they strategize and make decisions. It should be noted that Adam Smith, the author of *The Wealth of Nations*, the intellectual platform for capitalism, was not an economist but a philosopher. He was, in fact, chairman of the Moral Philosophy Department at Glasgow University when the book was written, suggesting the premises that Smith envisioned were a new framework for interpreting how the world works. One could surmise that he envisioned a society of competing interests that would, he hoped, serve all of mankind. This was a presumption based on and influenced by his other noteworthy work, *The Theory of Moral Sentiments*, in which he hypothesized a commercial society where economic thought is inseparable from ethics, politics, and justice.

As this book was being finalized, the necessary reediting caused me to reflect on ethics as an academic inquiry in the study of business via the techniques of applied research. I came across comments by Jeanne Liedtka. She states,

> The notions of 'scientific' detachment and objectivity in ethics research appear illusory at best…. Yet, if all truth is subjective and shared meanings are impossible, are we wasting our time as scholars, conducting studies to satisfy our own selfish pleasure in the discovery of the particular—with no hope of finding something of value to say to those who inhabit the world we examine? If that is the case, shouldn't we perhaps move to a more productive line of work—writing fiction or making widgets?[2]

While Professor Liedtka's contention—investigating ethics in the pursuit of knowledge—may be scholastically self-indulgent, it nevertheless has value in the real business world where missteps and errors in its application have positive and negative implications. This book is written not to engage in a philosophical discussion of the subject but to allow managers to appreciate the influence of ethics on their strategic determinations and their operational and administrative tactics. It is a discipline that must be considered especially in the era of modern globalization, and therefore it is a managerial skill to be acquired. While managers aim to boost their company's influence around the world, businesspersons must recognize that their commercial conduct is part of global life and impacts not only their organization but also the lives and environment of all it touches—a reference to Adam Smith's aforementioned contentions. Whether the term *governance*, *social responsibility*, or *ethics* is used to define managerial conduct, the subject has emerged as a leading-edge discipline in contemporary management studies.

The connection between business and society in general has always carried a stigma, an unethically stained label. Outside of the atrocities of war, a history of human rights abuses has cast a long shadow over the profit motivation of the commercial imperative. The dark side of humanity has been revealed in many of the global ventures that business enterprises have taken. Throughout time, trading initiatives have been riddled with practices and events that have saddled businesses with the scars of oppressive behavior in respect to their worldwide dealings. In domestic settings, the early use of apprentices to master craftsmen placed such individuals in a long-term, indentured-servant status. As the commercial process developed, the ill treatment of employees toiling under dangerous factory conditions or in harsh, repressive agricultural environments, with meager life-sustaining wages, plagued those caught in the lower echelons of commercial venturing. But as the process moved internationally in the search for new resources, the infliction of harm and the absence of respect for human rights intensified in scope and degree. Notwithstanding the great strides made in national laws coupled with an empathetic public awareness, the historic malfeasance of MNCs is a legacy that continues to fuel today's discussions on the ethical behavior of commercial institutions and their social responsibility.

The greatest wholesale abuse of human rights occurred during the colonization of the Western Hemisphere by European powers. Tens of thousands of native Africans were sold into slavery and transported across the Atlantic. Placed in perpetual bondage, they labored just one step above domesticated animals on plantations in the American South and the Caribbean region. In South America, they supplemented indigenous populations in the mineral-extraction process, with both groups considered as savages and thus not worthy of human dignity and no better than the beasts of burden they replaced. As the world developed, remnants of this oppressive, commercially induced behavior were repeated all over the world. Historical records abound with horrific descriptions of the treatment of imported and local labor. David Grann in *The Lost City of Z* recounts a vivid portrayal of atrocities committed by the British-registered Peruvian Amazon Company in the extraction of rubber as verified by the 1904 UK government's Casement Report. He recounts how genocide was used to control the native population. Public beheading was a common punishment, while rebellious Indians had gasoline poured on them and set on fire, or were simply drowned, or were fed alive to ravenous dogs.

Further, they were castrated, physically mutilated, and starved to death. Company henchmen raped women and young girls, and smashed their infants' heads on the ground. Similar vile actions have been attributed to commercial ventures for centuries. While thankfully not to the same degree and scope, less severe but just as reprehensible remnants of such despicable actions have been reported as some MNCs outsource to the sweatshops of today's underdeveloped countries and directly or indirectly partner with repressive governments to limit and suppress human rights.

Many early philosophical and religious teachings decried the unscrupulous nature of merchants and the money lenders as taking unfair advantage of their clientele. The Latin phrase, and an often used legal principle, caveat emptor—"let the buyer beware"—comes to mind. In the modern era, the fraudulent dealings of financial firms with the investing public, as well as the use of false advertising and the production of knowingly harmful consumer products, has continued to contribute to this poor image. Damage to the environment by MNCs, both in the harvesting of resources and in the manufacturing process, continues to plague commercial institutions. The need to regain the trust and admiration, no less the goodwill, of the population at large is a burden that modern business enterprises carry with them. They are beginning to understand that their reputations are an intrinsic prime asset that can add continuing value if handled properly. But if their practices are judged unethical, then it can also subtract value.

A new era of applied capitalism has accompanied globalization and it is represented by a variety of terms. Deepak Chopra, professor of management at the Kellogg Business School at Northwestern University, uses the phrase *conscience capitalism* to describe the idea that commercial institutions must work to improve the quality of life on the planet for all stakeholders in a company as opposed to the narrow agenda of increasing shareholder value. John Dunning, emeritus professor of international business at the Universities of Reading and Rutgers University, refers to a new process in making globalization good (in his book of the same title) as *the moral challenges of global capitalism*. Neville Isabell, recently retired board chairman of Coca-Cola, calls the idea as *connected capitalism*. Whatever term is used, a fresh approach to the commercial initiative that includes a wider horizon of its defined mission is taking shape. It will shape the global advancement of MNCs as they incorporate into their strategic decision making the elements of acceptable ethical conduct and practical social responsibility as equal synergetic components alongside their historic charge: value creation. Global business institutions will not only remain results oriented but also will be held accountable for getting things done right, striving for a balance of all interested parties, and regaining the trust of the public. This book is dedicated to helping firms achieve such new goals.

The object of this book is to assist in the creation of a reasonable, workable floor of universal ethical standards and its collateral issue corporate social responsibility (CSR) while recognizing that the ceilings of a company code of conduct will vary according to the political, social, and economic environments of the firm's headquarters country and those in which they operate abroad. As with all texts on the subject, only guideposts can be suggested and their rationales explained because in the end moral decision making is individualized, deeply influenced by the personal cultural-value determinants that one is exposed to in life. Therefore, not all will agree with the guideposts proposed, a point best illustrated by a quote from English poet William Blake (1757–1827): "Both read the bible every day and night, / but thou read'st black where I read white."

It is enough therefore that the text promotes discussion and debate, as these are the starting points of illumination and the eventual engagement of ethical dilemmas.

Many of the book's subjects are introduced with quotations to set the stage for what follows. The reason for such preparatory remarks is twofold. First, to show that moral empathy and ethical behavior are embedded in man's history and are not the result of our modern-day reaction to globalization. And second, they are included as a tribute to my father, Irving Beer, who collected sayings of wise men and used them in my education. He taught me that one's life is a reflection of one's deeds. I remember him for his life and not his death.

The shortest and surest way to live with honor in the world is to be in reality what we would appear to be; all human virtues increase and strengthen themselves by the practice and experience of them.
                                        —Socrates, Greek philosopher

My scholastic friends always remind me that for an attorney to write about ethics, especially in an academic text, is an oxymoron and that William Shakespeare's line "The first thing we do, let's kill all the lawyers" is the only way to ensure just sanity in the world and provide for moral clarity.[3] The writings that follow, however, are not meant to promote the mandate of a few on the majority. They are intended to lay a foundation for informing those who decide the fate of others, for such is what ethical behavior is really about.

> *An honest man can feel no pleasure in the exercise of power over his fellow man.*
>
> —Thomas Jefferson, U.S. president and statesman

As readers move through the text they will notice that subjects are revisited or re-presented and expanded upon. This writing technique is deliberate because ethical decision making on a global scale is a complicated issue composed of numerous components. Each time a new ingredient is introduced into the ethical mix, with its collateral agent and social responsibility, the entire matrix must be restored, be reconstituted, to preserve a proper continuing universal blending of all elements.

The second edition of the book is intended to update and expand on the ever changing field of business ethics. Although published in early 2010 the original manuscript was constructed over a few years. It drew on the then historical and current state of affairs concerning strategic and tactical maneuvers for managers to navigate the exiting ethical environment. While the underlying principles remain intact in just a short period of time, the subject matter has exploded to the point of being a required skill for commercial leaders to master.

The evolution of ethics from its position as a hovering mechanism over business dealings to its important place in the planning and administration of organizations and their operational activities is due to a variety of interwoven issues. The revised edition highlights these factors. Ethics has become unabridged. Its traditional application in the business world has morphed into a full-fledged component of managing a successful enterprise. Contributing to its new positioning are:

- *Duel public transparency.* Firstly scandals, mistakes, and errors in judgment by corporations are not just reported but have become the subject of in-depth investigations. It is impossible to cover-up such events and the negative public impact has affected the performance of companies like never before. Secondly, firms themselves have been pressed to issue a periodic description of their socially beneficial activities as an adjunct to the financially oriented annual company report. Such information has become a new judgment mechanism while valuing a company's success.

- *Change in terminology.* The term ethics has been replaced by a new lexicon that both incorporates and expands the traditionally accepted and applied definition of a moral conduct. CSR has exploded on the scene and its emotionally charged make-up has altered the competitive environment global companies operate in. It has transformed ethical philosophical principles into a real element in the marketing mix to promote the historic selling of products and services. Alongside this contemporary terminology has come the expression *responsible leadership* a newfangled take on how managers are evaluated that includes a wider determination of supervisory accountability.

- *Ethics as an industry.* The subject of ethics within the orbit of altruistic motivation has moved from being a moral imperative to an actual practical functional application in the business process. From business school courses to nongovernmental organizations and to professional training programs, managers are inundated with an array of guidelines on how to be ethical—be socially responsible and in the end be considered a responsible leader. A new recognition of corporate managerial performance has surfaced—the good corporate citizenship award. Books, articles, magazines, and a host of supplemental materials flood the marketplace with advice on how to be ethically savvy in the commercial sector. The personal initiative and discipline to act within a socially acceptable virtuous manner toward people and the environment is no longer an internally manifested imperative. It has to be taught, injected into commercial operations, and materially rewarded and worn as a badge of honor. Ethics no longer falls within the purview of an area of study, a branch of philosophy, dealing with behaviors adjudged as morally right or wrong. It is celebrated with social responsibility company and man of the year awards. Ethics is a business unto itself.

The aforementioned alterations in the ethical climate have altered the landscape that corporations and their managers need to contend with. The field of ethics within the context of commercial dealings has moved beyond the traditional constraints of moral turpitude and into the wider arena of social welfare. The noticeable transformation has taken ethics out of the closet. It is now akin to the proverbial elephant in the room and cannot be ignored. As such, today it occupies a greater presence in structuring the strategic and tactical approaches one must take to successfully compete in the globalized world.

A reflection on the changes in the societal landscape in respect to corporate responsibility and a challenge to the historical capitalistic view that shareholder needs are the prime obligation of management comes from the comments of Jack Ma, founder and CEO of Alibaba, the Chinese internet giant. When interviewed on "60 Minutes," a USA TV show, following the company's successful public debut on the New York stock exchange, he made the following statements.* "If you want to invest in us, we believe customer number one, employee number two, shareholder number three. If they don't want to buy that, that's fine. If they regret, they can sell us." When further queried by Lara Logan, the program interviewer noting that, "In the U.S. the shareholder is usually first." He replied, "And I think they were wrong. The shareholder, good. I respect them. But they're third. Because if you've taken care of the customer, take care of the employees, shareholder will be taken care of." Ma's comments signal an unorthodox approach to traditionally accepted corporate objectives, with the focus on investors, and towards an emphasis

---

* Retrieved on October 22, 2014 from http://managment-quotes.net/author/Jack_Ma/quote/10116

on consumers and employees. It may be indicative of a new direction that the CSR initiative has produced; a move to a wider more inclusive social agenda driving corporate strategy. This rapidly emerging issue for executives is more extensively treated with practical tactical approaches in the second edition.

One of the hardest things to do when writing about ethics and its companion offshoots, social responsibility and responsible leaders is to keep away from personal beliefs, attitudes, and feelings. To offer inspection and commentary in a purely objective fashion is difficult to maintain, as there is a natural human tendency to exhibit some subjective judgments to the issues presented. We all have an internal moral compass that points us in a particular principled direction. A magical Jiminy Cricket (the character of conscience in the children's tale of *Pinocchio*) that whispers what is right and what is wrong, delineating for us life's good and bad. I ask the reader to appreciate this dilemma not only in the mind-set of the author but to recognize it in themselves.

While the manuscript was being typesetted, the American seasonal holiday period had begun and I found myself sitting with my grandchildren watching a recent movie. Directed primarily at children it was titled *The Lego Movie*. It featured a key bad guy called President Business, the unscrupulous CEO and president of the massive Octan Corporation intent on world domination via a company whose diverse operations touches consumers everywhere. He is referred to as Lord Business, the most evil of tyrants who oversees a robot militia attempting to take over the LEGO universe. The hero of the story is a Lego mini-figure prophesied to save the world from the wicked big business executive. While watching the movie, I reflected on a section of my new Chapter 4 which examines the public's prejudicial view of the business and its principles as villainous personalities due to their portraits in theatrical and literary works. I was reminded that even young children, exposed to such fictional characters in fairytales, are programed to think of corporations as destructive elements, desirous of hurting people.

Also left out of the references in Chapter 4 of films characterizing businessmen as immoral individuals are two of the most famous iconic movie classics shown repeatedly on television during the holiday season. *A Christmas Carol*, a 1938 American film adaptation of Charles Dickens'

1843 novelette by Chapman & Hall is built around the character called Ebenezer Scrooge. He is an elderly miser who learns the error of his ways on Christmas Eve when his past, present, and future are collectively revealed to him. Whereupon the mean old businessman undergoes a radical change of heart and awakens on Christmas morning a new man. The infamous Scrooge character has come to symbolize the greed of a capitalist whose obsession with earning money trumps all other virtues. Widely considered as a typical Christmas movie, *It's a Wonderful Life* is a 1946 fantasy comedy-drama based on the short story *The Greatest Gift* by Philip Van Doren Stem written in 1939. The plot line features a personality called Henry Potter, a crabby old banker motivated by money and greed, whose actions lead to unpleasant repercussions for the financially struggling residents of a small town. Such fictional portrayals only add to the public's indoctrination of the destructive nature of business concerns and their principles; devoid of ethics and lacking any social compassion.

This book is dedicated to my wife Karen, who always said if you have something to say that could benefit others, put it down on paper and find someone to publish it. Then let the reader decide.

Lawrence A. Beer
December 14, 2014

Executive Summary

Ethical practices, those corporate policies historically programmed as subservient to the core responsibilities of commercial enterprises, have begun to emerge as an important antecedent in the strategic global planning process. The engagement of socially responsible moral standards in the determination of international managerial behavior and decision making has come under increasing pressure. Beginning with public interest groups and moving to the exposure by the press and legal review of actions and statements as well as consumer pressure, the resulting effect has pushed this traditionally subordinate core competency to the forefront. Multinational firms are being driven to construct and implement a universal code of conduct as part of the globalization imperative. Central to such undertaking is the development of crystal-clear definitions and unambiguous statements of intent in their codes to act as a protective shield for their reputations and as a guide for global managers. Built around the principles of absolutes and relatives, a blueprint for a practical universal code of conduct is provided.

This guide is constructed in seven chapters. The first begins with a definition of ethics as a dilemma, touching on whether it is prudent for global commercial companies to compose a code of conduct. It then sets the stage for environments in which firms find themselves today. Chapter 2 advises managers to consider incorporating ethics into the strategic planning process so that initial tactical decisions do not come back to haunt them in the future. It also profiles the influence on firms to further consider ethical behavior as part of their planning initiatives. Chapter 3 sets the stage for the development of a code of conduct by reviewing and commenting on how ethical values are developed and further impacted by public perceptions. Chapter 4 expands on the rise of prejudicial societal assessments of commercial entities due to increased transparency on two levels, external and internal, while showing how corporate social responsibility has been integrated into managerial strategies and tactical maneuvers. It ends with comments on the concept of responsible leadership. Chapter 5 reviews the attempts at creating a universal code of conduct while also presenting ideological input from theological and secular moral philosophies. Chapter 6 describes a model outline for actual code construction, its verification and monitoring requirements, as well as organizational structuring for its proper administration. Chapter 7 summarizes alternative ethical routes for companies to consider, along with inspectional guidelines and frameworks for making informed ethical decisions. It concludes with the determination that ethics is an imperative that must be incorporated into a firm's strategic intent and global planning process for companies entering the international arena.

CHAPTER 1

Ethics in Commerce

Ethics Defined

When I do good, I feel good; when I do bad, I feel bad. That's my religion.

—Abraham Lincoln, American president

Ethics is a branch of moral philosophy. It is a set of principles to govern human conduct as practiced by a particular person as well as in concert with a specific society or culture group. It therefore includes institutions and organizations. Ethics within a commercial setting are reflective of rights or wrongs as defined by the business organization as it pursues its strategic objectives. The study of ethics is basically concerned with identifying, assessing, and selecting the appropriate values to be used as standards of judgment and then applying such determinations to achieve acceptable results. Ethical strategies are planned courses of action, a tactical decision making, that do not violate such principles and in fact promotes them. The book has a prime objective: to induce managers to incorporate an ethical imperative into the corporate strategic process and to provide guidance so this can be achieved. Such a process is especially relevant today, when global operations are coming into contact with more and more varying cultural and economic conditions. Applying ethics on a global scale involves a matrix of informed values applied to changing conditions; the result is ordered flexibility.

The Ethical Dilemma

With the increased expansion of firms operating across and between nations of the world, the modern globalization phenomenon, the definition of ethics takes on a broader horizon and a wider application. Therefore, the search for universal fundamental human rights values that all men can subscribe to becomes a more complex matter. Given the vast differences in social laws, cultural- and religious-influenced codes of conduct, and economic and environmental conditions, not everyone has a uniform mind-set as to the right course of action to be taken when a moral question arises. Conflicting values are always in play. This is the ethical dilemma: The need to choose from one or more acceptable courses of action, each one evaluated as viable. The choice is made more difficult when one choice prevents the selection of another. How can one properly evaluate two totally dissimilar potential paths—the fork in the road? Is it possible to clearly see both sides? This is a difficult exercise and the dilemma is best illustrated by a quote from F. Scott Fitzgerald: "The true test of a first-rate mind is the ability to hold two contradictory ideas at the same time."

Embedded managers of multinational corporations (MNCs) in foreign markets are more often impacted by the ethical dilemma than their domestic or headquarters compatriots. Back home these executives are conducting their activities and therefore making ethical decisions in uniform national environments with prevailing acceptability. Managers abroad must increasingly look to their parent corporations for guidance and assistance on such matters. Too many times ethical decisions are made by default and not by intention. By initially recognizing that such issues will arise and that they will require an informed calculated response, and by incorporating an ethical component into the strategic planning process, the potential for a best-results scenario increases.

The Code-of-Conduct Debate

The decision by multinational firms as to whether or not to establish a code of conduct that utilizes some underlying moralistic or philosophical approaches to the subject and creates universally applied workable guidelines for their worldwide activities is one that companies are already making or will have to make in the future. Some scholars and global corporate chief executive officers (CEOs) feel that the subject is driven by an American or Western obsession with ethical conduct and that the global commercial community does not support the importance of the subject matter.

Still others see the topic as transient in nature. They note that the occasional public disclosure and dissemination of a case of questionable or inappropriate ethical behavior by a global commercial entity fuels public sentiment and promotes interest but is soon extinguished. Still others view the subject as one of the prime responsibilities of commercial entities and believe that determining its place in corporate decision making is a valid inquiry. It is against the backdrop of such different approaches within the era of modern globalization that the issue is approached. We start by examining the place of ethics in the global commercial world and show how the worldwide strategic planning process could be impacted by including ethics as an additional element to be considered. Its value and impact on companies are reviewed within the growing spectra of the public-interest imperative. As the social responsibility of companies closely parallels ethical conduct, although the issues are separate, an examination of how commercial entities impact the local human condition requires one to address these linked matters. While any company does provide an economic and therefore a quasi-social benefit to the community in which it operates, its activities do not always offer the publicly perceived value additions such as increased liberty, promotion of good health, and general welfare, nor do they target the absence of violent behavior inherent in good societies. The question therefore arises if in fact commercial entities are endowed with the moral challenges of ethically minded institutions. This crisscrossing of social responsibility and ethics, one driving the other or vice versa, requires both be considered in the text.

The competitive and financial consequences acting in unison as qualitative and quantitative drivers behind a firm's decision to implement some form of ethical conduct are examined next. The initial efforts to construct international codes of commercial conduct are presented and an examination of their wording and definitions is offered. Moral philosophies are revisited to provide some additional guidance, along with specific references to religious teachings in regard to man's obligations to his fellow men in order to present a wider underpinning and direction for incorporating ethics in the global function of managing a diversified workforce. However, an in-depth discussion of the philosophical frameworks of ethics and morality across all segments of a business is outside the scope of this limited investigation.

A comparison of the company codes of two firms, Nike Inc. and Gap Inc., is used to illustrate some practical approaches to the issues. A template for construction of a reasonable global code of conduct for multinational companies using the principles of *absolutes* and *relatives* to guide embedded international managers in the making of ethical decisions is presented to allow the reader to reflect on a practical approach. The text then summarizes charted avenues of global ethical decision making, a series of checks listing various optional routes international firms can choose to utilize. Absent from the book is an in-depth discussion of the accusations of lying and cheating leading to potential criminal and civil lawsuits targeting executives involved in false public reporting of their firms' financial activities. We are mainly concerned with value creation for the company and the place of ethical conduct in its construction as practiced initially during the strategic planning process and later in its tactical implementation, which requires a clear and concise definition of its objectives. From a purely economic stance, the ethical question involves the evaluation of the efficient allocation of corporate resources to justify its place in a global moral ecology.

Social Responsibility

A man is truly ethical only when he obeys the compulsion to help all life which he is able to assist, and shrinks from hurting anything that lives.

—Albert Schweitzer, global humanitarian

This view of a commercial enterprise expands the jurisdiction of firms beyond their internal organization, their shareholders and employees, and asserts that a wider, more global circle of stakeholders and the worldwide communities they touch need to be considered, as well as the demands of the consuming market. This expanded arena is *corporate social responsibility* (CSR) and is a subject collateral to ethical decision making. While they share some common characteristics they are separate terms. *Social responsibility* is considered an ideological theory based on the concept that business institutions should not just function amorally (the ethical component) but should contribute to the general welfare and social improvement of the communities in which they operate. In simple terms, companies have a corresponding duty to the societies that utilize their products and services, a give-and-take scenario. Such responsibility, however, moves in two dissimilar directions, a duality of obligations. First, firms should not act in a negative or harmful fashion; they have a responsibility to refrain from doing anything that is damaging to the social environment around them—a resistance stance or sustainability factor. Second, firms must act responsively by instituting positive actions that promote improvement in the social environment around them—a proactive stance.

CSR may be the generic umbrella under which a code of conduct is constructed. CSR broadly directs us to care about the societal surroundings we operate within, but it does not provide specific directional choices in order to confront and assist in solving precise ethical dilemmas. The magazine *Corporate Responsibility Officer* publishes an annual list of the "100 Best Corporate Citizens" along the lines of *Fortune* magazine's "Most Admired Companies" and "100 Best Companies to Work For." *Corporate Responsibility Officer* uses a scoring system for publicly listed U.S. firms that was developed in 2000 by Marjorie Kelly, Samuel P. Graves, and Sandra Waddock. The system combines eight categories of stakeholder interest: shareholders, community, governance, diversity, employees, environment, human rights, and product. Such a diverse accounting criteria underscores the fact that social responsibility is not a simply defined term but a subject with many influencing determinants. Notable, however, is the absence of the term *ethics* or *moral conduct* in this applied analytical approach, as such judgments have a subjective component that is not easily qualified or quantified objectively. The subject of social responsibility is handled in a more in-depth examination later in the book, as it is an issue collateral to as well as embedded in ethics for the global business and global manager.

Roots of Globalization

In this world everything changes except good deed and bad: these
follow you as the shadow follows the body.

—Unknown

As the reader begins to move into the various sections of the book, the question "why are these issues being raised today?" might arise. The initial process of globalization, according to researchers in anthropology, occurred during different periods when various societies and their commercial agents—first crown merchants, then entrepreneurial traders, and later companies—were commercializing their then known world. The ancient silk and spice trade routes crossing continents and stretching from England to China, first by land and then by sea, may have begotten the globalization of the world. Some would argue that the first true global era was inaugurated during the time that the British and other European nations set up their vast overseas empires, established colonies, and practiced mercantilism, and that the current period is an extension of this older process. Certainly multinationals have been around for some time. Moore and Lewis in their book *Birth of the Multinationals* examined the linkage of history and the world economy by tracing the development of transcontinental enterprises through the four great empires of the ancient world, Assyrian, Phoenician, Greek, and Roman. Such early motivation to trade across borders and promote foreign direct investment (FDI) was attributable to the desire to seek out natural resources to be used in the home market, to sell domestically made goods in new markets and to "rationalize a [then] global division of labor."[1] All these historic incentives to globalize still induce modern firms to internationalize their operations and activities. Even the commonly accepted definition of a multinational enterprise, one that "engages in foreign direct investment (FDI) and owns or controls value-adding activities in more than one country"[2] is as apropos today as it was thousands of years ago.

As the ancient world grew, occupying a growing number of people involved in the commercial process both within and without their territorial boundaries, historians tell us that the business endeavor was not looked upon with favor. Early philosophers like Socrates, Aristotle, and Plato, commenting on the activities of their societies, dismissed "trade as petty and vulgar." They "saw honest profit coming from farming or using natural resources."[3] Merchants were portrayed as those who greedily took advantage of others, cornering markets and accepting bribes with little concern for the welfare of the society. While the Europeans viewed the trading exercise with disdain, the Japanese regarded those who engaged in commerce at the bottom of the social ladder. Adding to their low positioning in Japan and their poor public image was the fact that traditionally local merchants collected royal taxes, skimmed off a profit, and sent the balance to national merchants, who presented the balance to the king. The resentment of the commercial process and its intrusion on society may have been rooted in such a consideration.

Commercial Ethical Behavior

The success of any great moral enterprise does not depend upon numbers.
—William Lloyd Garrison, American journalist and
social reformer

Throughout history the commercial imperative has been labeled as a contributor to society's ills and misfortunes. The contemptible practice of slavery, both the process of trading in human bondage and the ownership of forced labor, as noted earlier, had a commercial motivation. The rise of employees demanding their rights via unionism has been portrayed in both nonfiction al and fictional literature as good against evil. Wealth accumulation and the rise to power by the robber barons of commerce monopolizing and controlling not only the local factory town but also national and perhaps world industries are also depicted in emotionally charged, critical rhetoric by commentators of the day in history books. It is against this backdrop of historic distrust and greed inherent in the commercial process that the modern era of globalization has emerged. Is it any wonder that many of the opponents of globalization cite the immoral actions of today's multinational firms, as they cross borders and take advantage of a more open world, as purveyors and beneficiaries of the destruction of environments and the rights of indigenous people? Historically, nations that grew to be commercially efficient battled internally with ethical issues, thereby erecting laws and regulations to reengineer their social climates to reflect their own codified moral imperative. Today, as these morally progressive countries engage developing markets via their MNCs, a conflict arises. Do such firms going abroad bring with them a packed-at-home suitcase of domestic laws and regulatory codes and press them on alien social environments, or do they wait for these improvements to be visited upon emerging regions in a more natural progression of time?

Proponents of globalization argue multinational firms that embrace an ethical program, whether by subscribing to a published code of responsible conduct or creating one themselves with real doctrinal direction, cushion the negative effects and become champions of more democratic freedoms in the lives they touch. They become ethical prophets. Opponents argue that this is *ethical imperialism*, a form of cultural orthodoxy and ethnocentrism, the colonization of the emerging world, that interlopers in an alien society have no right to impose their will on others. As invited visitors, they should accept the status quo and practice *cultural relativism*. They should allow developing societies to passively change when they themselves feel a new direction is warranted. It should not be forced on them as even good intentions can produce unforeseen consequences and possibly unravel social structures.

Questioning the ethical conduct and perhaps immoral activities of today's large global enterprises is therefore nothing really new, except for the fact that in the modern era the wide public dissemination of such indiscretions and its potential influence on the buying decisions of global consumers has drawn such issues to perhaps a high level of importance. It is beginning to affect the bottom line of public corporations and therefore is impacting their strategic planning and everyday activities.

The idea of linking ethical behavior with commercial dealings can be traced back to transactions in ancient Egypt, where a code of conduct was proclaimed in the name of the then revered deity:

> Do not move the scale, do not change the weights and do not Diminish the part of the bushel…. Do not create a bushel that contains Tow, lest you will near the abyss. The bushel is the eye of Re. He loathes him who defrauds.[4]

The Greek and later the Roman civilizations placed their commercial weights and measuring devices in their temples at night to ensure against tampering, although the actual transactions were carried out outside such holy structures during the day. Such solemn practices were indicative of man's early desire to have commercial dealings blessed by the gods and to ensure that men treated each other in a fair and equitable manner as overseen by a higher authority. During the Aztec Empire in Mesoamerica, the city administrators of Tlatelolco, which housed the ancient world's single largest marketplace attended by 60,000 people daily, sent patrols among the thousands of vendor to enforce the use of legitimate weights and measures and to settle disputes; collateral but necessary to their primary role was collecting taxes. Ethical conduct in the business environment has always shadowed mankind. Those that engage in commercial dealings are advised in the teachings of Buddha "to engage in harmless occupation" according to the *Mangala Sutta*. Confucian philosophy encourages one who manages or employs people to do so with the intent to treat them with care—so no harm befalls them, as a system of ethics is based on loyalty, reciprocal obligations, and honesty in dealings with others. Islam preaches similar sentiments, exhorting those who engage in trade to be fair and equitable and not to take advantage of circumstances. The Koran speaks approvingly of free enterprise and of earning a legitimate profit through trade and commerce. The prophet Mohammed was once a trader.[5] German sociologist Max Weber argued that Protestant ethics emphasize the importance of hard work and wealth creation to glorify God. While it is difficult to exactly link religious teachings with business practices, most would agree that human ethical actions are based for many in the world on a belief system emanating from the dominion of the sacred, a spiritual base, and a divine reverence that has been with us for thousands of years.

Modern Globalization and the New Ethical Imperative

There is not moral precept that does not have something inconvenient about it.

—Denis Diderot, French philosopher

Why at this time in the history of mankind is the matter of ethics generating so much attention? The answer may lie in the simple factors that have propelled globalization into the modern era. The scope and degree of the process of globalization as practiced today reaches and affects more people than ever before. The advances of modern technology have allowed the world to be reduced to a smaller place. Communication and travel are faster and easier. Commercial firms have expanded all their value-creating activities across borders at a rate never seen before. A true global marketplace for goods and services has been created. This new economic system has fewer of the walls that historically insulated national societies. The world's population now interacts at an ever-increasing pace, and more players are being drawn into the global economic game. Transnational commercial enterprises have become the explorers of the world. With their economic strength, they have opened new territories and linked them with the rest of the world. By their very power, which rivals that of great armies that once conquered the known world, their actions affect all of us to a degree never before experienced. These massive global firms can be ambassadors of change or conservers of the status quo. Many multinational firms are larger than countries themselves. A report issued by the Institute for Policy Studies in 2000 claimed that of the 100 largest economies in the world, 51 are corporations and 49 are nation-states.[6] Some feel such MNCs are even sovereign entities unto themselves, rivaling nations in power and reach. No wonder their decisions and actions are carefully watched, recorded, and reported. Whether one is a consumer of the products and services offered or is touched in some way by their expanding supply and value-chain activities, multinational firms affect us all. It stands to reason therefore that their conduct is being examined and even judged, as having dominion assumes a responsibility and duty toward those feeling their presence. Working in combination with such consideration is a rise in public awareness of the reach of such global entities and their effect on the world. People, as they are drawn closer together, are realizing that no man is an island unto himself. The actions or inactions of those with global commercial power are controlling the destiny of mankind. It therefore follows that questions of ethical equitable propriety are legitimate queries to be made of such institutions.

More and more people are concerned with such issues as the development of basic human rights or the protection of the fragile environment. Hence the onus to examine them has emerged at this time, and firms that pursue a global agenda best take heed. It seems the world is watching, and such is the tenor of the times we live in.

Ethical Reach

All behavior, including commercial endeavors, has an ethical component.
—Lawrence A. Beer, global ethics explorer

As noted earlier, the general study of ethics, and the moral principles that emerge, is a branch of philosophy dealing with values relating to human conduct and the rightness or wrongness of certain actions. It is often viewed in its positive definition as generating a set of standards that, when applied, generate virtuous and admired conduct. Correct application brings honor to the user and results in gracious satisfaction to the receiver. Ethics therefore is not limited to the creation of a corporate code of conduct by global enterprises as examined in this book but personally resides in all of us in our one-on-one interactions and relationships with others.

Ethics, when defined as an inquiry into moral judgments, standards, and rules of conduct as practiced in a commercial setting and therefore guiding the behavior of the participants in the process, is the circumference within which the book is constructed. Such a wide view encompasses breaches of corporate fiduciary responsibility from accounting fraud and falsifying of documents to insider trading. It concerns itself with deceptive advertising, misleading promotional programs, price rigging, defective products, and other forms of consumer injury. It also covers forms of proper employee treatment and behavior, as well as bribery of influential third parties. The constituency it affects is wide, with stakeholders dispersed across all that the firm touches, directly or indirectly, and in varying degrees and on numerous levels.

However, we will be investigating one slice of the ethical business pie: those aspects devoted to moral decision making within the international domain. The intent of this book and the chapters that follow is therefore limited in scope and application to a commercial organization operating within a global environment. It is not a guide for individual determination of one's moral actions, which remain deeply personal, but readers will certainly find themselves reflecting on their own ethical compass as they move through the text. The book aims to investigate the establishment, if firms deem necessary and to what degree, of a universal code of conduct. It is intended to guide the practical decisions and procedural dealings of commercial multinational enterprises as they cross borders and encounter differences in ethical approaches. It targets managers by furthering an understanding and appreciation for the potential need to develop uniform declarations of acceptable conduct for their embedded worldwide managers, as well as their overall ethical positioning as they enter alliances with commercial third parties, come in contact with unfamiliar native people, and operate under alien governmental authorities.

The Ethical Imperative

The dual notions of parties acting ethically in trade and commercial exchanges and the idea that business institutions contribute to the public good have always been part of the social order of organized groups. Throughout history, as the power and reach of merchants and industrialized entrepreneurs increased, their moral behavior and relations with the communities they operated within have always been the subject of inspectional commentary. With the dramatic rise, however, of modern globalization and vastly expanded global development in the early 1990s, the pressure on public companies to behave ethically and to pursue elements of basic social responsibility has seen the bar of acceptable conduct rise. Awareness of ethical concerns is coming from a number of venues, with the subject fueled by the magnification of operating in a wider world arena where different moral directions exist. Multinational companies are falling under the inspectional lenses of many stakeholder groups demanding greater scrutiny and transparency of the corporate publicly perceived moral actions. A worldwide press follows all allegations of potential commercial misconduct, with the reading public eager to denounce the commercial sector, a group they already believe is morally bankrupt.

While it would be good if managers heed to the seemingly biblical refrain as interpreted by Edmund Burke—"For evil to triumph it is enough for good men to do nothing"—and be motivated by altruistic intentions, the realities are that more is involved. Beyond simply being admonished or praised for acting in a socially acceptable manner, commercial institutions, especially MNCs, have found that their ethical actions, either real or perceived, have financial ramifications that impact the bottom line. Ethics is no longer a sidebar issue but a critical part of a firm's operational activities. As such it is an important element that must be incorporated in the strategic planning process and the tactical actions that support it. Mismanaged ethical behavior or misapplied CSR activities can deeply influence a firm's continuing success, while proper application of a code of ethical conduct and use of well-received CSR programs can sustain as well as improve the competitiveness of companies. When companies are publicly reprimanded for their misconduct or even rumored to have behaved unethically with or through others, they face a number of potential consequences (some of which are noted in the following list and will be covered in detail later in the book).

- Loss of sales or service revenue.
- Damage to a company's intangible capital asset: its reputation or brand image.
- Increased cost to reverse the first and second point as well as to settle accusations of improper conduct along with the attention and involvement of key managers, taking them away from their normal operational functions.
- Alliance partners with ethical problems causing a disruption in company supply chains and an expensive interruption in business networks requiring nonbudgeted switching costs.
- Placing operations in a country whose government is deemed ethically repressive.

However, projecting a social caring image, with appropriate cooperative programs, and taking proactive measures to assure no missteps in ethical decision making throughout the firm's operational reach has its rewards.

- Consumers wish to feel that the purveyors of their needs and wants are honest in their dealings, so if a competitor falters, those with a clean record are granted an advantage.
- Consumers see societal cause marketing as added value to a brand or product and are more likely to patronize firms that contribute to the benefit of the society via such combined promotional programs.
- Associates like to do business with commercial partners they perceive as having a high social status in the community, thereby attracting more useful alliances.

- Employees like to work for companies that have a good ethical reputation, so firms can use such assets to attract the best talent.
- Some shareholders only wish to invest in ethical companies, while other stakeholders, from communities to nongovernmental organizations (NGOs), are attracted to companies with a good public standing, as this attribute adds to their status and prestige.

The potential positive and negative effects of ethical decision making, as well as the CSR programs of firms, have made these tandem subjects rise to a level of importance never before seen in the commercial sector. Today, the ethical imperative is a driving force that global companies and their managers must be concerned with. It is gaining a more prominent position in strategic determinations and the actionable activities of firms both at home and abroad. The issue necessitates an increased obligation on the part of managers to introduce ethics into their thinking matrix, integrating it with the other disciplines of managing a business. Management is a practice combining science and art, while ethics merges the rational with the emotional. Grafting an ethical imperative onto the managerial system, while complex, is a required skill set in 21st century globalization.

Managerial Reflections

1. The subject of ethics within the modern era of globalization presents a series of ethical dilemmas for MNCs and their embedded managers. Can a universal code of conduct really be constructed? Consider this issue now and as you read through the book continue to reflect on this central question.
2. Ethics is collateral to social responsibility; the terms are not synonymous. What exactly is the responsibility of business organizations to the world around them?
3. Commercial activities have always been suspect, as the goals of business institutions and the needs of the societies they impact are not always in unison. Can MNCs balance their strategic intent with the

requirements of a global community, no less between the individual markets they interact with?

4. Ethical conduct reflects a personal choice as per the quote by Lincoln. As such can one be appreciative and empathetic of another's moral direction and resultant ethical determinations?

CHAPTER 2

Ethics and the Strategic Determination

Ethics in the 21st Century

For many men, the acquisition of wealth does not end their troubles, it only changes them.

—Marcus Annaeus Seneca, Roman orator

The global process was first begun as domestic companies following the traditional product life-cycle theory pioneered new markets for sales expansion after reaching plateaus in their originating market. Via limited historic entrance vehicles, first export and later the licensing route allowing for the transfer of distinctive core competencies, firms first expanded their revenue-growth imperative overseas. The companion use of importing cheaper raw materials and components for local home-market production was initially utilized as firms tended to keep their prime activities and secondary operations concentrated in their headquarters or country. A restrictive international strategy was practiced. However, in this era of globalization international companies are driven to make fuller use of the extreme global value chain in order to remain competitive, both at home and abroad. They are therefore highly motivated to establish their primary and supportive activities in numerous geographical locations in order to create and sustain value creation. Too often, globalization, whether in ancient times or in the modern era, is characterized as a race to the bottom by companies, a contest to see who can source or make what is cheapest by cutting corners with little or no regard for the ethical consequences.

Today's globalization race is not a commercial fad nor an economic trend but a permanent alteration in the global business landscape. The process of modern globalization, having its roots in ancient trade, is a change in substance but not in form. It is an alteration in the extended geographical radius upon which the procedure is practiced, with the effect that more markets and therefore more people around the world are drawn into the circle. John H. Dunning, in the role of editor of a collection of essays titled *Making Globalization Good*, describes the current process from a variety of viewpoints. An anthropologist sees it as "the connecting of individuals and institutions across the globe," while economists would define it as the creation of a global market "referring more specifically to the flow of goods, services and assets across national boundaries."[1] The critics of globalization, commenting on its potentially negative consequences, view the phenomenon in a narrower sense as the spread of capitalism, which they would describe as "a better instrument for the creation of wealth than it is for the equitable distribution of its benefits."[2] Perhaps globalization is simply a new world system as Thomas Friedman postulates in *The Lexus and the Olive Tree*.[3] It may have no moral significance as it is a mechanism, a progressive natural occurrence embraced by mankind as a tool toward a material end.

However, with the expanded use of foreign-subsidiary production facilities, offshore joint-party manufacturing ventures, and alternative sourcing from third-party contractors in foreign countries that offer the most cost-efficient labor pools, new strategic directions are under way that are forcing firms to engage in a world of diversified people and their ethical differences. Today, such overseas expansion has begun to encompass a wider array of firm activities, including outsourcing of back-office functional services and even the primary development of value creation, research and development (R&D) via global alliances, and establishment of satellite laboratories in global centers of excellence. Such practices bring companies into contact with an increasing multitude of different values and beliefs, which generate varying moral practices.

In the development of such ambitious international-supply programs and other global service renderings, the added baggage of ethics and social responsibility has begun to grow and seems to be a natural accompaniment to overseas expansion. As a new criterion for country and partnership evaluation, ethical conduct may no longer be an auxiliary consideration but an integral part of a firm's strategic planning process. Whether such corporate strategy is an international one, a multinational series of country-specific entrances, or a global or fully integrated transnational involvement, firms must begin to internally dialogue and decide whether or not they should incorporate a workable code of conduct collateral to such strategic preparation. If an affirmative decision is made, they need to test their strategic decisions against a set of agreed principles—be they signatories to existing compacts or ones of their own construction.

All the tactical tools to engage a worldwide corporate strategy and facilitate its successful operational effect will bring the organization into direct periodic contact with third-party foreign individuals. Whether partnering via joint ventures, alliances, and licensing; using independent distributors, agents, and franchises; engaging new employees in a greenfield or brownfield direct foreign investment; or developing relationships with arm's-length contractors for offshore manufacturing or service outsourcing, the prudent application of the firm's ethical determination and resulting conduct will be tested.

The alien entities that international firms encounter will possess their own separate, inherent, corporate ethical culture that reflects the specific moral compass of their individual societies. Potential conflicts could appear when questions of ethical choice emerge. The decisions that firms make in advance of such possible contested issues may also be challenged by other stakeholders in the firm such as consumers, public-interest groups, stockholders, and other institutions. The perceptions and opinions of these parties could also affect the business operations and financial outcomes of companies. It follows, therefore, that the ethical choices of firms may include a wide array of interested onlookers. Hence, the context in which these ethical decisions are made may go beyond the immediate parties affected, with the added judgment of a wider constituency. As the activities of firms globalize at an increasing rate, their managers will have to integrate themselves into varying societies. As social behavior and attitudes, the framers of moral conduct, are embedded in a particular milieu of a nation, it is a given that differences in ethical decision making will arise. Working with people whose unique and distinctive cultural values and beliefs, the underpinnings of moral applications, vary around the world requires firms to recognize such differences. Failure to consider such wide variations could result in costly misunderstandings and business problems that not only extend to internal operations but also can deeply affect corporate external profiles via perceptions of impropriety by customers and other stakeholders. Ignoring or mishandling diversified approaches to ethical and social responsibility issues for a global corporation is emerging as a key consideration in the strategic planning process. Mismanaging ethical matters might render otherwise successful enterprises and their activities ineffective and troubled.

There is a dangerous supposition taking place in the world. It is wrong to assume that, with the advent of modern globalization and its related progress toward more uniform commercialization standards with increased shared, homogeneous consumer needs and demands, the formation of a global society with shared ethics is beginning to take hold. The world is still more tribal than universal, with individual national state systems imposing varying political and economic differences as well as continued splinters of cultural and religious values. Societies remain diverse; hence, the dispersed reasoning of ethical issues will remain a problem for MNCs as they segregate their value-creating activities around the globe while trying to integrate such competitive advantages on a global scale.

Moral behavior is still fragmented, and balancing right and wrong is a difficult process. In the modern era of commercial globalization, operating across and between such boundaries of differences therefore involves navigating a complex set of ethical dilemmas. When effectively approached with careful consideration and made part of the criteria in the development of corporate strategy, ethics can serve as a value-creating ingredient and, alternately, a deflection of value reduction. Although the development of corporate codes of conduct, which provide guidelines for dealing with ethical and social responsibility issues, is clearly an area of increasing vigilance for global firms, it is a most difficult subject to present. Morals, because they are so deeply tied to personal interpretation and individualized emotional application, are hard to discuss and present objectively. Ethical conduct deals with decisions and interactions on an individual level, whereas social responsibility presents issues that are broader in scope, tend to affect more people, and normally reflect a pooling of decision makers resulting in a general stance taken by a company. Corporate social responsibility (CSR) goes beyond legal obligations and compliance regulations. It is associated with a firm's commitments to investors, customers, suppliers (and their networks), and the community at large and their general welfare—a collection of stakeholders. It is more externally and socially directed, as opposed to ethics, which is internal and personal to the practitioner. There is a considerable overlap and integration between the two decency motivators of judgmental actions even though their differences may be of scope and degree.

The idea that the current global-economic system, in its modernized enlarged form, must begin to adjust to social needs with additional moral responsibility is a theme emerging in the academic field. In new editions of textbooks on international business and management,[4] the authors are presenting whole chapters on the subject as opposed to including such issues under cultural differences and political or legal environments, while also offering instructional cases to supplement conceptual development. Renowned international scholar John H. Dunning, whose work has previously been mentioned, concludes that the challenges in the coming global society require an adjusted institutional-structural design to support a new moral science. He notes such changes need to be brought about not only by multinational firms but also by the combined work of nongovernmental organizations (NGOs), national governments, and supranational agencies. But as Jonathan Doh observes in his review of Dunning's book, the essays offer a "persuasive argument for what is wrong, some general principles that could guide an improved form of GC [global capital], but little in the way of specific guidelines as to who must do what to achieve this transformation."[5]

For ethics to be successfully applied by firms at the initial planning process and to make them later applicable in the field where they are truly tested, they must be presented with clear, consistent, coherent, and complete language—a most difficult task given the various, diffuse areas of input used to construct them.

Because ethical determinants are influenced by religious indoctrination and subject to the pressures of one's peers, the subject also becomes one of strong cultural sensitivity and subjective group rationalization. Nevertheless, it is a subject worthy of inspection, as the decisions and actions or nondecisions and nonactions that flow from its considered application affect the performance of global entities. And it all starts with the strategic planning process.

Integrating Ethics in the Strategic Planning Process

Affairs are easier of entrance than of exit; and it is of common prudence to see our way out before we venture in.

—Aesop, renowned teller of fables

Strategy determines firm performance and as such it profoundly affects the success or failure of a commercial enterprise. The simple object of strategy is value creation that allows firms to achieve sustainable competitive advantage. Most of the literature on strategy offer models of evaluation, or SWOT (strengths, weaknesses, opportunities, and troubles) analyses, that focus on how companies can (a) leverage firm core strengths, making effective use of firm resources and competencies; (b) brace or shore up weaknesses; (c) take advantage of opportunities; and (d) avoid troubles. Such analysis is traditionally conducted within the context of specific industries or business segments. International strategy adds the dimension of conducting firm activities in multiple geographic centers or national markets that offer diversified value-added benefits. While the use of a global strategy has certainly been magnified in the 20th century due to rapid advances in technology, it could be argued that cross-border trade was the imperative for an international strategy. Such an idea has been part of the commercial process since ancient trade routes were first used to obtain rare and exotic products from foreign lands. Today, the economic value of an international strategy to gain access to the riches of new territories has become a sophisticated search for value creation beyond merely unique and exceptional merchandise. In the current era of globalization, firms look for suppliers of low-cost raw materials and components, cheap and efficient labor, and pockets of specialized technology, as well as learning-curve opportunities. One of the key original motives for exploring foreign sites was to take advantage of low-cost indigenous labor pools in underdeveloped countries in order to gain a competitive advantage over domestic rivals. This international strategic initiative has been expanded to include offshore sourcing for traditional, routine back-office support functions. More recently there has been a trend to place R&D activities in global centers of excellence where developmental costs are lower. Collateral to the movement abroad of the

R&D function is that firms want new, innovative techniques and product designs to be placed closer to the production sites so that the time frame to incorporate revolutionary ideas into the final manufacturing process and then through the channels of distribution is shortened.

In many new textbooks and revisions of old ones devoted to the study of strategy, the opportunities of operating in a global arena have begun to emerge. While most traditional works on the subject are devoting separate chapters to globalization and its effect on the external context that strategy is developed within, the ethical imperative as an implication for managers to appreciate in the process seems to be lacking. Much of the literature on international business has just begun to paint an outline of how firms should respond to globalization and the strategic gains to be had from such consideration. The prime advantages of market and production factors are emphasized. Increasing market size, as firms expand beyond the home country into the greater consuming world, is a key driver for firms to globalize. Utilizing location advantages by moving into low-cost manufacturing sites due to an abundance of cheap labor pools in emerging nations is the other side of the globalization coin. When taken together they form the perfect motive for firms to internationalize their strategies. If the additional advantages of receiving a greater and faster return on capital investment while improving economies of scale and moving up the learning curve are added to the motivational equation, the incentive to develop a global strategy is only magnified.

Once companies identify the aforementioned basic impetus to go global, they are traditionally presented with a series of corporate business-level strategies to choose from—international, global, multidomestic (also called multinational), or transnational. A key consideration in choosing from such alternative strategies is the extent to which the industry requires a greater degree of local responsiveness versus a need for low cost and global integration of operations. This normal process of strategic determination is followed by the selection of modes of entry or tactical tools used to cross into national territories as previously noted—exporting, licensing, strategic alliances including joint ventures and franchising, turnkey and management contracts, acquisitions, or greenfield subsidiary creation. The advantages and disadvantages of such market-entrance methods follow the initial corporate design stage in the strategic decision-making paradigm. Management problems and risks are usually presented next, focusing on political and economic matters that could have a negative effect on the firm's efforts to globalize its activities. Collateral to such analysis are differences in institutional, governmental, and cultural conditions around the world. Further evaluation tends to focus on the effects of a firm's marketing mix on the corporate strategy and the entry mode(s) selected. The unintended consequences of the moral global deployment of a firm's assets and the company's organizational ethical positioning in an expanded world are seldom included in the evaluation process. This may be because traditionally firms operated in a single domestic environment and tended to share the same moral mind-set and resultant ethical indoctrination. Hence, historic strategic models and procedures never required such additional considerations be applied to them. When firms began to expand beyond their borders and looked around for new strategic models to base their decision upon, the constructors of new planning and evaluation methodology for global operations just followed suit and never introduced an ethics factor. They may have simply viewed the expanded geographical territory as additional space to leverage the resources and capabilities of companies applying basic tools of strategic decision making across a wider market of nations. While barriers and differences were noted that could affect operational decisions, impede performance improvement, and perhaps limit opportunities for value creation, the ethical component was overlooked.

Whichever market tactical-entry method is chosen or whatever value-producing activity is transferred overseas, companies need to recognize that it will be carried out with the use of foreign citizens and in the framework of alien environments. Such simple realization means that different ethical conditions will be encountered. However, the internationally integrated strategic decisions firms must consider when operating across and within national boundaries rarely include a reference to the varied value and belief systems that form the resultant ethical issues global firms will face.

Take the simple example of Nike. Their founding strategy involved creating a more competitive market positioning in the United States by using "low-cost, high-quality athletics-shoe production in Japan. As costs increased in Japan they moved to other low-cost producers in Korea, Taiwan, Indonesia, and Thailand... to maintain... competitive advantage."[6]

From the outset the Nike strategy embraced the global location advantage factor. This key cost driver provided the tactical imperative for continuing country-entry decision making with respect to their manufacturing operations.

At the heart of Nike's location advantage strategic imperative was the use of indigenous low-cost labor in emerging nations along with lax governmental regulations on employment practices and the desire of such governments to provide employment for their unskilled citizens. Yet such a visionary strategic imperative never included an ethical factor concerning the treatment of potential workers. Low cost was the critical feature, with such key intent trumping all other collateral issues that impacted the decision.

If Nike had incorporated in their original strategic decision-making process an ethical ingredient, many of their posttactical moves might have avoided the numerous problems that later haunted their envied successful growth and tainted the firm's position as the world's number-one athletic apparel maker. Their poster-boy image as the very embodiment of the term sweatshop might have been avoided, as would all their costly and very public efforts to defend such operational activities with third-party contractors accused of violating basic labor rights and taking undue advantage of their workers. The conventional mechanisms used to construct corporate strategy need to introduce an ethical factor in such analysis, especially for firms contemplating any type of offshore or cross-border activities to create value. The basic SWOT initiative, to measure a company's relative positioning, as a prerequisite for strategic determination might include an ethical component in its inventory of measured elements.

Corporate Strengths

An initial evaluation of a company to gauge its inherent properties and hence the platform upon which its strategic plan can be generated is the SWOT analysis. It begins with an examination of the firm's core competencies—its strengths. It is a given that a good name supports and amplifies the strengths of a company. Being perceived by all stakeholders as a moral institution is a strength often not viewed as a core competency, but it is.

Sometimes overlooked in the analysis is that a company's key strength may stem from a strong connection to social issues and human rights objectives. Take, for example, the Body Shop, an English retail-franchise chain specializing in skin-care products and toiletries. It promotes itself as a champion of nature, using natural ingredients in its products and thereby acting as a preserver and caretaker for the global environment. They see the world as their garden and stress their adherence to community trade, supporting the producer's whole community and not just the growers themselves, to affect real social change. These are the key strengths, or proprietary competences, upon which the company was strategically built. Collateral to this moral imperative is their announced strategic desire to "passionately campaign for human and civil rights."[7] Such image positioning gave the enterprise a value-added perception among consumers from its inception. The company's statement of values in an undated corporate literature release states,

> We will establish a framework based on this declaration [reference to Universal Declaration of Human Rights] to include criteria for workers' rights embracing a safe healthy working environment, fair wages, no discrimination on the basis of race, creed, gender or sexual orientation, or physical coercion of any kind.[8]

An image and reputation of a *doer of good deeds*, a wise and charitable patriarch like the Wizard of Oz, may result in a meritorious reward bestowed on companies that practice and announce their moral initiative. While such desire may have at its core a real moral conviction, the commercial result was to place the company in a most enviable position vis-à-vis its beauty-industry competitors. A case can be made that a "social-accountability audit" is not just morally correct but in the end can add economic strength and magnify core competencies.[9]

Amanda Tucker, director of business compliance at Nike, has stated, "If you work with factories to make them better places of employment, quality improves, productivity goes up, there's less waste and you retain workers longer."[10] These are strengths every commercial entity would like to have in its arsenal of competitive advantages. Global firms have begun to covet the banner of caring and protection in a remake of their public persona. British Petroleum (BP), in a desire to strengthen its image as environmentally friendly, changed the company logo, a valued asset, to a softer emblem with the all-important shade of green incorporated into the symbol.[11]

Walmart openly portrays its support for social programs in local communities with television commercials evidencing the activities of their employees on behalf of charities and welfare programs to enhance the company's appearance as a socially conscious neighbor. Positioning a company as a contributing caretaker of the earth and the general society is an intangible firm asset and a positive creator of an image that only enhances the company's reputation as the type of organization both consumers of products and users of services want to associate with.

Corporate Weaknesses

If one accepts that the portrayal of a company as a moral do-gooder is a positive driver, it logically follows that any opposite indictments of poor conduct may result in a drag effect on a firm, a weakness holding it back from a smooth, uncontested path. Negative publicity attacking an organization's ethical conduct can become a permanent stigma. A firm is weakened by any continuing perception by consumers of moral wrongdoing. Take the alleged violations of labor conditions and the long-lasting saga of Nike. In 1990, a photo published in *Life* magazine of a 12-year-old Pakistani boy stitching a logo-embossed soccer ball, captioned by a statement revealing that such effort took a whole day with the child being paid $0.60, has always plagued the company. This pictorial portrayal and the accompanying caption resulted in public condemnation that still haunts Nike today. It has become a proverbial thorn in their side, a stigma placed on their brand name and hence a weakness directly traceable to their questionable ethical actions.

Twelve years later, Nike's spokesman at a seminar on corporate responsibility at the American Graduate School of International Management was still pressed to outline the company's plans to monitor working conditions throughout their 900 overseas factories. Even though they utilize 86 compliance officers as opposed to just three staffers in 1996, their ongoing actions are still subject to constant review and comment.

The shame of past deeds remains with the accused and dogs their existence forever.

Nike still is viewed as a poster child for unethical treatment, and the label continues to plague the company as noted by a civil action brought against them quickly reaching the U.S. Supreme Court. Many legal scholars felt that a decision on the matter would have far-reaching implications not only in California but also across the country and around the world. A plaintiff suing Nike alleged that the company made false and misleading statements pertaining to its ethical activities, in essence denying participation in foreign sweatshops. Via news releases, full-page ads in major newspapers, and letters to editors, Nike commented on its own moral conduct. Under California state law an action was brought, citing violation of the law prohibiting unlawful business practices. Nike countered by claiming their statements fall under the protection of the First Amendment—free speech. The state court concluded that a firm's public statements about its operations have the effect of persuading consumers to buy their products and as such equate to advertising. By sustaining and promoting a company's reputation, the consuming public is motivated; hence, such commentary is part of the sales-solicitation process. The majority court opinion summarized its finding by stating that

> because the messages in question were directed by a commercial speaker to a commercial audience, and because they made representations of fact about the speaker's own business operations for the purpose of promoting sales of its products, we conclude that these messages are commercial speech for purposes of applying state laws barring false and misleading commercial messages.[12]

Statements by a business enterprise to promote or even defend its own sales and profits are factual representations about its own products and its own operations; therefore, the business has a duty to speak truthfully about such issues. Such case precedent could present a minefield of potential danger for commentary by global firms as to their ethical behavior. It would effectively elevate statements on human rights treatment to a corporate marketing theme, not affording company spokespeople the shield of public debate via free speech. If the appeal was upheld by the U.S.

Supreme Court, commercial entities will be hard pressed to defend any allegations of human rights abuses and would have to be more proactive, assuring that their worldwide activities from the start are well defended by construction of specifically defined and properly implemented codes of conduct. (While it should be noted that this case was settled by the parties before final determination by the court, the arguments presented at the state level should be well noted by global companies in drafting their responses to allegations of ethical misconduct.)

Allegations of inappropriate activities by global companies are always popping up. Some arise via a highly publicized legal route while others are dramatically portrayed by television investigative news programs. Still other incidents find their way to websites devoted to such reports, as the self-appointed watchdogs of corporate improprieties are always on the prowl for questionable behavior. While such possibilities could fall into the threats category of the SWOT analysis, they have at their heart a weakness for firms that fail to shore up their outstanding ethically deficient areas. Partnering with the wrong party, operating in a country with a repressive government, and even not having a qualifying corporate process for the public venting of pronouncements are all inherent weaknesses. In essence, firms, by not paying careful attention to their ethical stance, can make themselves vulnerable to such potential assaults.

Corporate Opportunities

The analysis of a firm's opportunities may include strengthening its human rights reputation with consumers, especially in industries that watchdog groups have targeted for inspection, such as clothing manufacturers in regard to maintenance of sweatshop conditions. Companies that are involved with oil and mineral extraction or the potential chemical polluting of the environment might be wise to consider public dissemination indicating that they are taking a lead from the bad publicity fallout of the *Exxon Valdez* incident. In 1989, an ExxonMobil oil tanker making its way to California ran aground and began spilling oil, with significant quantities of its cargo of 1.26 million barrels entering the environment. Following the incident and the inability to contain the widespread devastation, the company took a defensive position. Its chairman, Lawrence

Rawl, was very suspicious of the media and reacted accordingly by shunning interviews and responding he had no time for that kind of thing. The company simply provided no evidence that they cared about what happened, appearing quite indifferent to the environmental destruction. The immediate consequence of their response—beyond the financial cleanup repercussions and fines of over $5 billion—was a loss of market share, slipping from the largest to the third-largest oil company in the world. Even more important was the damage to their reputation that, although hard to quantify, resulted in the symbolic entrance into the language of the name *Exxon Valdez* as a synonym for corporate arrogance and massive environmental damage. Even when Rawl decided to do a television interview and was asked about the plans of his company to explain their cleanup activities and other strategic planning moves to prevent further catastrophes, he responded that such areas of responsibility were not in the purview of the chairman. The company lost an opportunity to be socially reactive and morally proactive in responding to the crisis and perhaps take an industry leadership position that might have resulted in a strategic competitive advantage in the mind of consumers. The event was a wake-up signal for the general public as it provided the first major skirmish in the battle between environmentalists and MNCs that still exists today. The United Nations (UN) Global Compact, international labor accords, or the slew of other recognized charters on such issues, including environmental matters as well as industry-specific proclamations, are proactive opportunistic imperatives for firms to consider. Being perceived as a caretaker of the community is a value-added benefit to companies that raise their positive perceptions across a wide group of stakeholders. It can be a definitive opportunity that all global firms might wish to pursue.

Corporate Threats

The threat of an allegation of ethical impropriety or poor moral judgment is a reality for many global companies in today's politically correct society. The National Labor Committee (NLC), a public watchdog and advocacy organization, is continuously on patrol for misconduct in regard to worker rights. One of their unique methods is to focus on celebrities who license their well-known names to further the marketing recognition of various consumer goods as such a technique results in faster public awareness. In 1996, the NLC publicized the sweatshop conditions of contracted Honduran women working on the clothing line of television personality Kathie Lee Gifford. The negative publicity generated by the extensive news coverage damaged the sales of the designer collection. It also severely injured Ms. Gifford's public persona and overshadowed her repeated statements that she personally had nothing to do with the offensive actions taken by the unknown suppliers of her licensed partners.

In December 2004, the NLC resurfaced with yet another attack on celebrities, targeting the Olsen sisters, Mary-Kate and Ashley. The activist group claimed they failed to qualify their position for supporting paid maternity leaves for Bangladeshi working women manufacturing their trademarked line for the Walmart retail chain. Failing to respond to NLC's request that the twins said they never received, they were issued a statement noting their vendors comply with rigorous safety and health standards. This pronouncement did not allay organized protests adjacent to the university the sisters attended in New York. While this incident was reported in a few publications that deal with the lives of Hollywood personalities, it does not seem to have adversely affected the large consumer adolescent following that purchases the products these two celebrities endorse. The ability, however, of activist groups to force commentary on ethical practices, even without allegations of deliberate worker injury, is a specter hanging over all commercial endeavors. It potentially cannot only affect individuals and their manufacturing operations but also reach up and into the channels of trade that support such endeavors, tarnishing any association with a company.

The potential threat at any time from any avenue of concern of an accusation of human rights infringement or environmental damage is the ethical sword of Damocles that menacingly hangs over the head of all commercial entities. It is, however, a more pronounced concern for global corporations as their worldwide exposure brings them into contact with such possibilities on a daily operational basis. The threat can strike over any issue, be it of a concrete nature or a mere desire to reaffirm a human rights position.

Porter's Five Forces Infused with Ethical Considerations

Strategic analytical programs like Porter's Five Forces may also require an update to include an ethical element.

To evaluate the state of competition in an industry and the ultimate profit potential in terms of return on invested capital, managers use the collective strength of five forces as a diagnostic tool. The five forces are the bargaining power of (a) suppliers and (b) buyers; the threat of (c) potential entrants and (d) substitute products; and the (e) rivalry among existing firms.[13]

Supplier strength in an industry may be affected by adherence to human rights matters. A consolidation or narrowing may take place with those being anointed with a factory-inspection verification shrinking the pool of potential suppliers in an industry adding to their bargaining strength in the industry. The additional criteria used to evaluate the competencies of suppliers may be some type of certification process proving that they comply with a set of universally established standards in respect to their treatment of the labor force. Those not able or willing to pass such a test may fall out of the supplier pool for selected industries.

Final consumers may become more conscious of the social responsibility and moral obligations of available intermediary trade merchants that deal in products or services the industry offers. Such attitude may lessen the number perceived as sensitive to proper ethical practices, thereby increasing buyer power in the industry. Pressure may be exerted by general consumers on their retailers to become purveyors of merchandise that carries a label noting their manufacturer observes good ethical practices. Stores that have such a policy may be more limited than ones that do not, creating a consolidation in retail channels of trade. A more limited segmentation of retailers for the industry to sell to may emerge.

New entrants to a particular industry may find that additional capital is needed to offset costs associated with making sure their startup factories comply with more stringent and up-to-date social initiatives. Industry newcomers may find that existing members have been able to gain a competitive advantage and strong current positioning via economies of scale due to previous weak enforcement of human rights violations. Those firms wishing to enter the industry may face closer examination of their ethical principles than those currently operating in them. In the end, such concerns may limit the threat of new entrants and consolidate power in existing industry participants.

The search for substitutes might intensify, as it is fueled by the consuming public's need to move away from morally tainted industries and the products they produce. Those that are perceived as potentially harmful to the environment, such as logging industries in the rainforests or woodlands, strip mining operations that devastate the surrounding land, or chemical plants that pollute the atmosphere, may find their products susceptible to consumers switching to more environmentally friendly substitutes.

Rivalries in selected industries may also become more intense as firms position themselves with a stronger, pronounced ethical code of conduct, each trying to prove to the public their attention to such matters. Competition may differentiate itself not by product attributes or low cost but by the added value of being ethical, proactive, or at least sensitive to such issues.

Country Scanning with an Ethical Infusion

Global environmental scanning following the adoption of a corporate strategic plan could require omission of countries whose human rights records are questioned. Nations that are signatories to Organisation for Economic Co-operation and Development (OECD) guidelines have signified their intention to abide by principles to govern multinational operations in their territory. Adherence to such principles of acceptable conduct may create a more moral environment for global corporations to house themselves within.

The energy-extraction industry, which must often partner with national governments in the exploration of resources, has come under investigation for joint venturing with repressive and corrupt administrations. An often-cited example is the regime of Equatorial Guinea, wherein the ruling family has supposedly enriched themselves at the expense of the human rights of their citizens vis-à-vis deals with ExxonMobil and other global oil firms. Reports from this country indicate that the government has granted these companies what amounts to eminent-domain rights over valued oil resource lands. Such governmental fiat has allowed these firms to displace local tribes without compensation and even treat the labor extracted from these areas as virtual slaves. Equally disturbing, and the subject of in-depth examination due to a very publicized court case, were the allegations leveled against Unocal. It involved the firm's compliance in the mistreatment of workers and their forced labor in the construction of an oil pipeline as an investment partner with the Myanmar government. In 1996, a U.S. civil court action was brought under the Alien Tort Claims Act (ATCA) of 1789 by local citizens, with the prime allegation against Unocal citing they not only were aware of such human rights violations by the government but also directly benefited from them. The suit alleged that Unocal turned a blind eye to atrocities (rape, murder, forced labor, and wholesale destruction of villages) committed by military forces protecting the construction of the company's $1.2 billion gas pipeline across the country.

Possibly prompted by the continuing lawsuit and the resultant publicity, the company announced in 2003 the adoption of new corporate principles covering fundamental rights of workers, including freedom from discrimination in employment, elimination of child labor, freedom of association, and collective bargaining by employees. The move to such reforms was welcomed by Amalgamated Bank, a key investor in Unocal and prime sponsor of the investor lead resolution. Amalgamated itself, even in its passive role of investor, had come under public criticism for the questionable activities of a company they merely invested in. Unocal continued to deny any allegations of complicity in the longstanding legal action, citing that the alleged atrocities, if true, were in fact carried out by their quasi-governmental partner and not Unocal. They, nonetheless, reached an agreement in principle to settle the matter in December 1993. Concluded a year later, Unocal agreed to pay compensation to the villagers affected while also funding general education and living condition improvements. It should be further noted that although the U.S. government banned corporate involvement by American firms in Myanmar in 1997, Unocal continues to operate in the country via a waiver provision that excluded contracts predating the enactment of the prohibition. Unocal has weathered strong public criticism for continuing involvement with this country's repressive regime that their initial strategy in the early 90s never anticipated or planned for.

It is noteworthy to appreciate that the obscure 1789 ATCA grants federal jurisdiction over suits alleging commission of a tort on an alien. A tort is a wrongful act that results in injury to another person, their property, or their reputation and for which the injured party is entitled to compensation. The act does not speak of human rights violations but actions brought under its jurisdictional provision have been painted with such emotionally charged rhetoric. The act was originally enacted to afford legal protection for American ship owners against marauding pirates. It has surfaced, however, as a modern-day instrument to increase corporate accountability for international operations, especially with respect to foreign-citizen grievances when global firms partner or act with foreign national governments in a commercial endeavor. The actual act is produced here.

Alien Tort Claims Act (ATCA)

928 U.S. Code, Chapter 85, Sec. 13500
Adopted in 1789 as part of the original Judiciary Act
Sec. 1350—Alien's action for tort

The district courts shall have original jurisdiction of any civil action by an alien for tort only, committed in violation of the law of nations or a treaty of the United States.

The Torture Victim Protection Act of 1991 (H.R. 2092/Public Law No. 102-256) expanded the historic ATCA by defining the elements of the actual damage caused by the alleged actions of responsible parties. The *actionable offenses* are "civil action[s] for recovery of damages [result] from an individual who engages in torture or extrajudicial killing." The definition of an *individual* is one "who, under actual or apparent authority, or color of law, of any nation" subjects another to such aforementioned treatment. It qualified the relative standings of the parties involved and the tort committed.

The risk of being attacked for even historic unethical indulgences seems like a constant threat lurking in the shadows for multinational companies. *The New York Times* reported on November 27, 2003, that the Ford Motor Company was named in a criminal complaint accusing the automaker of aiding in the suppression and torture of workers during Argentina's *Dirty War* from 1976 to 1983. Their subsidiary is said to have allowed the government to set up a detention center on factory grounds and allowed nearly two dozen workers to be rounded up and kidnapped off their premises. Ford was further charged with supporting the military by producing trucks and vehicles to round up dissidents and carry them off to prison and presumed murder. General Motors and Daimler came under a similar allegation for their relationship with the historic apartheid South African government and their supply of vehicles to the repressive regime in the 1970s. It seems that ethical conduct does not have a public statute of limitations.

Mobil Oil found itself the target of a similar allegation to the one posed to Ford Motor Company. Investigative reports have questioned the company's knowledge, and perhaps tacit complicity, in regards to actions of the Indonesian army and other government-sponsored human rights abuses that allegedly took place in proximity to their joint ventured (35 percent ownership) operations with the state-owned monopoly Pertamina. Reports indicated that a processing plant was used as a torture site and company machinery was used to dig graves for Muslim separatist guerillas executed by the military.

A case in Switzerland was recently allowed to proceed wherein the litigants claimed that IBM helped the Nazis 68 years ago to commit genocide by providing them with punch card machines that enabled the methodical tracking and killing of Gypsies. A similar allegation against IBM has also surfaced in South Africa regarding the company's information-processing systems being used to enforce historic governmental apartheid policies. Caterpillar, a supplier of specialty armored bulldozers to Israel, has been sued by relatives of an American activist killed during military operations directed at the demolishing of Palestinian homes using such machines. The legal action alleges that the firm knew the purpose of the specially constructed equipment and its potential danger to individuals in the proximity of their use. A separate suit was brought in Israel against the state and military segments for the actual incident, which they defend as an accident. The company received criticism over the sale, with UN human rights official Jean Ziegler expressing "deep concern" in a letter sent to Caterpillar chief executive officer (CEO) Jim

Owens. Activist groups have claimed the action was in direct contravention of the firm's corporate responsibility policy. Given the company's wide global revenue stream and the growing percentage coming from many developing nations, such adverse publicity directed at their ethical conduct may have prompted Caterpillar to state on its website that it "shares the world's concern over the Middle East and certainly have compassion for those affected by political strife." Further comments by the company, and a defense used by other firms alleged to have indirectly assisted questionable governmental actions, is that they have neither the legal rights nor the means to police individual use of their equipment once sold. They argue that such alleged legal responsibility would be equivalent to indicting a car manufacture as a criminal accomplice or placing civil liability on them for a purchaser's use in a robbery getaway or vehicular death, standards that have not yet been applied in case precedents to date. The court of public opinion, however, may still view such actions as repugnant and immoral.

While civil suits of this nature may be troublesome, the initial strategic decision to place the firm in the middle of an emotionally charged global issue with moral overtones is a matter that companies like Caterpillar might have considered in their earlier stages of decision making. If ethical considerations were a factor placed in the ongoing strategic-planning evaluation process, perhaps the incidents encountered by these global companies might have been avoided.

In March 2005, a federal judge dismissed a lawsuit brought against U.S. chemical companies, including firms such as Dow Chemical and Monsanto, accusing them of participating in war crimes during the Vietnam War. The plaintiffs (the suit was brought on behalf of millions of Vietnamese) alleged that the companies' supply to the American government of the defoliant Agent Orange resulted in illness, birth defects, and deformities of those innocent civilians exposed to the poisonous substance. Even the supply of a product via a sales transaction with one's own domestic government has legal consequences that flow from ethical strategic decisions that may run to the heart of a company's business. Certainly both chemical firms knew of the eventual use of their supplied products.

The perception of a government as amoral with respect to its relations with its own citizens plays an important role in strategic selection of nations for entrance, as well as the choice of regime partnering for multinational firms. Guidance for multinational companies in developing a model for corporate codes to deal with repressive governments may be found in the International Council on Human Rights Policy statement. It addresses four actionable areas that may result in companies being considered as complacent in human rights abuses.

1. Directly or indirectly assist the perpetrators of human rights abuses.
2. Go into joint ventures with a government where it might be reasonably foreseen that the government, or its agencies, is likely to commit human rights abuses in carrying out its part of the agreement.
3. Benefit in any way from human rights violations.
4. Maintain silence or inaction in the face of human rights violations.

The Porter Diamond Model presents four interlinked components to determine the competitive advantage of nations contributing to the successful development and growth of selective industries in their respective countries.[14] One of the criteria is factor endowment, a nation's position to offer human, physical, knowledge, and capital resources as well as infrastructure systems. A prime factor of production is the ability to offer an effective and efficient labor force necessary to compete in a given industry. Beyond evaluating quality of workmanship, inherent skill, and labor cost, the element of ethical treatment of workers may be a required adjunct to such investigated determinants. The direct investment by U.S. firms in foreign manufacturing sites has increased in the last 20 years, while subcontracting work abroad, a difficult figure to quantify, has most certainly expanded at an amazing rate. The large emerging nations of China, Indonesia, and Malaysia and even small countries like the Mariana Islands, as well as the developing markets of Singapore, South Korea, and Taiwan have benefited from offshore production. But activist groups like the NLC periodically issue reports on conditions in factories in such countries, noting the use of girls in the age group of 17 and below (sometimes as young as 10 to 14) and 25 being pressed to work 60 to 90 hours per week for less than $0.20 per hour. They are denied normal bathroom and work breaks, placed in overcrowded mandatory dormitories, and fed a poor diet they are required to pay for, while operating unsafe machinery.

Incidents of sexual harassment and even rape by managerial personnel have also been alleged. Many watch-dog groups have periodically accused well-known U.S. clothing designer labels and retailers of utilizing such facilities via subcontractors, forcing companies to defend their knowledge of and compliance with such alarming conditions. Such exposure is forcing more and more firms to adapt active codes of conduct with verification procedures when engaging the indigenous workforce. Armed with a workable code to begin with, many companies might have altered their strategic plans, revised tactical decisions, and alleviated these situations.

Porter also asserts a "final value"—that of government as an improvement to or detraction of national competitive advantage. Regime policies toward the workforce, be they citizens or imported aliens, may influence the managerial decision to enter a country on an foreign direct investment (FDI) or joint-venture basis as well as with third-party contractual manufacturing.

Just operating in a country that oppresses the freedom of speech can produce an ethical dilemma down the road. The 2006 entrance decision by Google into China was made in full acknowledgment of existing state censorship laws, enacted under the realm of national security, that would require its domestic search engine to purge specific subjects and not offer user access to banned topics. Citing such requirements, as well as allegations of cyber espionage resulting in the infiltrations of Gmail (Google's e-mail service) accounts of human rights dissidents, Google announced in January 2010 that it was considering halting its cooperation with Chinese governmental Internet censorship and effectively closing down its operations. Varying estimates place the current value of its Chinese operations between $300 million and $600 million, a small percentage of the firm's approximately $22 billion in worldwide revenue. In four years, the company was able to achieve a one-third share of China's 340 million web users, with the local firm Baidu holding the majority of the market.

While now been praised for taking a higher moral ground and reemphasizing their nearly evaporated ethical standards, Google is attempting to repair its image, which was tainted by being a complacent partner to Chinese autocratic, repressive policies in respect to curtailing civil rights and civil liberties. This belated realization may be a reaction to worldwide watchers, as policy and practices in one market in the era of globalization influence the way consumers, advocacy groups, and governments view companies as favorable or unfavorable in other markets. Google knew full well the governmental prerequired operational conditions, but initial rhetoric indicated that even a government-filtered search engine was better than none at all. Perhaps this was a rationalized ethical position, but at some point management had to be aware that their decision would be critically challenged. Knowing the host country's political environment and using it to evaluate the extent of ethically based considerations inherent in a targeted entry market requires that such a component be placed in the strategic decision-making process on par with other valued qualitative and quantitative measurement variables. Whether there exist restrictions on human rights and free speech would be a core issue to a global information delivery system such as Google. If such functional promise is compromised in one country, the value of its global service is diminished, with its perception as providing quality, reputable performance worldwide called into question. Not considering this underlying issue in its global strategic plans has resulted in a current ethical dilemma for Google. It impacts its future revenue stream in China, the unrecoverable loss of historic investment assets in the country, as well as potential damage to its reputation and image in other global markets, which can have negative financial implications attached to it.

Such critical decision making may require the introduction of a strategically induced ethical quotient beyond the traditional risk factors of governmental intervention, social unrest or disorder, and expropriation, as defined and qualified by public opinion of a government. An investigation of global consumer perceptions as regards the key markets that a company plans to associate itself with, no matter what the extent or form such contact takes, may come into play in the strategic decision-making construction.

Guarding Reputations in Volatile Arenas

Associate with men of good quality, if you esteem your own reputation; for it is better to be alone than in bad company.
  —George Washington, U.S. president and statesman

The reputation of a company takes years to build and is an intricate part of a firm's marketing effort to induce the buying public to support its products and services. Trademarks have been measured as to their proprietary value in surveys of the top 100 brand names in the world by *BusinessWeek* magazine and the annual reports they have published for last nine years.

Corporate names, on the other hand, are often given an intangible assessment known as goodwill as referenced in accounting terminology in takeover transactions—one company buying out the other. Essentially, goodwill is reputation, an estimation of the esteem attributed by the public to a company. It is made up of many contributory factors. Objectively it can be classified as to the quality of products and services offered, cost-price benefits as perceived by consumers, and other tangible values such as being a leader in technology. Subjectively one's reputation is also tied to meritorious conduct that produces favorable repute as judged by the general public. Damage to the objective criteria can be corrected; for example, a bad product is pulled from the marketplace and refunds are offered. The injury to subjective criteria is more difficult to reverse as it destroys years of construction as opposed to reacting to a singular event. In the subjective arena affecting reputation, the most volatile element is the potential allegation of human rights violations. An allegation of ethical misconduct where people are concerned strikes a strong emotional chord. When such charges are leveled at a company within the context of a specific statute like the ATCA, public sensitivity is increased because personal injury is alleged and the conduct is perceived as bordering on a criminal act even though the act allows only for civil action. The global resource-extraction industry tends to be most vulnerable as their operational activities, in order to accomplish their strategic goals, must be partnered with foreign governments in order to secure such rights. As earlier noted, many companies have been accused of being complicit in human rights violations because of their commercial relationships with not only repressive governments but also the quasi-military actions of nations.

Paul Tarr, writing in *Business Ethics* magazine,[15] proposes a set of guidelines based on a case authored by Gare A. Smith exemplifying an approach taken by BP in the operation of a gas pipeline project known as Baku-Tbilisi-Ceyhan to proactively shield firms from charges under the ATCA. He sets out seven practical steps to combat charges of human rights violation and to protect a firm's valuable reputation. A summary of his points with explanatory comment follows:

1. *Establish governing standards.* At the outset companies are prompted to work with the host government and major stakeholders to erect governing standards for projects—including mechanisms for addressing human rights and environmental concerns—that not only encompass local laws but also inject global standards that go beyond domestic regulatory requirements. Firms have a marked tendency to initially consider the commercial aspects of the association, but such new direction places ethical issues in the strategic forefront of negotiations.

2. *Engage key stakeholders.* Extend an invitation for interested parties such as NGOs, community organizations, and all associates, including third-party contractors, supply-chain participants, and institutions financing the project to be consulted in the process. Such extended contacts allow firms to see broader issues and, if handled properly, could alleviate criticisms from such groups in the future.

3. *Be transparent.* Periodically volunteer updates with a wide dissemination via a website devoted to project news. Provide such information early in the project development and throughout the process, using disclosure as a shield against potential problems.

4. *Create supplemental legal frameworks.* As legal systems in developing countries are often not sophisticated nor do they conform to the regulatory laws of advanced nations, create a supplementary set of technical, legal, and fiscal policies to govern the specific project that acts as an ancillary agreement between the parties as to corresponding rights and obligations. This is the next step to point 1.

5. *Set security guidelines.* The parties should commit to the Voluntary Principles on Security and Human Rights, a compact negotiated by the U.S. and UK governments and several global oil companies in 2000. This document defines corporate *aiding and abetting of* violations by state security forces while also setting out the proper conduct expected from security personnel.

6. *Establish monitoring.* Firms should create independent verification committees, with outside members, to monitor compliance with the

principles set forth in prior points and hear grievances in connection with the project. Again, an expansion of interested parties to oversee operations could deflect the appearance of wrongdoing by a firm and add credence to the transparency factor, point 3.

7. *Create philanthropic programs.* Companies should contribute to local communities impacted by the project as part of a social responsibility program. Such efforts should consist of stimulus for economic opportunities for local business along with other charitable benefits that touch the social, health, and educational needs of the region's citizens. In essence, a good neighbor policy that incorporates the policies of NGOs and other recognized international developmental agencies should be implemented.

While these seven steps were targeted to improve and sustain the reputations of the global extraction industry partnering with governments, specifically oil and gas companies, the guidance offered is a valuable tool for all firms to consider.

Foreign National Labor Practices

The cost of a thing is the amount of what I call life which is required to be exchanged for it, immediately or in the long run.
—Henry David Thoreau, American writer

The fundamental rights of [humanity] are... the right of freedom of labor.
—Albert Schweitzer, global humanitarian

By their action or inaction, nations that condone mistreatment of labor and permit sweatshop conditions to exist or foster debt bondage of a foreign workforce could find themselves on the list of reprehensible countries. For instance, Taiwan by law allows factories to charge foreign workers for room and board with little or no inspection of how the law is applied to wage deduction. South Korea allows foreign workers to be considered trainees and therefore exempt from minimum-wage and overtime-pay guidelines. Chinese domestic migrant citizen workers are forced to surrender their prized travel documents permitting them to move from their residential province to that of employment to their employers. The result is to restrict their movement in the provinces they work in and literally force them to be confined to factory compounds.

Countries like Myanmar and others accused of government-sponsored forced-labor conditions could be boycotted by multinational firms that do not wish to run the risk of public condemnation. Nations may find that their attractiveness as low-cost producing centers or even those containing an abundance of the positive attributes of Porter's Diamond Model in the global value chain may have their destinations as a prime location resource for global firms diminished by a failure to assure human rights protection within their borders.

The Ethical Push from Other Sources

Civilization can only revive when there shall come in being a number of individuals a new tone of mind, independent of the prevalent one among the crowds, and in opposition to it—a tone of mind which will gradually win influence over the collective one, and in the end determine its character.

—Albert Schweitzer, global humanitarian

The Influence of NGOs

NGOs are composed of nonprofit organizations whose prime agenda is social change via political influence. They provide social and humanitarian service in highly politicized cross-national contexts and are an emerging modern force in policing global moral standards. These organizations are composed of individuals and donors committed to the promotion of a particular (set of) issue(s) through advocacy work or through operational activities whereby services are delivered. To the public at large they are seen as watchdog groups that bring attention to questionable or unethical practices of global commercial entities, celebrities who trademark their names on products, and repressive governments. Such groups have emerged from a variety of avenues. Traditional primary organizations whose names are publicly recognized like the International Red Cross tend to operate in the open with a consistent agenda of humanitarian concern. Splinter groups like the bands of protesting advocates of the antiglobalization movement that disrupted the 1999 Seattle World Trade Organization meetings often arise against the backdrop of emotional awareness.

Crossbreed organizations like Save the Children and CARE mix their charitable efforts with public dissemination of their causes. Labor groups such as the NLC target commercial misconduct of the world's workforce and promote employee rights. Quasi-NGOs composed of industry companies in an alliance network aim to pool resources to offer education and instructional guidance in dealing with similar social issues around the world.

From whatever background these NGOs materialize, they have begun to develop as third players in the global socioeconomic system along with national governments and multinational enterprises. Beyond their introduction on the world stage containing a separate and pronounced vision to promote social change, they are also seen as mediators between business interests and authoritative governmental direction. Their emerging influence as new actors in the global drama has prompted the worldwide consuming audience to place a greater emphasis on their pronouncements, as they are viewed as having a bit more accountability and legitimacy than their corresponding rivals whose agendas are suspect. Their ability to sway public opinion and draw greater attention to global human rights issues and environmental concerns is a strong reason for commercial institutions to pay attention to them. Companies would be wise to consider the effect of NGOs on their strategic decisional plans, as the specter of their presence will not diminish in the future. Firms might even find it valuable to take some direction from their codes of conduct. When it comes to globally recognized NGOs, none is more widely known and respected as a socially responsible organization, primarily cited for humanitarian efforts in the face of disaster relief, than the International Red Cross and Red Crescent Movement. The introduction to their own code of conduct recognizes that agencies, whether experienced or newly-created, can make mistakes, be misguided and sometimes deliberately misuse the trust placed on them and as such they are susceptible to internal and external pressures. Given such a consideration, these venerable organizations encourage other NGOs around the world to consider abiding by their published code of socially responsible conduct. Their guiding principles may serve as a good reference guide that could assist many global commercial firms in the construction of the underlying tenets that their own codes of conduct should contain. Although their code contains 10 operating principle commitments customized to their special activities, those pertaining to universal commercial interests have been extracted and are presented in the following list.

1. Aid is given regardless of race, creed, or nationality of the recipients and without adverse distinction of any kind. Aid priorities are calculated on the basis of need alone.
2. Aid will not be used to further a particular political or religious standpoint.
3. We shall endeavor not to act as instruments of governmental foreign policy.
4. We shall respect culture and custom.
5. Ways shall be found to involve program beneficiaries in the management of relief aid.
6. We hold ourselves accountable to both those we seek to assist and those from whom we accept resources.
7. In our information, publicity, and advertising activities, we shall recognize disaster victims as dignified human beings, not hopeless objects.

Growing Ethical Awareness from Additional Avenues

A special advertising section in *Fortune* magazine headlined "Corporate America's Social Conscience"[16] devoted space, normally used to promote products, services, and government incentive programs, to issue a suggestion to executives to develop "a list of commandments imbedded into the corporate mission statement that guides an organization down a moral path so it can rise to the challenges of today's global economy." The mere fact that the subject of ethics is directed to such a wide dissemination level is a testament to the subject's importance.

A key quotation as printed in the advertisement from Andrew Savitz, a partner in PricewaterhouseCoopers, seems to sum it up: "They [U.S.

companies] realize that just one insult to their reputation can cause significant damage to their business." The linkage of acceptable morality to commercial success by admonishing firms to consider ethical behavior in the global strategic planning process has begun. It is also interesting to note that a 2005 television commercial created a new corporate title, that of chief courage officer admonishing firms to appoint a corporate moral administrator who dares to steer companies in an ethical direction. Both advertisements may be indicative of a trend to place the subject of proper conduct by commercial entities via their strategies and tactical actions in the public light.

Perhaps the precursor to such integration of ethics and strategy is the inclusion of a viable policy embedded in a firm's mission statement. A corporate vision that recognizes to some degree the organization's social responsibility across their operational environment and relationships with all stakeholders may serve as a compass to help navigate ethical global decision making. Providing a beacon of morality, the signal sent by the corporate mission statement may light the way for the company ship. It helps to set and adjust the firm's strategic sails and makes sure they move the firm in an acceptable ethical direction.

While it may be hard to extract the specific quantitative value in terms of sales loss or gain provisioned on perception of the ethical standards of a company, surveys have shown that good corporate citizenship is on the mind of American consumers. Ranked on issues of importance of potential buyers of products and users of company services, environmental pollution and human rights were numbered 1 and 4, respectively. Consumer response indicated that in the past, corporate citizenship was seen as something unique, a differentiator for business and their brands. Increasingly, however, the public is viewing corporate citizenship as an expectation, and companies are seeing it as an opportunity, demonstrating that doing good is a smart, pragmatic business strategy for doing well.

The Trust and Transparency Factor

As noted earlier, for nine years *Business Week* magazine has published a survey of the "100 Best Global Brands," a list prepared by Interbrands to determine brand value, a key corporate asset.[17] This 2009 collateral title to the ranking of companies is titled "The Great Trust Offensive," as such consideration describes a new prime criteria customers use in evaluating their perception and hence support of brand names. Of the top 10 brands, eight are American, with one each from Finland and Japan. Coca-Cola leads the pack, a position the company has occupied for many years, followed by IBM, Microsoft, GE, and Nokia.

The term *trust* is difficult to define, and in fact the *Business Week* article itself does not specify its meaning. It seems to be made up of a number of contributing elements. But what is most evident is that consumers have a basic distrust of business organizations as a whole. Such a feeling may be a subset of a general public distrust of all institutions, whether governmental, religious, or commercial—an idea that has been circulating in the late 2000s. The article cited a phone survey conducted over the summer of 2009 by the Edelman public relations firm, showing that 44 percent of Americans trusted business, as opposed to 58 percent in the fall of 2007.

The trust factor is, however, a meaningful component, says Larry Light, CEO of brand consultancy Areature, as it "drives profit margins and share price."[18] In the words of Mary Dillon, global chief marketing officer of McDonald's (number 6 on the list and up from number 8 last year), "Trust and transparency [are] more important to us than ever."[19] It seems that in the latest economic crisis consumers, the ultimate judge of company behavior, have placed blame not only on the financial sector but also on business in general. They are distrustful of businesses' motivational intent.

Although not specifically singled out in the article, consumers seem to be saying that proper ethical conduct is what they expect from the companies behind the leading brands, that companies should be open and honest in all their dealings. Their sales and marketing efforts should not be misleading but provide true consumer benefits; their financial integrity should not damage their stakeholders and their far-flung global activities should take into account environmental concerns of the planet—these are just a few of the areas consumers are concerned with. In essence, there is an underlying desire by the public for firms to operate with a moral conscience in order to achieve and sustain brand recognition. A firm's reputation can easily be tarnished by inappropriate or bad behavior or even by the perception that the firm hasn't been forthright (the transparency factor) in responding to allegations of misconduct.

What we are seeing is an ethical imperative injected into the consumer purchasing decision. While price and quality, innovation, and customer support are important parts of the consumer motivational puzzle, a new piece has been added. Companies would be wise to heed this often overlooked part and incorporate it in the strategic planning process.

A Specter of Change: Potential Employee Inquiries

Even potential managers, the future constituency of corporations, have morality on their minds. In a survey of "The Best B-Schools," the importance of incorporating ethics in MBA (master of business administration) programs was one of the key criteria in the rating system of the top business programs[20] and this measurement index continues today. Other studies polling graduating students and those seeking better employment situations have increasingly cited the desire to seek firms that have good track records with respect to ethical conduct. Kelly Services Inc., a firm devoted to the global placement of employees, in a survey released in October 2009,[21] concluded that firms benefit in attracting top talent by the perception of their ethical and social responsibility actions by potential candidates. The extensive workforce survey covered 100,000 people in 34 countries with 90 percent of respondents in the study saying they would be more likely to work for an organization they viewed as acting ethically and in a socially responsible manner. The survey further reported that 50 percent of those in the 18 to 65 age bracket, presumably coming from differing cultural, ethnic, and national backgrounds, would even forgo a pay increase or a promotion to work for a company that possessed a good reputation in the communities in which it operated.

Rushworth M. Kidder, president and chair of the Institute for Global Ethics, outlined a series of questions that potential interviewees could use to distinguish those firms that really practice ethics from those that have the external trappings but not the internal substance. His article[22] came on the heels of Martha Stewart's conviction for stock-trading violations, the Marsh & McLennan accusation of unethical conduct, Citigroup setting aside $5.2 billion to cover costs arising from its alleged role in numerous questionable deals, and the Enron financial scandal—a time when public opinion of executives and the commercial sector was negative. Kidder makes two assumptions in putting forth a path of inquiry to uncover the real inner workings of corporate ethical systems. First, potential employees are so deeply concerned with the issue that they turn the proverbial tables on the interviewer and in essence interview the company. He reasons that new personnel in a firm have a vested interest in joining companies with a good ethical track record as morally careless CEOs could be "lugged off to jail," thereby damaging one's career due to exposure to "unethical subcultures" or placing one's retirement in jeopardy due to being caught up in a "vortex of scandal and bankruptcy." He places a measurable value on the inquiries, a point many interviewees may not consider, but fails to stress that individual distress upon being involved or associated with unethical practices may also come into play—the personal factor. Second, he assumes one is interviewing with a firm that already has in place a code of conduct, an ethics office, or a designated department to oversee stated principles, as well as a large international operation across which ethical conduct is required to be enforced. Kidder avoids commenting on the fact that if no such programming exists to begin with, this may be an indication of the firm's ethical positioning, hence it might be one to be avoided or questioned as to why it doesn't exist.

Kidder's five questions are rated in order of their intricacy and the required density to answer, and as such offer a good insight into how firms really approach the matter. His initial inquiry generally gauges the surface issues that permeate the organization and exert control over its basic activities. His follow-up gets more specific: He asks if their personnel see their code principles as a general statement of intent or if actual compliance enforced. The next question is a bit more philosophical as it tries to determine how diversity in the world affects code language. Is it based on home-country values that are then projected on the world (ethical imperialism) or does it take into account differences (cultural relativism), the *when in Rome* approach? An example of an individual's corporate loyalty via a lie versus truth telling to an associate about potential company downsizing that affects him is used to illustrate reaction to a moral dilemma in the framing of the fourth question. The final inquiry deals with whistle-blowing policy, questioning company policy that while morally correct may also be damaging to the firm.

One may agree with the areas covered by the Kidder model or may choose to create their own line of ethical inquiry when being interviewed.

Either way, the concept of integrating ethical content alongside other employment concerns at the outset of employment seems like a new and valid consideration that may begin to impact the subject of ethics as practiced by MNCs.

Historically, it was normally in the purview of the employer to query candidates on their values and moral stance so that honest employees would be hired. Today, the interview wheel has rotated 180 degrees, with the prospective entrant raising such issues of the company. Such reversal of the question-and-answer interview session may be attributable to changes in general public opinion.

Golin/Harris International, a public relations firm providing professional counsel and strategic communications programs to clients around the world, is a leader in both reflecting and formulating the attitudes and outlooks of the public at large. Their vision for global firms is that good deeds are in fact good business. As such they take a social marketing approach, advising their clients of the value of positive social action to build trust relationships with their stakeholders. In a number of surveys, the importance of a firm's public persona in regard to the perception by consumers of their positive communal social actions is well indicated. Many statistics indicate that a majority of Americans were inclined to begin or enlarge their relationships with companies practicing good social citizenship, an increasing trend in the past years. A large number of consumers feel that corporate citizenship, led by such indicators as environmental pollution, conservation of resources, and enforcement of equal human rights, were instrumental in establishing a trust relationship with commercial entities, a prime motivator of the patronage they afforded them.

The reputation of a company in its international dealings is important. How stakeholders view the ethical activities and operational decisions of firms has a direct bearing on image perception, which in turn translates to relationship building, a necessary ingredient in a successful enterprise.

Ethics: The Impetus Toward Lawful Regulations

The old saying *there ought to be a law*, heard when people perceive an ethical injustice committed against them, may never have been truer than with the enactment of the U.S. Sarbanes–Oxley Act. The outrage within the investment community and general shareholding public of the breach of fiduciary duty by executives at a number of large U.S. companies swept the country like a firestorm and pushed Congress into immediate legislation. The climate of ethical indifference, as exemplified by the outright misleading financial statements issued by top managers at firms like Enron and WorldCom, grabbed the attention of commercial institutions both in America and abroad. It again illustrated what many critics of business have long proclaimed: Corporations are led by individuals with suspect moral standards; a point noted earlier in the text as regards the ancient trading or merchant class. On the other hand, such events and the resulting public pressure, which in this case resulted in a new regulation, heightened civic awareness, especially in the United States, of the ethical conduct of corporations. Some observers have commented that these scandals of executive office improprieties are an American phenomenon, as is the obsession with ethical conduct in the commercial sector no less than the political arena. Citizens of foreign countries with longer histories than the United States seem to be more accepting of such conditions, discounting such behavior as part of the process. They are not outraged to the extent American culture exhibits and accuse Americans as being a bit too self-righteous. Testing such theory might make for an interesting investigation. Given, however, the economic influence of U.S. multinational enterprises on the global market (they dominate the Fortune 500's largest world companies) and the fact that the American marketplace is still the world's largest, appreciating the current environment of the U.S. community is appropriate even for offshore firms that compete with U.S. firms either overseas or in the U.S. domestic arena. Knowing the ethical baggage that may accompany American firms abroad or appreciating the climate in which American consumers view commercial behavior just increases their own learning curve in regard to competitive actions and market reactions. Whether such current attentiveness as shown in the United States is a fleeting trend or evidence of a more permanent desire for firms to be ethically transparent in the future is a judgment for all global commercial entities to make. How these aforementioned examples are perceived and treated by companies around the world could affect their strategic planning, internal and external operations, and perhaps their assessment of the need for precise ethical direction—a code of conduct.

Global Branding and Social Responsibility Revisited

The enviable value of erecting a sustainable global brand is part of the overall corporate strategy of all firms in today's world of globalization. (Note earlier references to *BusinessWeek* magazine, which every year devotes a front cover and an extensive article to evaluation of the top global brands and their value to the enterprises built upon their worldwide acceptance.) Based on such a survey an article in the *Harvard Business Review*[23] found that a key criterion in the next generation of global branding is social responsibility. As reviewed by Nick Wreden for MarketingProf.com, the article shows that global consumer focus groups cite three dimensions of global brands. The first two qualities signaling quality and positive international attributes were symbolic of a worldwide cultural sharing of common product perceptions. The third, however, indicated that global consumers demand more from global brands, specifically that they represent vehicles for social responsibility, a proactive characteristic. When the companies behind these global brands fail to live up to consumer expectations in regard to ethical practices, they are deeply tarnished, as they are held to a higher standard. The article also identifies four consumer segments, or how world brands are judged. The largest segment, some 55 percent of respondents, characterized brands as "global citizens."

This label identifies global brands in terms of quality and as *guardians* of consumer heath, the *environment* and *worker rights*. When the study was evaluated to determine strategies for future global branding, two interwoven implications were offered. Both evolve around the perception of a firm as being active in local communities as socially responsible citizens to negate their image as uncaring and only interested in themselves and their profit motive. The establishment of a global brand and the resulting benefits have an ethical and social responsibility component that companies need to appreciate in their marketing strategy.

The handling of the CSR issue is itself a growing business. PR News in late 2009 published a 200-plus-page book, retailing at $399, titled a *Guide to Best Practices in Corporate Social Responsibility (Vol. 2)*.[24]

PR News' logo includes the phrase "Building the bridge between PR and the bottom line." Such pronouncement recognizes that incorporating a CSR element into the marketing mix and using it as a contextual expansion of adverting through public relations proactive activities wins friends and influences people, in the end becoming a valuable contributor to profit generation. One of the book's chapter subheadings, "Shades of Green: Integrating CSR to Improve Business Performance," well states the concept and the financial linkage. Other specific tactics are identified, such as the expanded use of traditional cause marketing and cause branding and the support of social issues to enhance reputation and brand equity. Companies are advised that by practicing good CSR by partnering with NGOs they gain added leverage with consumers. Firms have learned that cross promotions incorporating company or specific-brand advertising with social responsibility issues help sell products and services. Whether it is a direct appeal such as announcing a donation to a charitable institution with every purchase or support by sponsoring a specific social cause through their activities (e.g., a walk, a run, or an event), the coupling allows the image of a socially acceptable foundation to rub off on the business. Using pronouncements of *going green*, an axiom for protecting the environment, blankets a commercial institution with vaulted values enhancing its reputation with the general public.

Also covered is communicating during a crisis to help defray the loss of the CSR asset. Other subchapter sections include how to globalize the message, as well as how to maintain social responsibility in a social-media world. The book provides planning steps and the incorporation of strategy into the process, using sets of diagnostic decision-making tools. The publisher's preface to the book admonishes firms for being behind the eight ball and promotes consideration of a global initiative or a local outreach program, whether philanthropic or environmental. The elevation of CSR on the global horizon as a more important element in the strategic process of firms has arrived. The beneficial marriage of CSR to corporate strategy is well evidenced by *CRO* magazine acting as chief sponsor of a November 2009 case-study webinar billed as "The Seven Secrets of Brand Strengthening via NGO Partnering." The web broadcast presentation focused on leveraging environmental social responsibility leadership to strengthen reputation with customers and stakeholders. By joining with NGOs that support actions to alleviate illegal logging and trade in forestry products, a positive CSR image could be gained by companies, enhancing their competitive advantage with the consuming public—a clear reference to cause marketing and cause branding as previously noted.

What is unique about CSR is the ability of firms to orchestrate with tactical, strategic moves to effectively use it as a value-creating resource. Firms can more easily be proactive in their pursuit of a CSR label than they can with ethics. By stage managing marketing efforts to take advantage of a social responsibility issue, firms can get out in front and actively promote the CSR allegiance factor. Ethics, however, are more difficult to control as it usually takes a negative episode to bring the matter to the forefront. While having a code of conduct in place may help to defray or create a handle for managing an ethical dilemma, the process tends to be reactionary instead of proactive as with CSR matters. Ethical concerns emerge and firms need to be in a strong reactive position to confront them with the proper policies in place. But even with programs to counter allegations of ethical misconduct, constant vigilance aligned with inspection and verification must be employed; CSR cause marketing does not require these added activities. Practicing good ethics is a semipassive value producer; it is expected. However, acting unethically, even to a small perceived degree, can result in a great negative value impact.

Environmental Issues

We won't have a society if we destroy the environment.
                    —Margaret Mead, American anthropologist

If we are going to carry on growing, and we will, because no country is going to forfeit its right to economic growth, we have to find a way of doing it sustainably.
                    ——Tony Blair, UK prime minister and statesman

In *Collapse* by Jared Diamond,[25] the Pulitzer Prize–winning author explores the fundamental reasons behind the decline, collapse, and eventual disappearance of societies due to self-inflicted ecological damage resulting in ecocide. He makes a most passionate case for modern man to learn from the mistakes of his ancestors in order to preserve the earth for future generations of mankind and not just to prevent the loss of rare and exotic animal, insect, and plant species. He concludes that man has a choice and that such choice is built around ethical decision making and the moral culpability of managers of today's controlling elite, the transnational corporation. Global firms, by virtue of their sheer size, multinational reach, and influence, may well be the anointed guardians of the world's environment. No other earthly entity, national government, super transgovernmental body, or NGO has the ability or the corresponding duty to equitably consider this issue.

There is no doubt that many domestic firms in developed nations, faced with costly regulatory-compliance laws in regard to the preservation of the local environment, have fled to foreign countries to conduct their operations. Because many emerging nations have neither stringent regulatory guidelines in place nor the financial and organizational resources to police and enforce the laws designed to prevent the rape of the environment, multinational firms find them attractive offshore alternatives. Instead of eliminating the dumping of toxic chemicals in rivers and streams by carting them off to safe and approved deposit sites or spending money to retard the polluting of the atmosphere by the emission of dangerous gases, it is simply easier and more cost efficient to locate such activities in global areas where no rules are in place. In fact, it might be argued that developing countries encourage such consideration to receive the foreign investment that global firms bring with them, mortgaging future environmental damage for the interim financial rewards that such immediate FDI activities afford them.

Because many countries do not have laws in place to negate or limit damage to the environment, a fundamental question of ethics comes into play. As morality is an issue that falls outside the legal avenues of punishable conduct, how should firms act in an environmentally lawless society where they have the ability to make their own decisions on this matter? Should they take a proactive stance and import regulatory statutes from other jurisdictions? And if so, whose rules do they follow, as countries around the world have different standards? Should they follow the most restrictive or most lenient ones? Should they choose to replicate their actions under the guidelines enacted and enforced by their own home-country governments? Should they feel free to do nothing and possibly dirty the host country's environment and jeopardize the health of its citizens for the sake of lowering expenses in order to sustain a competitive advantage over industry rivals? Or should they take a neutral semiactive position, deciding to follow some basic, acceptable control methods requiring minimal expenses while passing on other, more stringent and costly capital investments? The objectivity of the right or wrong of these ethical issues may dictate the degree of responsiveness by multinationals, a gray issue and not a black-or-white criterion.

These issues are quasi-hidden ethical dilemmas because, unlike direct actions that may immediately bring harm to employees on the job, causing the arousal of public watchdog groups in the labor or general human rights arenas, the danger of such actions is not always so evident. Environmental damage may occur over such a prolonged period of time that not until actual physical illness of the neighboring inhabitants—crops, animals, or humans—is confirmed does the physical danger surface. It may take sophisticated technical equipment to detect and experts to verify the destructive effects of an environmental injury and then link them to the serious illness they might have initially engineered.

One of the key elements behind such ethical questions may be the degree of knowledge and therefore resultant responsibility that multinationals may possess. If a company has reasonable knowledge that their production or manufacturing processes use or emit toxic chemicals commonly considered dangerous to the health and well-being of those potentially coming into contact with such substances, is there a predetermined duty to act responsibly and take appropriate actions to minimize or eliminate such potential damage? This simple test of public accountability might cause companies to take the proper ethical stand and institute the required internal and external actions. Certainly, among many industries such facts are easily recognizable, and these entities should be held to a higher standard of ethical behavior that should be inherent in the development of their global strategic planning operations and reflected in their corporate codes of conduct.

Many worldwide industries, like logging in primitive rain forests, open-pit mining operations, raw chemical production, and whale and dolphin harvesting, are internationally recognized as potentially damaging the national or territorial fragile, balanced environment, with effects that are felt on a global scale. Whether or not a specific host nation has regulated such activities, a higher authority, the common unified global initiative coupled with worldwide public opinion, has already placed such commercial activities on the danger list. Companies whose operational activities are already publicly acknowledged as potentially harmful need to take notice and consider acting in a socially responsible manner worldwide.

Bribery

Though the bribe be small, yet the fault is great.
—Sir Edward Coke, lord chief justice of England,
renowned jurist

It's often said that there are countries where bribery is a way of life and that's still the case.
—Laurence Urgenson, deputy attorney general of
the United States

Bribery is a subset of corruption, which itself is the abuse of entrusted power for private gain. It is considered an unethical activity and in numerous nations an illegal act. Parties to the bribe are guilty of harming the economic and social development of the society in which it takes place. The process distorts markets, stifles commercial growth, and destroys free market competition, often leading to monopolistic higher pricing and inferior quality of the product or service offered. It robs the local citizenry of proper control and value for their resources, be they asset land or people. The bribery problem has been combated by global conventions and national laws. Commercial institutions would be well advised to consult such declarations and instill such provisions in their own codes of conduct. Fundamental principles like those orchestrated in the 2003 UN Convention against Corruption and the 1997 OECD Convention on Combating Bribery of Foreign Public Officials in International Business Transactions are a good place to start. The UN Convention compels signatory governments, in accordance with their own legal systems, to develop and maintain anticorruption policies by passing criminal laws and establishing administrative enforcement agencies to effectively police governmental officials and the private commercial sector. Articles detailing the acts of bribery, the trading of influence, and the resultant undue advantage are noted but not exactly specified, so latitude in interpretation of its principles allows sovereign nations to construct their own detailed provisions. The OECD convention asks that subscribing parties adopt similar prohibitions as prescribed in the UN declaration. A host of regional, governmental, and associational guidance is also provided by the Organization of American States (OAS) and the Council of Europe.

Many individual countries have enacted their own laws on the issue, the most notable of which is the U.S. Foreign Corrupt Practices Act, which is covered later in the text. While private sector institutions cannot sign on to these sovereign governmental decrees, they are a valuable template source for constructing international accepted definitions and standards regarding involved parties and their nonpermitted activities for inclusion in company codes of conduct. In the private sector, the International Chamber of Commerce (ICC), the World Economic Forum through its Partnering Against Corruption Initiative (PACI), and Transparency International (TI) have all initiated supplementary, voluntary frameworks on the issue for companies to follow. Consulting such conventions and documents allows companies to incorporate into their own codes of conduct universally accepted and applied principles of ethical behavior in respect to their engagements with their own and foreign governmental bureaucracies.

Beyond adherence to such compliance principles, it is equally critical that governments, businesses, and civil societies along with NGOs assist each other in the battle against corruption in all forms. The addition of multinational banks as policing agents for such illicit cash flows has also been suggested as indirect alliance of partners in the fight. The key, however, is for MNCs to incorporate policies against corrupt activities into their strategic planning and place specific language prohibiting it in all its forms into their own individual codes of conduct with applicable monitoring of their employees and association partners for any violations. Furthermore, they should commit to sharing information on corrupt officials with respective governments, NGOs, and even within their competitive industries.

Masked Bribery: Government to Government

While the use of bribery by MNCs or extortion by foreign government ministers for such payments or favors tends to the norm in many cultures, one should not overlook the fact that unscrupulous governments can offer incentives to other governments that benefit the private commercial interests of their domestic enterprises. These offset initiatives are harder to detect and more difficult to combat, but they are worthy of mentioning when discussing the subject, as a potential or perceived conflict of ethical interest might arise. An example of indirect influence peddling by a government to allow for the undue advantage of its state-owned commercial agencies and perhaps private sector recipients was the issue of scholarships from the Chinese Education Ministry to study in China secretly awarded to the children of nine top officials, including the president's daughter, in Namibia. China has been aggressive in courting entrance into many African nations to receive rights for mineral-resource exploration as well as to place their state and private companies in a position to garner trade deals. They are not alone in this commercial endeavor, as numerous countries harbor the same goal for their respective home industries with underdeveloped nations on the African continent. The actions of China—influencing no-bid contracts, receiving lucrative trading rights for strategic import and export products, as well as getting approval of residence and work permits for their own citizens by issuance of the noted scholarships to decision-making officials in Namibia—illustrates a type of corruption, government to government, not technically covered in any of the aforementioned conventions.

While it may be reported as a new wrinkle in unethical global practices, nations have always used their influence to gain commercial advantages in foreign countries. Whether it's the outright granting of most-favored-nation status to lower import tariffs or direct economic assistance packages, as well as a host of other enticing incentives, the idea is not new. Governments have in their stable of agencies and ministries numerous ways to indirectly pressure and sway foreign governments. In 2009, the United States extended for another year a duty-free importation program, first implemented in 1976, to 132 developing countries covering over 3,400 types of products. Such grants can act as a *quid-pro-quo* to such nations to give American firms competitive leverage in their respective markets—which is, essentially, indirect bribery.

In the aforementioned example, China used a unique influential conduit and just got caught. Historically, companies went abroad on the heels of the national interests of their respective home governments and used the political-diplomatic links established to launch their private enterprises. European exploration was an alliance of sovereign royalty houses and merchant traders, and it was blessed by religious orders. Early trading companies were granted chartered rights to operate in government-controlled colonies. The Dutch East India and British East India companies, although private investment vehicles, were deeply tied to their respective home governments as the national economies of their home markets were interwoven with the foreign interests of both companies. In the era of modern globalization, the influence of governments to promote the strategic plans of their homegrown commercial institutions cannot be overlooked. Their potential actions as straw men in the bribery area raise ethical concerns, and as such MNCs should be careful to neither directly nor indirectly benefit from such actions.

Further Thoughts on Bribery

Almost every textbook on international business and management devotes a section to bribery because it is normative practice, a fact of life in many cultures. For expatriate managers and the organization in general, it is a troublesome issue as from a relativist viewpoint it seems appropriate, while a strict moralist would interpret the action as wrong. The act of bribery falls into a number of categories that international commercial firms tend to experience in their domestic and global operations. The first class of bribery is the *gift* consideration to show respect and gratitude to a person in a relationship. It is common in Western societies to offer business associates presents on Christmas and birthdays, with other cultures following suit. The tradition in Japan, and practiced by other civilizations, of offering introductory gifts of appreciation upon first greeting commercial guests is an accepted custom. Within this context social meals and other entertainment occasions that provide opportunities to pursue business interests in more informal environments are a business expense recognized in the tax codes of numerous countries.

The second class of bribery is the *facilitation*, or grease-the-palm payments, that are offered to lesser governmental employees to assist in the efficient and expedient processing of routine bureaucratic actions, such as document registration or timely clearance of imported shipments. Such payments are considered tips or rewards for good service and in many countries are viewed as a normal business disbursement. Bribes in this arena are seen as a device for augmenting the salaries of government-service personnel when the local government cannot afford to provide adequate compensation for such normal and required activities. Those who study the economies of developing countries have often commented that such underground nonreported income contributes to and helps sustain the financial stability and even growth of such markets.

Perhaps the third class, and the one that begins to cross the ethical line, is the *intermediary fee*, or middleman payment, to agents, consultants, and business facilitators to help in commercial connections. In many countries, this is viewed as a regular expense when professional organizations are utilized to help establish a local relationship. But such payments often serve as obscured conduits to government officials, with payment masked by a straw man pass-through. *Political contributions* to national parties, the fourth class, while on the face are not illegal, are in many countries akin to extortion payments with the promise of preferential treatment or freedom from inspection implied in the receipt. They are made under the guise of responsible democratic action but may be due to intimidation and threat of reprisals. The fifth class of bribery is *outright cash payments* to influential governmental administrators to receive a contract or generous tax ruling, rig a bidding process, or cause difficulties to a competitor; these may be coupled with *exorbitant gift giving* that takes the form of purchased assets for others to entice a quid pro quo action. Vacations (or vacation homes), cars, shopping sprees, tuition for children, medical procedures, or even charitable contributions to favorite organizations are basically disguised cash payments. Such deflected or semiobscured personal assistance is illustrated by the following situation. During protracted negotiations for mining rights in an African nation, a member of the MNC team was approached during a social break by a government minister involved in the discussions. The official had a personal matter and he asked his executive friend to help. It seems his son, enrolled in a French university, needed tuition assistance. His own country's foreign exchange rules did not allow him to send such funds abroad. Could the foreign company loan his son the money and he would guarantee its repayment? Such scholarship assistance would be warmly welcomed by him and he would not forget the act of kindness that their relationship produced. What does the company do? Other forms of *preferential treatment*, while outside the specific class of bribery, are nonetheless questionable ethical practices. Preferential treatment targets important buyers, often taking the form of special discounts or promotional activities, first-launch rights for a new product or line, or simply tagging advertisements with their store identification to keep them happy. Such activities may also involve assisting the family members of clients in achieving their personal community or business projects.

Many books, however, treat the subject matter within a more narrow reference with discussion of the American lead initiative and the passing of the Foreign Corrupt Practices Act in 1977. The act is reproduced on the following page because it is an attempt by a sovereign nation to construct a code of acceptable and unacceptable conduct for prescribed actionable offenses outside of its territory and by parties who may not be citizens—in essence a universal borderless ethical instrument.

[As of July 22, 2004]
    Anti-Bribery and Books & Records Provisions of
    The Foreign Corrupt Practices Act
    Current through Pub. L. 105-366 (November 10, 1998) UNITED STATES CODE
    TITLE 15. COMMERCE AND TRADE CHAPTER 2B SECURITIES EXCHANGES
    § 78dd-1 [Section 30A of the Securities & Exchange Act of 1934]. Prohibited foreign trade practices by issuers
  (a) Prohibition
      It shall be unlawful for any issuer which has a class of securities registered pursuant to section 78l of this title or which is required to file reports under section 78o(d) of this title, or for any officer, director, employee, or agent of such issuer or any stockholder

thereof acting on behalf of such issuer, to make use of the mails or any means or instrumentality of interstate commerce corruptly in furtherance of an offer, payment, promise to pay, or authorization of the payment of any money, or offer, gift, promise to give, or authorization of the giving of anything of value to—

(1) any foreign official for purposes of—

(A) (i) influencing any act or decision of such foreign official in his official capacity, (ii) inducing such foreign official to do or omit to do any act in violation of the lawful duty of such official, or (iii) securing any improper advantage; or

(B) inducing such foreign official to use his influence with a foreign government or instrumentality thereof to affect or influence any act or decision of such government or instrumentality, in order to assist such issuer in obtaining or retaining business for or with, or directing business to, any person;

(2) any foreign political party or official thereof or any candidate for foreign political office for purposes of—

(A) (i) influencing any act or decision of such party, official, or candidate in its or his official capacity, (ii) inducing such party, official, or candidate to do or omit to do an act in violation of the lawful duty of such party, official, or candidate, or (iii) securing any improper advantage; or

(B) inducing such party, official, or candidate to use its or his influence with a foreign government or instrumentality thereof to affect or influence any act or decision of such government or instrumentality, in order to assist such issuer in obtaining or retaining business for or with, or directing business to, any person; or

(3) any person, while knowing that all or a portion of such money or thing of value will be offered, given, or promised, directly or indirectly, to any foreign official, to any foreign political party or official thereof, or to any candidate for foreign political office, for purposes of—

(A) (i) influencing any act or decision of such foreign official, political party, party official, or candidate in his or its official capacity, (ii) inducing such foreign official, political party, party official, or candidate to do or omit to do any act in violation of the lawful duty of such foreign official, political party, party official, or candidate, or (iii) securing any improper advantage; or

(B) inducing such foreign official, political party, party official, or candidate to use his or its influence with a foreign government or instrumentality thereof to affect or influence any act or decision of such government or instrumentality, in order to assist such issuer in obtaining or retaining business for or with, or directing business to, any person.

(b) Exception for routine governmental action

Subsections (a) and (g) of this section shall not apply to any facilitating or expediting payment to a foreign official, political party, or party official the purpose of which is to expedite or to secure the performance of a routine governmental action by a foreign official, political party, or party official.

Source: http://www.usdoj.gov/criminal/fraud/fcpa/fcpastat.htm

The simplified direction of the act is that it outlawed the paying of bribes directly or indirectly via agents to foreign government officials to obtain a commercial reward—(a) mentioned previously—and provided penalties to both the company and the individuals convicted of violating its prohibition section. The law does, however, recognize that it does not pertain to "facilitating or expediting payments" to "expedite," speed up, or improve the efficiency of "routine," standard actions or processes that a business would normally receive from a foreign government authority— (b) mentioned previously.

Protests from a number of U.S. firms operating abroad followed the enactment of the law, as they felt such prohibition would place them at a competitive disadvantage with foreign companies whose host countries did not have an equally effective statute governing their actions. It has even been mentioned that in some countries the paying of bribes as outlawed by the act can be taken as a legal business expense, which fueled the complaints of American firms. No precise surveys exist to prove the contention that the act specifically damaged U.S. enterprises, but rumors persist around this initially controversial legislation.

Twenty years later, the member states of the OECD adopted a convention on the bribery of foreign governmental officials. Its provisions mirror, to a degree, the American act with its criminal considerations while also excluding payments designated as routine facilitations. Although the document became active in 1999, each member nation must take individual action to incorporate it into their respective country's body of laws. Corruption through bribery is still a problem, as the practice can have the effect of destroying a level commercial playing field and providing an unfair advantage—both moral considerations. It may also impede the ability of a country to prosper and advance when its governmental administrative personnel award lucrative contracts not to the most qualified or the most cost effective but to those who reward them. If such ineffective public servants add to the cost of governmental service projects by demanding bribes, such additional expenses are a drain on the public funds as the beneficial entities just add the costs back into the bid quotation. Even beyond bribes to elected or appointed governmental officials, global firms may make such payments to those in opposition to such institutions. The U.S. Department of Justice recently announced it was investigating a report that a subsidiary of the Chiquita banana company made cash payments to a Colombian terrorist organization when they came under pressure to ensure the safety of their local employees. Such reports of multinational firms offering substantial payments to opposition parties, no less revolutionary groups, often emerge in developing countries throughout the world.

While the public official category of the bribery issue has technically been made moot by legal mandates in many countries, it does not alleviate the need to further examine the morality of enticing commercial associates by the offering of monetary inducements. A fine line exists between lucrative entertaining and outright cash payments. If an executive offers two front-row tickets to a world-class event for a prospective global client or buyer, it tends to be viewed as an entertainment expense, both ethically acceptable and tax deductible. But if the cash equivalent was placed in an envelope and slipped into the pocket of the associate, the payment might be hidden in corporate accounts as petty cash, but the action itself might be labeled a bribe. The danger in such a case is evident. Corruption breeds corruption and may end up injuring commercial entities because they may be lulled into a false sense of competitive security when in fact their products and services are not being sold based on the quality and price of performance or inherent sustainable company competencies but on misleading pretenses. Firms would be wise to consider this potential masking of the effectiveness of their sales activities and institute a policy of prohibiting payments, gifts, or exorbitant entertaining by anyone in order to obtain or retain business. Bribery is therefore an issue that needs to be addressed in a firm's code of conduct as its culturally induced inconsistencies, seen as alternating values of right and wrong, are part of the ethical equation.

Traditional Cultural Relationship Obligations

Collateral to the bribery issues is a matter often found in national cultures—the rewarding of special relationships via preferential treatment. While cash payments are not normally associated with such practice, reciprocal obligations and family ties play an important part in how business is conducted in many global societies. In England, the *old boy* network in the halls of exclusive clubs greases the rails of commercial transactions in the country. The practice of *guanxi*, or connections, in China is the way deals are made. The custom "incorporates an element of graft" but it can help "get things done faster and more efficiently if used properly."[26] In strong family-oriented societies, commercial transactions with relatives often reveal that special discounts, unique promotional tools, or limited inventory not offered to others is reserved for them. In India and South America, it is not uncommon to find that employee vacancies are normally filled by those whose family members already work for an organization. The American idea of hiring the most qualified is replaced by a different, socially induced imperative: The employment of those with whom one has already established a record of loyalty and trust; hence, a family relative or close friend. While such practices tends to be prohibited or frowned upon in the United States, the acceptance abroad of this alternative hiring criteria is a cultural bend in the ethical road that must be appreciated and acknowledged.

The Ethical Linked Identity Factor

Global commercial entities have always been identified with their home-nation origins; sometimes benefiting from the symbolic allegiance and sometimes regretting such labeling. Foreign-embedded businesses have always been viewed as national flag carriers, and whenever local citizens demonstrate against the policies of their home-country governments, they run the risk of being symbolically attacked. The lesson for MNCs is not to get embroiled in their home government's malfeasance. They could be labeled as beneficial co-conspirators even if they neither engineered nor directly participated in the unethical activity, such as in the case of the aforementioned masked bribery. Perceived immoral conduct does not follow an even, logical path back to the initiator, as once unleashed, innocent bystanders can get pulled into its flow. While MNCs, with the exception of state-owned companies, do not directly partner with their home governments when going abroad and may not be prone to the bribery charges by their governments, they do carry with them a linked national identity that can affect their international operations. On the global, political front, countries themselves have behavioral traits evolve into reputations and images that are connoted with their home country institutions that are born in such environments. Therefore, American, as well as Chinese, British, and Japanese firms, are considered as representatives of their national home country when engaged in foreign commerce. The global public attaches the repute and general ethical positioning of countries to their international commercial envoys. Foreign citizens often see a specific nation's MNC as an economic conduit for the political policies of their home governments, whether warranted or not. When countries are accused of unethical conduct, such visions are associated with the MNCs who originate from them, and guilt by association may evolve. MNCs are always vulnerable to displays of anger or contempt by the local citizenry for the real or perceived immoral actions of their home countries. Boycotts of the goods of a specific country may be orchestrated to show displeasure, but in some cases, outright protests and violence may be inflicted against the property and even the employees of their foreign subsidiaries along with their domestic, host-country, joint-venture partners. Especially susceptible to such actions are product-branded lines and franchisees whose marketing programs are built on or emphasize a connection to a foreign country—Colombian coffee and French wine are promoted with a home-field advantage over foreign competition. The trademarked beverage Coca-Cola is deeply associated with American tastes and cultural identification even when the company has gone to great lengths over time to present the drink as a domestic choice. McDonald's restaurants, even with local menu adaptations, remain as an icon of American service ingenuity—the fast-food industry. Japanese and German cars still contain the allure of their nations' precision engineering skills, first demanded in the home market, as a selling point in going abroad in spite of localized production. Whether the association is classified as a tangible or an intangible property, a linkage to the home countries of MNCs is part of their image. MNCs may therefore find that they may be called upon to renounce or distance themselves from the actual or perceived unethical conduct of their home nation so that their private reputation and appearance abroad is not damaged. This is a difficult dilemma, as ethical judgment may be demanded of an MNC regarding the actions of their home government, which exercises legal jurisdiction over their headquarters. By being critical of their home governments, they risk possible domestic governmental or consumer backlash, but if they take a defensive position, they could jeopardize their foreign operations. During the period of apartheid in South Africa, a number of embedded companies were prodded by their home countries' foreign policy to pull out and thereby exert economic pressure on the existing local government to change their immoral activities. Many MNCs did leave, while the American company General Motors remained. While their decision was criticized, it resulted in the creation of the Sullivan Principles, the grandfather of modern-day codes of conduct for global commercial institutions (covered in Chapter 5).

Firms are caught in the middle when these issues arise and need to consider their responses even when the unethical accusation is not specifically directed at them but rather symbolically placed on them. As much as MNCs would like to stay out of this arena, avoid guilt by association, and lay low, they may be compelled to address these accusations. This is a matter best decided by the CEO with the advice and consent of the board of directors. It should not be handled by local embedded managers, as the issue transcends local political and societal considerations and is a consideration found in neither international conventions nor corporate codes of conduct.

Managerial Reflections

1. Ethical determinations have emerged as a stronger issue in the modern era of globalization. Will firms as they enter more emerging markets be faced with additional challenges?

2. SWOT analysis, usually a precursor to strategic planning, needs to have an ethical component, while Porter's Five Forces industry evaluation requires a new element in the mix. How can moral-based contingencies be incorporated into these assessment models?

3. Market-entry considerations need to be infused with an ethical determination. What investigatory mechanisms are available for such a process beyond the arena of public opinion?

4. Be aware of the ATCA, a law whose original intent has been expanded for U.S.-based civil liability suits to impact foreign territory. Do civil liability insurance policies cover such potential risks?

5. Foreign labor laws, especially in emerging nations, tend to be lenient compared to those of developed countries. What exactly are *sweatshop* conditions and unethical labor practices? How does one balance traditional, acceptable local practices, domestic regulations, and economic conditions against pressures from outside critical agencies?

6. The sustainability of corporate reputations and the value of global brand names seem to be more susceptible to allegations of ethical misconduct. Are consumers genuinely concerned about this issue or is quality and value still their prime concern? Can companies promote their ethical qualities and social responsibility in their marketing programs, and if so, how?

7. Companies do gain a competitive cost advantage by placing operations in environmentally lax countries. Whose regulations should
control: those of more restrictive developing nations or those of the
foreign country? Should economic development precede environmental concerns?

8. Bribery in many countries is an acceptable form of business expense
and part of the cultural relationship way of life, a form of client
gratification. Is the U.S. Foreign Corrupt Practices Act an American
legal encroachment on the rest of the world?

CHAPTER 3

Ethical Value Development

To care for anyone else enough to make their problems one's own, is the beginning of one's real ethical development.
—Felix Adler, intellectual, social reformer, and founder of the Society for Ethical Culture

The actions of men are driven more by the fear of negative consequences, and the resulting penalties, than attracted by the prospect of doing good and being rewarded.
—Lawrence A. Beer, global commercial ethics explorer

Ethics as practiced by international managers, when viewed from a global vantage point, develop on three planes. When traveling abroad we often pack a moral suitcase with those principles that fit comfortably at home. But when we encounter a new ethical climate such well-appointed ideals may not fit the different social environments we are placed in. Adjustments may have to be made.

The Personal Principle

The basic or core plane is a personal one, as each individual decides for himself his own private moral compass. The influence of one's cultural society including religious teachings tends to form values and beliefs, which become the underpinnings for the development of one's own ethical dynamics. It is often difficult for individuals to qualify their moral stance and quantify their thresholds of ethical observance. We do not go around with a preprinted card announcing our personal code of conduct. Instead, we usually find ourselves reacting to a given situation or set of circumstances in which we are asked to reply according to our internal ethical code. In essence, one cannot always explain or put into words a full and complete definition of an ethical imperative. Many of us would proclaim that when we see a wrong or an injustice, we just know it. What we are experiencing is an emotional reaction that often is not accompanied by reason. In other words, the heart reacts before the brain rationalizes. Our ethical stance therefore begins on a deep personal plane and although we may be drawn to observing the ethical approach of others, such internal criteria of right and wrong are a silent umbilical cord that remains attached to our subconscious decision making.

The Diversity Principle

Given our exposure to an ever-widening global interaction with others, our personal moral stance tends to be assaulted with values and beliefs that form the ethical systems of others. There is a marked tendency for those of similar backgrounds, cultures, and religious training to develop common ethical approaches. However, when we venture beyond the borders of our domestic society a diversity of ideas on life is encountered, and we find our ingrained moral concepts may be challenged. We find ourselves encountering circumstances, events, and problems whose solutions must be generated in the context of an alien environment that is vastly different from our home-structured surroundings. The criteria to judge our actions of right and wrong can no longer be applied, as the playing field upon which they are practiced has changed. This diversification of ethical principles that international managers find themselves in is the second plane.

The Motion-Leveling Principle

Global ethical conduct is constantly in motion. As international managers take their personal moral interpretations and practices abroad with them and encounter new approaches, a new set of integrated ethical principles may emerge. Cross influences of acceptable behavior may produce current, universally acceptable concepts of ethical conduct, but such principles are continuously subject to alteration. As more people from more places come onto the global-economic playing field, the contextual nature of ethical decision making swings back and forth. The setting of ethical standards tends to move from one leading group to another. In this modern era of globalization, driven by the economic strength and therefore by the influence of multinational enterprises, current global ethical direction in the commercial sector is originating from Western societies that gave birth to such institutions. But as the world begins to level out and the large human capital communities of China, greater Asia, and India enter the labor and consumer marketplace, the influence of their ideas, values, and beliefs will alter the existing uniformity of global ethical principles. As Thomas Friedman postulates in his book *The World Is Flat*, a new global scene is unfolding, a "flattening of the globe."[1] Those institutions previously serving as models of authority and persuasion as regards acceptable ethical conduct may give way to a different and adjusted universal morality. This may be especially true in the global commercial arena. With entrance into the worldwide labor force of the massive populations of emerging countries, the notions of the proper number of hours worked per day or week; acceptable minimum age of workers, general factory conditions, and labor rights; as well as other aligned issues affecting the workplace may be flattening out. Such standards as pushed on the world by dominant Western influences and practiced by multinational firms may in fact recede from the prevailing global benchmarks their prior policies aimed to establish. While this new competition has already placed a brake on or diminished labor salaries in certain industries and service areas, their ability to promote new standards of acceptable ethical conduct in regard to the whole area of labor rights and moral practices of employers toward them may be on the horizon. Therefore, acceptable global ethical conduct is constantly in motion and may result in the leveling out of ethical practices around the world as depicted in Figure 3.1.

This idea serves as a third plane of inspection in the understanding of this complicated subject. It is against this backdrop of levels of global ethical development that the construction of a workable approach needs to be discussed and tested.

Practicing Ethics in the Global Environment

The interlinked principles of global ethics and social responsibility cover a wide range of issues as well as an ever-increasing circle of stakeholders.

Stricter Standards
(Industrialized nations)

Looser Standards
(Emerging or developing countries)

Figure 3.1 Global ethical converging scale: global standards in motion moving to a converging, leveling plan—a balance of ethical applications

It is the application of moral principles among the growing number of those affected by them that is most difficult. Aiming to both construct and eventually implement a universal code of conduct in a world of diverse and conflicting approaches is a hard task.

Driven by current public awareness, especially in respect to violations of human civil rights (those actions that are physically or mentally injurious to people everywhere regardless of national identity), global firms are being pressured to adopt a pronounced ethical direction and come up with a corporate code of conduct to guide their actions. Lizabeth England, writing for the U.S. State Department, projects that "in the 21st century, the role of ethics in international business transactions and interactions will receive more attention.[2] The global market presents firms with more complex ethical issues than they experience when operations are limited to one country with a single set of acceptable moral standards. Historically, enterprises operating within the confines of a codified domestic market were able to apply uniform standards of ethical behavior to their operations. A common thread of cultural understanding tends to run through a country, with the simple result that basic tenets of social responsibility are spread more equally throughout and within the borders of a specific nation. Due to a more unified societal initiative, the view of morality tends to take on a uniform persona. As companies extend themselves across borders they encounter societies whose behavior varies with the home headquarters culture. Such conflicts in applying alternating principles of morality and responsibility create a dilemma that global enterprises will face on an increasing scale in their strategic decision-making process. What will be required, according to Ms. England, is "an international code of ethical practice, and not a code based on each individual culture's unique norms and practices… [as such] is essential to global survival in the 21st century."[3] Such a code is difficult to construct due to morally global "gray areas,"[4] as ethical behavior is not universally applied nor equally defined across world borders.

Transnational firms are being pressed by global watchdog groups to appreciate the lesson of George Bernard Shaw that "indifference is the essence of inhumanity." They have begun to pay heed to the previously noted and perhaps religiously inspired direction by Edmund Burke that "for evil to triumph it is enough for good men to do nothing." Plausible deniability may no longer be an option in today's more socially conscious world, with the specter of public opinion focused on worldwide corporations. The prime beneficiaries of the globalization process and the numerous value-creation advantages that have flowed from them have tended to be utilized by firms originally grown in industrialized nations. As firms go abroad, there is a natural inclination to plant the seeds of imperialistic morality in these new areas based on their own heritage and hence ethical perceptions. American corporations are portrayed as the *new sovereigns* in the age of modern globalization. Their commercial *imperial conquests* are documented in the pages of current business textbooks, but such characterization can be applied to any company whose operations now encompass cross-border activities. Because the prime goal of such world monarchs is to maximize public stock price, managers are thought to use corporations narrowly and amorally in their march to achieve domination, perhaps forgoing the best interests of the global workforce used to support such initiative. In their pursuits, multinational enterprises may carry the stigma of acting in a manner that exempts them from any of the normal constraints we expect from governments or individuals.

As they engage new societies, companies have an understandable tendency to apply an ethnocentric view of morality to their overseas operations, relying on a singular or preordained culturally induced set of values and beliefs. Such thinking results in molding codes of conduct in their own image. The companies inadvertently create statements of intention that utilize precoded words and terms and language based on the tenets of their own society. Such ethical platforms are prejudicial and therefore suspect when applied to foreign environments where concepts of ethics not only ride different trains but also travel upon contrasted tracks built on alternating levels of socioeconomic development.

The Commercial Enterprise as a Social Institution

When morality comes up against profit, it is seldom that profit loses.
—Shirley Chisholm, member, U.S. House of Representatives

Popular myth portrays a good business firm as a financially successful and economically efficient enterprise that combines profit making with social responsibility. A social idealist, however, might refine such a simple portrayal, exclaiming that such a stereotypical, idyllic firm should begin by providing stable and well-paid jobs with generous benefits to its employees. They should philanthropically support culture and the fine arts of the community in which they operate while paying their fair share of taxes with great pleasure as contributing to the social good. Furthermore, they should encourage employees to become involved in their communities and present themselves as good corporate citizens to the world. Nobel Prize-winning economist Milton Friedman[5] stated,

> In a free-enterprise, private property system, a corporate executive is an employee of the owners of the business… to conduct the business in accordance with their desires, which generally will be to make as much money as possible while conforming to the basic rules of society.

The Friedman canon of commercial social responsibility—to be continuously profitable while staying within the bounds of the law and common decency—is often cited as indicative of the immorality of unscrupulous business firms and of their unethical behavior. Friedman, however, is not commenting on ethical decision making but the inter-play of commercial organizations and the society in which they operate. A profit-making entity contributes to society by paying taxes and employ-ing people. It further provides global consumers with needed or beneficial products to improve their lives and make them more enjoyable. It should be noted that Friedman's commercial social responsibility doctrine does have a built-in ethical factor. He notes that in the pursuit of profitability the activities of the firm should be conducted "in open and free competi-tion without deception or fraud."[6] Certainly, acting in an honest manner free of deceitful activities carries with it a moral tone of correctness. While this declaration seems to be appropriate under a definitive socioeconomic model, it may stumble when applied to a nation where an open-market initiative collides with alternating systems that impact the local human condition.

Theoretically the conceptual notion of the public corporation, or its French equivalent, the SA—société anonyme (anonymous society)—supports the contention that a company is a legal fiction devised by entre-preneurs. Therefore such vehicle is technically not endowed with human attributes and, it follows, may not contain concepts of morally endowed spiritual-like conscience. While the degree of involvement by commercial entities in promoting social responsibility and providing ethical direction can be debated, the Friedman school of thought, if taken to another level, could dismiss the idea completely. Some would argue that the capitalistic system exists as an instrument to create wealth and not for the equitable distribution of the benefits it produces.[7] Commercial firms, built to enrich their shareholders, do not have an altruistic intent. They are not charitable organizations with a not-for-profit motive. They are not mechanisms for applying morality nor are they a device to ensure respect and equality of the human condition around the world. Only individuals, through their actions with and reactions to others, are endowed with such virtuous char-acteristics. As a contrived legal fiction, public corporations have no soul, they have no heart. They are merely a commercially invented vehicle solely designed to insulate and promote the objectives of a group toward the sin-gular operational goal of receiving a financial return. The action does not result in a countermanding social obligation to act responsively, other than under the law controlling such organizations. If the decisions of the corporation in respect to ethical issues and social-welfare programs contribute to promoting the firm's prime goal—profit achievement—then such considerations are valid. If not, they are out of the purview of the commercial activity. If proper conduct, as perceived and judged by consumers of their products or users of their services, enhances the firm's competitive edge and thereby increases its ability to receive revenue, it is a valid strategy. If such practice helps to avoid problems or its nonuse puts the company at a competitive disadvantage, then again it is an area of concern. If its use results in a measurable and distinct contribution to furthering the aims of commercial entities, then it is worthy of investigation and it earns a place in strategic decision making. It becomes a price to pay for achieving acceptable performance. It is a marketing tool, a functional device with no purity of intent other than to support and promote an improved financial return. The *Kasky v. Nike* case in the state of California, noted earlier, would seem to affirm in a legal opinion that a firm's public statements about its ethical practices equate to advertising and corporate self-promotion. It is part of the sales-solicitation process, whether used to enhance or defend the image and public perception of the company and its products with consumers. Such expressions of motivational intent might be called cynical and some might say shameful, but they are still valid commentary on the place of ethics and social responsibility in the commercial world. To some, the use of proclamations of moral nobility attached to advertising cheapens and masks the true underlying meaning and objective. However, if such a strategy is tainted by a prime financial or market driver, does it still achieve a worthwhile objective? While ethical and social responsibility programs may have a noble root, their realistic use as a financial stimulator may be the true fertilizer for multinational corporations (MNCs). Given the tenure of today's commercial global environment, which has begun to count moral actions in the corporate-evaluation process, firms would be wise to consider its value.

Corporations are formed by individuals with their joint actions and decisions guiding such institutions. If each person is endowed with some form of moral responsibility to others, then why shouldn't companies reflect and mirror such attitudes of right and wrong? The reason they do not may have to do with the spiritual nature of humans and the divine salvation principle.

Individuals, via the dogma of Western religious indoctrination, are told that their proper and respectful conduct vis-à-vis their life interaction with others can result in self-redemption and let them achieve a heavenly reward. The consequence of failure can produce damnation and the prospect of their spirit being condemned to a hellish environment. Eastern spiritual teachings direct individuals to follow the right path so they can attain personal tranquility and reach a state of nirvana. In Buddhism the individual reward is freedom from reincarnation and constant suffering, while Hinduism promises the pious person a place where they will be oblivious to pain, worry, and the pressures of the external world. No such recompense is granted to groups; only the self can achieve such a specialized state of grace. Under the teachings of Buddhism, as interpreted by Alan Watts, a pioneering figure in domesticating Eastern philosophy for the Western mind, mankind is charged with finding ways to be wise and compassionate but not necessarily to act in a good way.

Public corporations do not die; they are dissolved or absorbed by other commercial entities. They do not have a group spirit that moves beyond the sell-off of their physical assets. They do not contain an assembled soul that has to be saved once the firm ceases to exist. They don't have clustered emotional feelings that are influenced by approval of their behavioral actions to do the right thing for redemption beyond the grave. While it can be well argued that a firm is a collection of individuals that produces a corporate culture or that the influence of the personality of its entrepreneurial founder provides direction that is akin to a spiritual path, a firm is not human. The punishment or damage inflicted upon a company for wrongful ethical actions or misguided social responsibility is not felt post mortem but only has discernible consequences during the life of the corporate entity.

This type of thinking does not alleviate individual motivations in regard to ethics or social responsibility; it just does not recognize that it should be channeled through a legal fiction, the corporation. Shareholders are welcome to donate their dividends or capital appreciation to worthy causes. Employees are welcome to give a portion of their salaries to charity. All stakeholders are entitled to treat others in a respectful manner and make their own choices. If such personal obligations are challenged via their duties within the confines of an organization, they have the right to voice their opinion. If the group does not agree with their direction they can always leave the association and pursue their own course of action. Simply put, the commercial entity and perhaps other connected institutions may not be the sole conduits of social change. It may be best left to representative governments and religious sects to bring about such outcomes. But if ethical strategies and the implementation of recognized moral actions coupled with perceived correct social responsibilities are practiced, the corporation may benefit, and such is the prime consideration.

A corporation is a collection of owners (shareholders) possessing a singular goal: Placing capital at risk for a return on investment—the profit incentive. That is why many organizations are denoted as not-for-profit institutions whose goals and therefore tactical charitable activities, helping fellow mankind, are alternatively different. However, creating a for-profit entity does entail financial considerations that affect ethical actions of others. The simple process of employing people and paying taxes allows other institutions in the public sector, government, and social organizations (religious sects and charities as well as special interest groups) to be proponents and guardians of the ethical and moral needs of a society. So, indirectly, corporations support ethical conduct and maintenance thereof in a society by contributing to their maintenance. But if in fact Friedman is correct, and profit is the chief social responsibility of corporations, one cannot ignore the fact that the revenue and expenses or cost, the prime contributors to the profit formula, may be impacted by ethical decision making. The moral actions attributed to such social associations of undistinguished owners have a direct effect on the firm's ability to market goods and services. The impact of the public perception of unethical or immoral behavior, even without the ability to squarely place such actions upon faceless or nameless decision makers, can impact the financial goal.

The previously noted quote by Friedman has acted as a beacon for executives who profess to separate social responsibility from the prime corporate interest to increase shareholder value. But if one takes a moment to dig more deeply into the economist's comment perhaps the true nature of the remark emerges. What Friedman sees as "conforming to the basic rules of society"[8] may simply require that the firm operate within the current public system but not be responsible for the reengineering of the social structure. He does not see corporations as the private forgers of change in the communal society. They are not the agents of moral transformation, nor the end makers of law that may flow from such direction. This exercise is left to representative governments and, in some theocratic countries, to spiritual leaders. But Friedman would be the first to champion the strategic embracing of ethical conduct and a firm's image as a positive contributor to social programs in a community if such activity by the corporation results in the creation of value for the enterprise. In essence, since Friedman points to profit as being the chief duty of firms, such enterprises might be wise to consider the financial impact of ethics on their businesses.

Financial Implications of Ethical Conduct: First Look

When it is a question of money, everybody is of the same religion.
                    —Voltaire, French writer and philosopher

If consumers are motivated and their purchase decisions are influenced by the actual or perceived notion that a firm is socially responsible and acts in an acceptable ethical manner, then the revenue of such corporation will increase, profits will be maximized, and shareholder value will naturally grow. For example, when a company engages offshore contracted suppliers whose factories either are certified as to the fair and humane treatment of their employees or receive a positive inspection record in regard to labor conditions, such differentiation from competitors creates a value-added element. When firms proactively work in a publicly perceived, reasonable manner to protect and preserve their community's environment, they send a positive impression of social responsibility that often results in consumer goodwill, creating an intangible asset. Ethical conduct could therefore be a creator of corporate worth, while immoral company behavior might conceivably diminish shareholder value.

Companies spend great sums of money creating an image, a reputation, and a name for themselves with the consuming public. Practicing immoral activities may lead to severe damage inflicted upon the reputation and image of firms, a loss of an intangible capital asset. The investment value of shareholders can be impacted by ethical improprieties. The morally tethered breach of fiduciary responsibilities in financial reporting, as exemplified in the Enron and WorldCom situations, destroyed the stock values of such firms, showing clearly that unethical practices can damage a firm. As noted earlier, television personality Kathie Lee Gifford licensed her name to a group, which in turn arranged for third-party manufacturers to create a brand of clothing for distribution in stores such as Walmart. When the poor factory conditions and sweatshoplike employee treatment in such contracted facilities came to the attention of consumers, the rapid demise of the line started. Even with explanations that did not tie Ms. Gifford to any of the deplorable conditions, the line soon went out of business, tainting any future association her good name could have had with the industry. The publicized legal entanglements of Martha Stewart, who built a media and merchandising empire out of tips for gracious living based on her personality, has impacted the brand's image and hence its salability of its products. Shareholders saw the company's business suffer by Ms. Stewart's indictment and criminal conviction on charges of lying to federal investigators about a stock trade. The value of the stock of the firm that bears her name diminished following a string of financial losses. While the consumer jury was still out on this matter, the interim results did not speak well of the commercial celebrity whose ethical conduct was questioned. While some famous personalities have seen the value of their name applied to products diminished, others have persevered and revived their business affiliations. Perceived unethical conduct of an enterprise or even a personality associated with it, no matter how far removed from the actual commercial entity, can however be damaging to shareholder value in the interim. It is interesting to note, however, that at Martha Stewart's company's annual meeting following her release from prison, she received warm cheers from a majority of the shareholders as she assured them that the company was well positioned for the long term and projected a financial recovery in the future. It may be that public sentiment, when it comes to ethical malfeasance by strong personalities, can be fleeting. Only a constant reminder of wrongdoing keeps the public fires of discontent burning, and if not stoked the issue burns out quickly.

It remains possible that consumer purchasing decisions may find an ever-increasing impetus to choose one competitor over another based on reports that the goods they buy are being manufactured by or assembled from parts made by workers who have been treated fairly by ethically responsible companies. Such positive actions may increase profits of one entity and reduce those of another whose practices are suspect. As the previously noted *Kasky v. Nike* case indicated, a good public persona, acting with moral character, can act as an advertising motivator. When a company's image is negatively perceived by consumers, the company might go to great lengths to reverse the perception.

When firms find themselves in court defending alleged human rights abuses, the costs associated with such legal expense can continue to mount. Many times a settlement is reached in cases that cause great sums of money to be contributed to charities with no admission of guilt. The Bloomberg News service reported in September 2002 that seven U.S. retail chains, including Target Corp., J.C. Penney, and Gap Inc. had agreed to settle a lawsuit over labor conditions brought by garment workers in Saipan. At a cost of over $20 million, these and other plaintiffs including 23 local manufacturers agreed to the creation of a fund to compensate more than 30,000 workers and to finance monitoring programs to combat claims of sweatshoplike treatment.

Coupled to the cost aspect of attention to the ethical issue is the increasing and frequent embarrassment of global firms being drawn into court for a public hearing of their unintentional wrongs. On December 2, 1984, Union Carbide's Bhopal, India, plant had a deadly toxic gas leak that killed 4,000 people that night. Over time approximately 14,400 more ultimately died. In subsequent lawsuits, the company, joined by the Indian government, claimed the tragedy was the result of sabotage by a disgruntled worker. Union Carbide was accused of failure to evaluate a developing country's ability to oversee the safe use of sophisticated technology[9] and to have behaved in an ethically reprehensible manner as to plant security in a manner different from what they would have done at home. Although owning a slight majority in the facility in 1984, the company paid a $470 million settlement, but still the suits kept coming. In March 2002, a federal district judge dismissed yet another lingering lawsuit brought in 1999, this time from a woman who had moved into the area years after the tragedy, but the plaintiff's appeal was denied. Time never ends for ethical improprieties, and such actions do not rely on a statute of limitations to be barred from being presented.

It seems that specific incidents of unethical behavior, especially those that kill or injure people, are neither forgotten nor financially forgiven. On the 25th anniversary of the Bhopal disaster, an op-ed commentary dated December 3, 2009, appeared in the *New York Times*. Written by Suketu Mehta and titled "A Cloud Still Hangs Over Bhopal," the Author recounts the incidents of the day in emotional detail and the torment of those still affected by the event. Over the years, Union Carbide, with the sale of its Indian subsidiary company, eventually pulled out of the country. Nonetheless, time has not allowed even the new owner of Union Carbide, Dow Chemical, to escape the morally tainted past of its acquired asset. The commentary chides Dow as "the maker of napalm married [to] the bane of Bhopal," a blatant reference to the phrase regarding the sins of the fathers visited upon the children with an extra moral kicker thrown in—that is, the old company's participation in asbestos production.

Companies need to learn from this journalistic example. Unethical conduct, whether real or perceived, is not easily erased. It is a scarlet-branded mark on a firm's reputation that continuously follows it, staining and contaminating even the acquirer of its assets with calls for continuing financial restitution. The importance of acting in a morally acceptable manner not only impacts a firm's current activities but also follows it well past its legal termination into the hands of a new owner who inherits, by innuendo, its obligations. It seems that ethics is both a tangible and intangible worth that transcends time and is always remembered. Its value, whether positive, as with an accounting for goodwill, or negative, as in this example, is always recorded and even runs the risk of being reassigned to others. It is an area where the sins of the fathers tend to be visited on the children.

The fallout of the WorldCom and Enron financial improprieties resulting from the unethical conduct of directors has proven most costly for both the companies and the individual participants. Ten former World-Com board members agreed to pay $54 million, $18 million out of their own pockets, to settle their portion of one of many lawsuits following the firm's bankruptcy and eventual collapse. Eighteen former members of the Enron board reached a $168 million settlement, including $13 million of their personal funds, with shareholders damaged by the financial shenanigans that resulted in the company's demise. It represents the fourth major settlement negotiated by attorneys in class-action lawsuits filed by Enron's shareholders. Senior executives of both firms also face criminal charges for their actions in grossly overstating sales and profits. Both situations deeply fueled the public's awareness of the immoral conduct of corporations as it touched their pocketbooks, individual shareholders, and pension funds, as well as their ethical conscience. Such revelations and citizen demand prompted the U.S. Congress to pass the Sarbanes–Oxley Act to bolster corporate transparency in the financial reporting arena. It should be noted that this federal law pertains not only to domestic firms issuing public financial instruments but also to all foreign firms that use the U.S. security system to raise capital. As such, it has far-reaching effects on the ethical conduct of MNCs across the globe. The Sarbanes–Oxley Act has been promoted as ushering in a new era of corporate responsibility via the construction of an official financial-compliance program for public companies. Such profiling language characterizing the law as advancing social responsibility is a bit misleading, as its enactment with noncompliance penalties takes the issue outside the realm of voluntary social action and places it within the regulatory system of the country. When questionable ethical actions become qualified and quantified in the law of a nation, they are no longer moral judgments. Perhaps the only real motivational impetus for firms to employ socially induced ethical practices is a resultant codified compliance ordinance in the territories in which they operate that forces them to be publicly transparent.

When accusations of misconduct are leveled at companies, a public relations effort may be needed to combat negative public awareness feedback. All these actions place a drain on profit. Gap Inc., historically accused of ethical improprieties involving labor practices throughout the numerous worldwide garment factories it utilizes, publishes an annual social responsibility report administered by the company's corporate public-reporting work group. This document, which aims to dispel notions of unethical conduct and present a public transparency to their actions, is a costly item filled with glossy photos, in-depth text, and charts. Its preparation by a dedicated staff is also an added corporate expense.

As firms uncover objectionable conditions in the plants of contracted parties, they face the added expenses occasioned by switching costs to other vendors while also responding to disruptions in their global supply chains—both occurrences depleting profit achievement. In the end, both proactive and reactive ethical practices can affect the financial results of firms. The Friedman social responsibility imperative of commercial entities—to make as much money as possible—could be influenced by a properly accepted ethical program that is openly disseminated to the general public.

Are Ethics That Valuable To an Enterprise? Another Look

The ethical conduct or perceived misconduct of firms, as highlighted by the Enron and WorldCom fiduciary responsibilities, received great attention from new reporting media spurring, as noted earlier, the creation of a federal law taking an ethical consideration into the regulatory stage. The Sarbanes–Oxley Act of 2002 targets individual decision making as it holds officers of publicly held companies, both domestic and foreign, personally responsible for the accuracy of their firms' financial statements and financial information. As such, it parallels aspects of the Foreign Corrupt Practices Act, piercing the corporate veil of the autonomous society, and it raises the ethical actions of individuals within an organization to a legal liability with personal penalties, both financial and criminally induced incarceration. The act, along with the investing public's desire for more transparent reporting of company transactions, has resulted in the revamping of numerous internal corporate-operating procedures and financial-disclosure documents. Behind the regulatory motivation is the general public's outrage at the unethical conduct of those having a fiduciary duty to others—a question of basic morality.

It would be imprudent not to ask whether such attention is a trend or a fashionable indulgence whose time will run out as public opinion wanes. While morality, one may argue, should be with us always, the consuming public is a fickle group whose attention and interest can be manipulated and swung in varying directions. Are we going through a period when the globalization phenomenon in general is being attacked, and moral improprieties targeting human rights and environmental harm simply add fuel to the fire of emotional discontent with the process itself? Does the subject of ethical conduct joining the agenda of those critical of globalization strike a current nerve with consumers that time will diminish? Should global firms be so concerned with the subject that their planning matrix and strategic decision making is affected by it? Should it be reflected in their immediate tactics and procedures but perhaps put on a shelf for the long-term strategic future? Does one gear up now, committing time and resources to current ethical projects, when the use of them down the road may not prove worthwhile? Such questions are proper, and international executives must deal with such matters. It took a few decades for the original Sullivan Principles, born out of worldwide press attention directed toward South Africa, to be re-reflected in the United Nations (UN) Global Compact. As soon as South Africa turned from its national apartheid policy, embraced reforms in its social order, and moved to more democratic principles, the Sullivan direction disappeared from the radar screen for global companies. The conduct, however, by a number of countries in respect to questionable treatment of their citizens did not disappear. The People's Republic of China, whose record of human rights abuses was dramatically highlighted during the Tiananmen Square incident, may have begun to sidestep such issues due to their newfound economic strength with more limited focus on them as a provocateur of unethical treatment. Certainly worldwide companies continue to invest in the country not only as a cheap production source and a newly found source for technology research but also for their growing domestic consumer market.

Although it is difficult to analyze the singular elemental impact of questionable moral behavior on the financial achievement of companies, a look at some examples reveals that a few firms, whose operational human rights activities have resulted in negative attacks, have weathered the public storm well.

The early 2000s was a period of increased public exposure and criticism of the foreign factories of MNCs in regard to sweatshop conditions. The prime targets of such allegations were American-owned clothing companies using third-party contractors to produce lost-cost products. Nike Inc., long an object of scorn to watchdog agencies and pushed to repeatedly defend itself against accusations in respect to its contracted factories and boycott attempts by consumer groups, reported record earnings in 2004, with a 14.6 percent increase in revenue. Beginning in 2000, the next four years of operations had sales improvements in every annual period, as did their EPS (earning per share) performance and return invested capital as reported in the Nike Inc. 2004 Annual Report.

Gap Inc., another company accused of sweatshop practices in the early 2000s, as they themselves note in their 2004 annual report, has nevertheless experienced sustained sales growth of 7.5 percent over five years beginning in 1999. Results for 2004 showed a 10 percent per annual growth, according to the Gap Inc. 2004 Annual Report.

Liz Claiborne Inc., a firm also under attack in early 2000 for unethical practices in their foreign supplier factories, garnered steady growth in revenue, moving to a December 2002 performance of $3,717,503,000 from $3,448,522,000, and in 2003 posting $4,241,115,000—an increase of 7.8 percent and 14.1 percent, respectively. Net income during such period rose by 20.4 percent and 20.1 percent. The question as to the effect of public opinion on the financial performance of public companies during a time when their ethical practices are challenged still remains open for debate.

At the other end of the ethical spectrum, during the same period when public sentiment was high for ethical concerns, consider the financial reporting of the Body Shop International PLC. This firm utilized a social responsibility marketing theme in promoting itself to consumers and, as profiled earlier, advertised their ethical treatment of suppliers in underdeveloped countries as a prime selling point. However, they encountered a flat revenue from 2000 to 2003 while their operating profit moved up and down over the four-year period in spite of store growth (number of outlets) increasing. Perhaps their core group of original targeted buyers, who respond favorably to products bearing a moral identity, had quickly reached a plateau or such patrons have lost their original affinity for social issues as reflected in product attributes and were looking for other added value characteristics. It is hard to qualify, no less quantify, the exact financial plus or minus effect of the singular factor of actual or perceived ethical behavior on the performance of companies. It might be fair, however, to conclude that a positive public persona of proper ethical conduct does not injure a firm; it may just not be a marketing strategy to ride exclusively.

The Ethical Dilemma Within the
Social Responsibility Orbit

The heart has its reasons that reason does not know.
—Blaise Pascal, 17th-century French philosopher,
writing in *Pensées*

There is a separation on issues of social responsibility and ethical behavior, though considerable overlap can be observed. The difference between the two is a matter of scope and degree. Whereas ethics deals with decisions and interactions on an individual level, decisions about social responsibility are broader in scope, tend to be made at a higher (grouped) level, affect more people, and reflect a general stance taken by a company or a number of decision makers (acting in unison). Social responsibility centers on poverty and lack of equal opportunity around the world, consumer concerns, the environment as well as employee safety, and (all culminating in advancing) the general welfare of society.[10] The onus of social responsibility is on the entire organization, while ethics seems to be practiced on a one-to-one personal relationship basis and is more internally orchestrated. Social responsibility focuses the resources of the company "beyond legal obligations to actively balance commitments to investors, customers, other companies and communities."[11]

Ethics are voluntary moral standards of behavior that are not governed by law. They arise from social pressure and culminate in the individual actions of citizens of a common group setting the acceptable standards for the human consequences of their actions. The measurement criteria, if such actions are tolerated or condemned, are determined by a particular society's cultural beliefs, norms, and values. It follows, therefore, that dissimilar cultures will produce different ethical dilemmas and pose varying moral issues for multinational companies. Although noted earlier, it is important to state again that historically, when firms operated within a single market, with shared societal attitudes born of a uniform culture, the subject of ethics was regulated to a diminished position. Today, however, as operations cross borders, it is normal to encounter vastly different values and beliefs.

As mentioned in the introduction, ethics is the study of morality and standards of conduct in general, while "ethical behavior tends to be a personal one"[12] with "each individual deciding for themselves what is right and wrong."[13] This idea was first presented as the personal principle, the initial platform in the three levels of ethical development discussed in the beginning of the chapter. Each of us processes (qualifies and quantifies) for ourselves what actions should be allowed and therefore condoned, and what actions should be prohibited and therefore condemned.

The sum of these individual decisions collectively results in a national consciousness that sometimes gives rise to the creation of legal doctrines being established as laws and regulations in sovereign nations. But at times, globally commercial entities may be challenged to erect their own path when a void is encountered in legal tenets. An ethical dilemma straddles polar moralities and presents itself when there are no right or wrong decisions, just alternatives, each of which may be equally valid, depending on one's own ethical compass heading. Such alternatives are encountered in international management as the view of an ethical approach in one country is often seen as unethical behavior in another country. It often arises when global managers aim to apply practices and norms they import from their home nation and find them in conflict with those of the local or host market they are operating within. Locally embedded managers are especially vulnerable to such considerations, as dissimilar cultures produce different ethical dilemmas that confuse and assault the treatment of subjects ethnocentrically held sacred. Any systematic corporate guidance on how to treat such matters tends to be welcomed.

Ethical direction emanates from within the individual and is difficult to articulate. When college business students are asked to define or state their moral values, they have a hard time explaining their precise standards of acceptable behavior. Many begin by referencing the Latin phrase *non aequus est*, exclaiming the roughly translated "it ain't fair" to describe a situation that bothers them. They then resort to rationalizing such a statement, acknowledging "when I see something wrong I just know it." In order to apply their moral criteria, they usually need to be challenged by an event, a problem, or an issue from which they can resolve the conflict. They need a concrete example in order to formalize their approach. They internalize the contextual circumstances and then take a moral position.

This process is fine for the individual making daily choices in life, but for international managers in charge of organizational policy across nations directing a code of conduct for use in numerous conflicting cultures the matter is much more complex. To provide for uniformity of decision making by far-flung managers over a vast global network, a corporation may need to enact and practice universal standards.

While the company's control over issues of ethics is more readily exercised when global-organizational structures include worldwide subsidiaries sharing an common corporate culture, the increased use, today, of international strategic alliances, joint ventures, and third-party, arm's-length outsourcing may make the matter even more difficult. The alternating moral principles of such varying independent entities can reflect on the company entering such associations, as accommodations and adjustments may be necessary to form successful strategic alliances with each separate entity. Some would argue that it is important that firms treat global situations in a like manner regardless of the commercial relationship between the parties, whether the offending entity is a wholly owned subsidiary, a partnered entity, or even a party to a contractual arrangement. The rules of the global engagement should be the same. Inconsistency breeds distrust and confusion when prejudicial applications of ambiguous principles are utilized.

Degrees of Separation

When a firm's operations include a number of independent, integrated vertical or horizontal contractors and suppliers, the ability to exert influence and control over such an elongated network of associations becomes even more complicated and burdensome. Firms in the competitive apparel and shoe business, like Gap and Nike, use such third-party manufacturing as the backbone of their global strategy. While some relationships, entrusted via a contractual document, can allow for exertion of obligatory references concerning human rights infringement between the noted parties, how far down the line must companies provide for compliance and verification? Take the allegation by Human Rights Watch, a New York advocacy group, whose investigation indicated that a Coca-Cola subsidiary in Central America supports child labor. Their findings allege that a refiner in El Salvador, Central Izalco—the nation's largest—from which Coke purchases sugar in bulk, processes raw sugar cane supplied by four plantations that routinely use workers under the age of 18.

Putting aside the theoretical discussion of what age exactly constitutes child labor, a culturally diffuse definition, the issue of how far down or back in the supply chain companies are required to extend and verify their stipulated code of conduct in their operations is a troublesome one. Does a code of conduct applied to a first-level provider automatically pierce and flow through their relationships with sublevels of supply? Must a company investigate and be held accountable for all commercial relationships that their transactions possibly touch? Where does such responsibility stop? If one contracts to have a shirt sewn at a factory, must they also track down the fabric supplier who wove the cloth, then in turn those that dyed and finished the raw material, and finally, the growers of the cotton in the fields to determine if all links in the procurement chain practiced acceptable ethical treatment of their employees?

Later in the book, the plight of workers subject to the unscrupulous activities of intermediary layers of labor brokers is described. This is a practice that is normally outside the purview of investigation and control of multinational companies using these resulting contracted labor pools. While debt bondage is usually entered into freely, its sometimes repugnant fallout subjects workers to slavelike financial burdens that deeply affect their lives while tending to further exacerbate the conditions of labor they must also endure during the debt service. A question arises for firms that may contract with third parties using such labor brokers. Are they required to verify employment practices of these arm-length parties and if so how far back in each individual's employment history must they investigate to determine that their own code of conduct, standards of fairness, and moral responsibility are being met by such parties? Even the foreign manufacturing firms that employ such unfortunates may not know the extent of the advantages taken of their own workforce, as these employees are reluctant themselves to share such information, fearing loss of a job or retribution from labor middlemen.

Corporate Social Responsibility Revisited: A Foreign Prospective

The division in terminology between ethics and social responsibility was initially presented in the introduction. The matter is worthy of revisiting, as the two concepts seem to be always joined in discussions concerning the moral implications embedded in the commercial endeavor.

Within the overall framework of developing ethical positioning for global firms, the general question of just what does corporate social responsibility (CSR) represent needs to be addressed from the outset. Different organizations have approached the issues within varying parameters as occasioned by their definition of the role of business in society—what are they required to give to the society in which a commercial firm operates? Therefore, ethical decision making in a global environment does include overtones of social responsibility. As such, it is prudent to revisit ideas of CSR.

Acting socially responsible while incorporating the notion of man's treatment of his fellow men, a moral judgment, is usually associated with charitable activities or programs conducted in the name of the corporation and dedicated to the local communities in which they operate. Commercial entities provide support via donations while prompting their employees to contribute their time to community events. They also offer public educational announcements and programs. Objective decision making takes place, as such activities are conducted to ingratiate citizens of the local region to the company. Studies have shown that employees like to work for firms with a good perceived social conscience and that consumers can be motivated to initially select or switch to companies that possess a socially beneficial image to the public.

Managers of companies, according to Milton Friedman (as presented earlier), have but one prime goal, that of fiduciary responsibility—creating a profit for their shareholders while conforming to the basic rules of society. The place of commercial entities in society and their relationship with the society around them is a subject that has been and will be debated for some time. As previously explored, public corporations are technically autonomous organizations (note the French SA—anonymous society) and were created via a legal fiction. As such, do they have an automatic duty to the society around them to support social causes? Are they endowed with a social conscience? Should they be engineers of social change?

It has been argued that if the singular objective of a corporation is to simply make money for shareholders, then why not let such individual recipients take their return on investment and decide for themselves if it is to be used to support charitable efforts or in other ways to benefit society and improve the general quality of life? Should the charter or articles of incorporation of companies endow them with the same social convictions as individuals?

Is a corporation just an artificial means or system for making money and nothing more? It might be helpful to view the opinion of a nonprofit website devoted to discussing the subject matter. At mallenbaker.net (http://www.mallenbaker.net), under the umbrella publication *Business Respect*, a periodic news monitoring and commentary report, CSR is viewed in the context of how companies manage the business processes to produce an overall positive impact on society. Such a viewpoint aims to induce global companies to take a proactive stance as their strategic intent emanates from a central philosophy, envisioning firms as social provocateurs. Simply put, commercial entities are asked to endow their managers with socially responsible agenda. This debated obligation is repeatedly well explained and illustrated in website commentary and with contributions from a variety of sources.

The issue is viewed by some as a stalking horse for the anticorporate agendas of those parties who proclaim big business as an evil, detrimental force, taking and never giving back to those they extort from. Others liken a lack of CSR to the original sin and see it as beyond redemption. To combat such accusations of malfeasance, Mallen Baker, the driving personality behind the website dialogue, prompts companies to take a dual approach when considering the role of business in society. In the diagram (Figure 3.2) depicting the required interplay between a company and society, he advises firms to work on two joined circles: an inner circle, the quality of their management in respect to the process of decision making, and an outer circle, the resultant impact on stakeholders. He sees external pressure coming from local communities; the general workplace as represented by unions; the marketplace itself as made up of customers, shareholders, and financial interests; and the need to safeguard the environment as influenced by nongovernmental organizations (NGOs) and the government. Management is instructed to gauge what the company has actually done, good or bad, by consulting the outer circle, as the public are the external judges of the quality of their CSR.

Figure 3.2 The integrated circle of social responsibility

Source: http://www.mallenbaker.net/csr/definition.php

While Baker's diagram provides an insight into the conditional are-nas and players having a stake in managerial decision making while also acting as evaluators of their resultant actions, it does not provide a clear definition of CSR. What exactly is it and does one size fit all?

To answer this perplexing question, the mallenbacker.net site refer-ences the World Business Council for Sustainable Development in its publication *Making Good Business Sense* by Lord Holme and Richard Watts. Using this reference it constructs the following definition:

> Corporate Social Responsibility is the continuing commitment by business to behave ethically and contribute to economic develop-ment while improving the quality of life of the workforce and their families as well as of the local community and society at large.[14]

Such a generic, all-encompassing statement is not, however, definitive. As it uses terms like "behave ethically," "contribute to development," and "improve quality," a very wide margin is left open to interpretation as to both qualitative and quantitative performance. It is noteworthy that the survey report supplied evidence of the varied and sometimes conflicting ideas of just how responsibly accepted CSR is viewed around the world. From an emerging nation like Ghana, a more economically directed imperative is related by stating, "CSR is about capacity building for sustainable livelihoods. It respects cultural differences and finds the business opportunities in building the skills of employees, the community and the government." In the Philippines, a simple phrase sums it up: "CSR is about business giving back to society."[15]

In the United States, the traditionally accepted model of social responsibility tends to emanate from our individual, cultural core values. We separate work-related activities from our personal social responsibilities. We make a living much as companies make a profit, and then we donate a share of our income or time to charitable causes. This is not to say that firms do not organize charitable drives acting as conduits for money or employee efforts on behalf of nonprofit organizations, they do. Americans just see social responsibility as an extension of their personal decisional obligation toward others and not part of their work product. For a majority of public U.S. businesses, CSR is peripheral to the main event—quarterly results that match or beat the expectation of Wall Street and their financial gnomes. For many companies the matter is relegated to a position of public relations, a subset of the advertising department.

The European approach is more in harmony with their general social outlook, a more collective, culturally induced progression. Europeans have a marked tendency to focus on operating their core business in a socially responsible way, complemented by investment in communities for solid business case reasons as such is demanded by what Baker would refer to in his diagram as the pressures of the external circle stakeholders. In Europe, government legislation is more primed to ensure the wellbeing of its citizens; hence, the business institutions mirror this social initiative. From an extensive array of blanket societal welfare programs such as national healthcare, to numerous laws protecting employees on the job with cumbersome dismissal regulations, to the French law mandating the number of work hours allowed reduced from 40 per week to 35, the social responsibility initiative permeates the commercial sector. Any American businessman wanting to reach, no less negotiate, a transaction with his European counterparts in July and August would be wise to consider that such periods are strewn with legally required, extended paid vacation time that well eclipses the American one to two weeks a year. Social responsibility is more deeply ingrained in European business entities and forms an integral part of their strategic intent and operational decision making. They see their managerial function on a much broader social horizon with a higher degree of responsibility owed to all stakeholders. CSR is considered part of the wealth creation process, with its measured accumulation containing more equalized portions of objective (money) and subjective (enjoyment of life) benefits.

The dispute as to the rightful place of public corporations in a society, as contributors or innocent bystanders, will continue as commercial entities increase their leverage on the global stage. Notwithstanding, however, is the fact that, like ethical decision making, CSR is housed within the varying complexities of social and cultural differences around the world. Just as the role of government in the lives of its citizens differs from country to country, so does the definition of social responsibility. In the modern era of globalization, the economic impact of MNCs operating in underdeveloped countries may be on a scale that eclipses the influence of national governments. In a number of markets, the foreign corporation or a cadre of such alien commercial institutions fuels its gross national product (GNP) or in some cases is their prime monetary engine. Due to globalization there is a marked shift in the power of national governments to effectively control their own domestic economies. As they are forced to abrogate this key responsibility, fostering the economic livelihood of their citizens, they may have no choice but to look to MNCs to take a larger role in sustaining and building their social programs as well. This may well be the challenge that corporations face in the 21st century as they need a stable social environment in which to operate and prosper.

Continuing debate ranges over the exact interpretation and hence the sustainable actions of companies to implement CSR. It is more than mere public relations efforts by well-meaning corporations? Does it require a continuing commitment by commercial organizations not only to act in an ethical manner (a dominating thread in the social responsibility cloth) but also to contribute economically to improve the quality of life of firm employees, their families, the local community, and society at large? To do so requires companies to recognize that

> the overarching components for translating CSR concept to reality is [embedded] in corporate strategy, because it takes cognizance of the internal and external analysis of the business and provides overall direction and necessary stimulus for the activities to be embarked on.[16]

In a country like Russia, beginning to taste capitalistic market initiatives as it moves away from a historic communist system, the definition of CSR directs companies to obey the law and pay taxes.[17] Such an approach may mirror the attitude of many totalitarian nations beginning to embrace democratic economic reforms, wherein the government is the sole source of authority and legitimacy and to which all social responsibility is due. As Schmida reports, "By politicizing the term, the Russian government risks making corporate social responsibility a code word for the subservience of the private sector to parochial state interests."[18] But under historic communist doctrine, the state exists for the people, so it is natural to assume that support of one automatically supports the other. The danger for Russian firms of viewing CSR running first through state government and then on to the greater society is that as their export-extractive industries, the chief drivers of the country's economic program, encounter increased global involvement they will fall under more scrutiny for their environmental and social practices. It is also noteworthy that as private Russian enterprises replace state national industries in remote and underdeveloped parts of the country, such new entities are viewed by the local administration as the prime resource for addressing the community's social and economic ills—a precious state responsibility. The same theoretical approach may be practiced by the Chinese government as they scramble to balance the transition from state-owned enterprises to privatization. They too may have to consider shifting a portion of their burden of social responsibility onto the shoulders of private entrepreneurial firms. This issue is already engaged as state agencies partner with foreign companies. One study points out a real implication for MNCs entering the Chinese market. It indicates that the Chinese society expects MNCs to help solve the country's problems in regard to "helping the underprivileged, education, environment and community."[19] Such consideration was echoed and its importance sustained as it was placed at the top of the agenda of the third plenary session of the 10th National People's Congress in Zhejiang Province, in line with Chinese President Hu Jintao's political slogan, "Building a harmonious society."[20] Chinese workers consider private enterprise as inheriting and extending the parental responsibilities of their former employer—the state, an institution that always integrated their social welfare with required labor.

In erstwhile and now independent communist-influenced countries, such as the former states that made up the Union of Soviet Socialist Republics (USSR) and at one time a number of Eastern European satellite nations, commercial firms may experience a duty far beyond just being lawful and paying taxes. CSR may be more important in these countries than in Western industrialized areas, as the citizens of these emerging nations see employment created by foreign direct investment (FDI) in the same light as the once state-controlled labor organizations—the provider of all community entitlements and benefits.

The CSR consideration is even more acute in underdeveloped or emerging countries where the corporate sector is probably the largest employer in the country. Getting companies to work more closely with communities for tangible improvement of their impoverished plight is the UK-based nonprofit organization Groundwork and its founder John Davidson. In Pakistan, Groundwork undertook a project where it encouraged children to interact with the managing directors of local companies to understand what business wanted from communities. In return, the children measured the impact of business on the local environment and advised the managing directors about mapping out plans to improve conditions. Both sides learned via dialogue how to balance the strategies of commercial institutions with the needs of society.

In Africa, private enterprises desirous of extracting the rich resources of the land have reengineered their strategies to encompass

the improvement of local infrastructures as part of their overall financial investment. Beyond capital funds for their factories and operational
structures, foreign firms have committed to building roads, airports,
hospitals, schools, and communication systems. Such an expanded
social agenda is a win-win situation. Firms need these upgrades to
function more effectively and efficiently, while the byproduct of such
projects targets the enhanced social welfare of the country. Such strategy contributes to national economic growth and improved health and
education conditions with the added benefit to the commercial sector
of helping create a local citizenry that provides them with more consumers and a stronger workforce. Some critics see this new corporate
social obligation as socialized blackmail by inept or perhaps repressive
national governments that cannot by themselves improve the social network, so they push this responsibility on foreign commercial entities.
Other commentators, who have closely followed the massive initiative
of Chinese semigovernmental firms moving onto the African continent
in the energy field, view such developments as having politically ambitious overtones—a way to ingratiate China with governmental leaders and to foster China's influence over the citizens of the region. In
October 2009, Guinea's military junta government, facing international
sanction and heavy strictures over a mass killing of unarmed demonstra-
tors, announced an agreement with a Chinese company (some specu-
late the China International Fund as a *semi-independent operator*, but
all companies operating outside China have governmental oversight)
to provide up to $7 billion in electricity and aviation infrastructure—
an enormous sum for a country whose gross domestic product (GDP)
barely approaches an inflated $4.5 billion. Although no compensatory
quid pro quo has been specified, observers believe the investment is tied
to rights for mineral extractions that will be granted to the company.
Such an example is cited as masked socialized bribery, masked as CSR,
behind which is an underlying, dominant profit objective (an issue first
covered in Chapter 2). Whether or not one shares the opinion that the
CSR consideration is tainted, there seems to be little doubt that the
marriage of social responsibility and commercial interests is an issue
companies must engage in their strategic determinations.

A Criteria Issue: Whose Standards?

While companies either develop their own codes of conduct or latch on to internationally recognized compacts as signatories and thereby incorporate such declarations of direction unto themselves, there are certain elements in each document that will always be problematic. One of the critical issues is the choice of the presiding authority to precisely define technical guidelines for universal standards or global common measurement criteria when no specific laws or regulations are in force. Certainly, firms must comply with the local governmental rules and agency directives of the sovereign nations in which they operate. But what if such authoritative directions do not exist? Should American firms incorporate the regulatory mandates of their government and borrow from provisions as expressed in the rules and procedures of their respective agencies, such as the Environmental Protection Agency for the environment; the Occupational Safety and Health Administration for employee rights and conditions of the workplace; or the Food and Drug Administration for product testing, safety, and manufacturing standards? Can global firms ignore their home-country mandates and graft onto other sources of guidance like European Union regulatory observations covering the same areas of concern? What if there is a conflict? Should the lowest standard be employed? Should the highest authority or knowledgeable expert be consulted and who or what is such a body? Where do multinational firms get their standards? Does a firm that possesses the latest technology and research in a particular field or industry have a world social duty to go beyond host-country laws and regulations, as proposed by the lawyers representing the injured in the Union Carbide Indian plant explosion case, as previously presented?

Many times, domestic companies deliberately leave the jurisdiction of one country for another just to escape a barrage of costly regulatory provisions to set up shop abroad. Surely such firms would not want to place such continuing burdens back on themselves via inclusion in a company code of conduct, thereby negating the very reason they crossed borders to begin with. When global firms leave a home nation that has a minimum hourly wage to obtain location economies around the world and settle in a country that has no such quantitative provisions, are they justified in proclaiming that offering jobs where none exist entitles them to pay whatever wage laborers will take, even if it is literally pennies a day? Must overtime be paid if local regulations contain no such provisions? Should daily labor time and weekly hours be administered with a universal standard? As global firms in many emerging nations have no accountability to governmental guidelines, are they therefore masters unto themselves? Does a countervailing duty and responsibility reside with those who make all the rules in a lawless society? Do globetrotting NGOs, with no jurisdictional legal authority but who set themselves up as a vigilante force, have any influence on multinational firms? The answers to such questions may lie only in a company's agreement to subscribe and be bound to the directional guidelines of universal codes of conduct or in the corporate codes of conduct they construct themselves. In both instances, global firms may in fact police themselves and make their own ethical choices.

The Judges of Morality

To be ever mindful of the obligation to be good global citizens, transnational companies are being forced to develop and implement codes of conduct for their worldwide activities. The need is being intensified as special interest groups and the media create more informed consumers. These potential customers of global enterprises are themselves beginning to focus on the issue and are perhaps motivated to make choices based on how they perceive the ethical conduct and social responsibility patterns of the firms they patronize. They may well become the world's judge and jury for offending global corporations. The reputation of a corporation is now interwoven with the degree of morality it practices in its operational activities as actually practiced and perceived by the public. A firm's ethical standards are no longer below a consumer's radar but may be on par with the traditional value-added triad of price, quality, and service in the motivational buying decision.

The issue is therefore as much a strategic issue as are the other aspects of business-management disciplines studied in the classroom. A mistake in this area may not be as reversible as other errors administrators make. The reputation of a firm and its managers in its social contract with mankind could possibly make or break an enterprise. It can become a destructive virus or a badge of distinguished honor. It is against this backdrop of potential importance that the formation of a code of conduct needs to be carefully acknowledged, constructed, or possibly discounted altogether.

A Stacked Deck?

In an earlier section of the book, a correlation between the trust consumers place in companies and the positive perceptions of their brand names was presented. The greater the trust, the better the impression of the brand name and hence the most value that is gained as the propriety asset for the company. Against such a backdrop is the underlying impression that consumers just distrust commercial firms in general. Michael Moore's 2009 documentary, *Capitalism: A Love Story*, drives such impression. The film serves as an indictment of capitalism, portraying it as not just a bad system but an evil scheme, implying an immoral personalization characteristic to an organized structural model. A similar theme was explored in an older documentary *The Corporation*, released in 2004. Both films use the Supreme Court's ruling in the 1800s making public companies a "legal person" and thereby vested with certain rights, ostensibly the right to defend themselves in civil actions like any other citizen, as a bridge to portraying companies with human characteristics. The premise in both films is to endow such legally created fictitious entities with a conscience—a heart and a soul. This approach allowed the earlier film to place the corporation on the couch of a psychiatrist, finding it to be a dangerous psychopath, one that acts without a moral conscience. This latest version follows the same reasoning but encompasses the whole capital system, making it the ethical villain of our times.

Both films fuel the public perception that the players, the corporations, and the system they use (capitalism) are not to be trusted. Therefore, when companies act or are perceived to act in an immoral fashion, possessing a suspect ethical compass, they face a prejudicial public audience that has been primed to find them guilty simply by association—they are part of the capitalistic system. They do not receive the revered presumption of innocence. They are constantly on the defensive, and as we all know, a good defense is a strong offense. The message of both these films is that a proactive approach to ethics is warranted by public commercial institutions or at best a continuing vigilance to the public perceptions of veiled impropriety that seems to shadow their existence. Feature films like *Avatar*, the all-time largest grossing film in history released in 2010, offers a prejudicial portrayal of corporations as sinister institutions. Its underlying theme is a condemnation of their continuing immoral actions 150 years from now. Set in the next century when supply chains extend to outer space, the story centers on a group of mercenaries hired by a brutal public mining company, with dialogue reference to increasing their share price at the end of the financial quarter and to drive humanoids on a distant planet out of their territory to get to the valued and unique minerals beneath their home. With the added overtones of preserving the environment and the disregard for local cultural moral values, the movie echo's the sentiments of modern-day critics of MNCs, specifically their invasion and destruction of the resources of underdeveloped countries and their people. It seems that the ethical sins of historic and present corporate policies are projected to remain even in the fictional future. These films and many like them portray corporations as evil institutions lacking compassion for the lives of people and the environment they touch, reinforcing the notion that such institutions are evil. They contribute to the public perception that profit is the only force driving commercial firms and hence their motives are not to be trusted. Such images plague even the best of companies in pursuit of their business objectives.

The Continuing Public-Interest Imperative

From the errors of others a wise man corrects his own.
                    —Publilius Syrus, Greek philosopher

Sunlight is the best disinfectant to absolve bad practices.
                    —Louis Brandeis, American jurist

Given the historic financial-reporting scandals involving Enron, World-Com, and Global Crossing and the recent economic crisis blamed on investment banking houses in the United States, which has spilled out into the world, a groundswell has been created for more corporate governance. Add to such events the Bernie Madoff scandal that also touched foreign shores, and the integrity of commercial institutions remains suspect. Such direction targets public financial reporting and other areas of information dissemination, which are internally generated moral standards. While such areas of concern touch ethics and social responsibility, they are limited horizons and are far from the basic human rights issues that firms going international must address. The positive result, however, is that public companies are being pressured to structure systems to address overall issues of moral responsibility. It has been reported that in 2002 the use of ethics officers was gaining prominence in the post-Enron world. Driven by the then-outraged public opinion, it was noted that in the last three months of that year alone, roughly 100 U.S. companies had hired ethics officers, a sign perhaps that conformance to the basic rules of society, as per Friedman, even in free-enterprise systems, needs constant vigilance by professional guardians. In the mid-1990s, 60 percent of American companies claimed to have detailed codes of conduct,[21] while one-third proclaimed they had ethical training programs or ethics officers.[22]

Global public corporations have begun to also affirm their commitment to ethical conduct. In a letter to shareholders back in 2003, Citigroup devoted an entire paragraph titled "Our Commitment to the Community" to the subject. They proudly cited then and continuously note their appearance on the Dow Jones Sustainability World Index, as they strive to meet the criteria relating to the environment and social performance as well as being a supporter of human rights.[23]

Globally, the consuming public has begun to learn of human rights abuses practiced with the tacit knowledge or even outright contribution of multinational firms. Reports by the investigative arms of the world press and some television documentaries have assaulted sensitivities of those who purchase products as they find that they are made under the auspices of slavery, child labor, deplorable and hazardous working conditions, exhaustive work sessions, and other reprehensible or potentially injurious conditions.

As prominent world brand names like Nike, Levi Strauss, Liz Claiborne, Ann Taylor, Brooks Brothers, and others have been publicly chastised for using subcontractors that do not pay overtime, house workers in crowded dormitories, feed them a poor diet, and operate unsafe factories, the pressure for change grows. The globally recognized retail chain Walmart has required its suppliers to sign a code of basic labor standards since 1992, but it still has not been immune to allegations of misconduct in specific countries. Saks Incorporated, owner of 10 major retail chains and 350 stores, announced a policy against sourcing products from Myanmar and that it would avoid goods private label and otherwise (from supplying manufacturers)—from a country that has seen ongoing issues around human rights abuses. They joined Walmart, Federated Department Stores, and Tommy Hilfiger, becoming the 39th U.S. company to ban goods from the country in early 2003.

Responding to the growing public interest as exhibited by consumer awareness in ethics and social responsibility causes might also bring a sustainable competitive advantage to a firm. Alternatively, having to combat such perceptions and defend actions diverts corporate attention and resources, placing such enterprises in a more difficult competitive situation.

Persistent Issues

Lingering questions remain. Does social responsibility equate to instituting social change? As global firms enter emerging or transitional societies are they required to alter their normal social development cycle? Would such intrusion rupture the fabric of a society and disrupt the normal progression of changes at a pace best left to internal circumstances and periods of adjustment? Can it positively be argued that real social responsibility begins and ends with acceptance of the status quo and not interfering in the society of another? Are multinational firms the modern-day evangelists, or are they cultural interlopers bent on imperialistic alteration in their own image? In today's world, two fundamental forces seem to be emerging: globalism and tribalism. Nationalistic groups and fundamental religious leaders are defending their traditional environments using emotional rhetoric to rally their citizens against the infusion of Western exposure. Forced changes in the commercial operations of local enterprises may be viewed as the precursor to wholesale transformation of the society around them. Resistance, therefore, may not be a simple question of different approaches to business ethics or acceptable moral principles presented on a labor-treatment platform but based on a resistance to change that undermines the basic social structure of a country.

Another View

There is a point of view expressed by human rights advocates that postulates the presumption that foreign influence vis-à-vis commercial
investment in a country by itself, without any ethical code of conduct
being pressed upon the local community, can be a force of positive change
and improvement. Many social economists feel economic development
in a nation can bring about pressure for democratic reforms. Fifty years
ago, sociologist Seymour Martin Lipset observed that more well-to-do
nations have a greater chance of sustaining democracy. More recently
Adam Przeworski reiterated such thinking by studying every attempted
conversion to democracy around the world, and finding that $6,075 in
per capita income is the level at which such a transition tends to succeed.
Those countries falling below $3,000 would probably fail in such an
attempt, and those in the middle have a 50 percent chance of sustaining democratic ideals in their society. The rationale behind the hypothesis is that as a country economically improves its GNP, the per capita
distribution of income and wealth is more widely dispersed among the
masses. The result is that a middle class begins to replace the elite, with
power being shifted to a wider, emerging group of citizens. A representative democracy takes hold, and the rights of all citizens are more fairly
enforced. In essence, as the dispersal of influence is widened in a society, individual entitlement rights are expanded. Such leveling adjustment
leads to more dispersed individual protections with the need for a more
representative government to be formulated. This in turn enhances the
opportunity for equality to mature and social justice programs to be
enacted. The message—a contribution to economic growth can foster
democracy—is often heard as a justification for firms entering China and
other historically repressive countries. This concept was cited as a motivation for General Motors to remain in South Africa during the apartheid
era and was the theoretical basis beyond the construction of the original
Sullivan Principles under which the company's continued presence in the
country was based. Perhaps, therefore, Milton Friedman's observation
that merely conducting a money-making enterprise while in compliance
with local society policy is enough. Any commercial activity that creates
jobs and converts resources, which improves the national economy, can

provide a platform on which democratic principles can be rooted and human rights can progress. A company therefore may not have to be semiactive and become a signatory to global compacts or even proactive and implement its own principles to have a positive impact on initiating social change in morally bankrupt countries. Their mere entry as the initiator of commercial activities in countries with historically repressive human rights conditions may contribute to the promotion and raising of ethical standards by their very presence. The burden of carrying the added baggage of morality as companies travel across borders may not be needed. Once their operations have begun, social change could conceivably be rooted in the economic improvement they bring to a country.

Such a rationale, as simple and compelling as it may sound, does not always play well on the stage of global public opinion. Companies are still criticized for setting up shops in nations with poor human rights reputations and are even chastised with the argument that their actions in fact support such reprehensible activities as opposed to altering them.

Workers' Right of Assembly and Organization

The history of the world is filled with the reluctance of monarchs and governments to allow their citizens the right to freely assemble and organize. Due to such conflicts, revolutions and wars erupted. In the business world, such confrontations periodically resulted in lockouts and strikes with violent ends, with governments often siding with commercial institutions. When societies in such countries embraced the local labor movement, they motivated their governments to enact laws and regulatory agencies to protect workers and provide them with the right to organize and choose their own forms of representation with employers. As multinationals engage the global labor pool, whether directly or via contracted third parties, the issue of recognizing the simple right of local laborers to gather, no less to form trade unions, is an ethical issue they encounter. In countries without formalized legal rights empowering local labor groups to form and negotiate on their behalf, the ability of global firms to control governments and even to influence the domestic society at large to suppress organized worker associations is strong. An inducement in fact for foreign investment in a country may be the capacity to operate without interference by organized local labor relations. It should be noted while most international labor human rights accords recognize the right of freedom of assembly by workers, the idea is not universal. This basic tenet is the civil-liberty platform upon which all other labor issues are constructed. It is the principle that separates free workers from slaves. It serves as the doorway for specific employee grievances to be addressed, including but not limited to the collateral elements of child labor, facility health and safety concerns, work hours, and equitable pay standards. Global commercial entities are therefore encouraged to include such fundamental considerations as they make ethical decisions affecting their worldwide labor networks.

Even communist-dominated countries have begun to press the issue of workers' rights on foreign investors. The founding doctrine of communism, to protect the proletariat, seems to embody the principle of recognizing worker rights but history has shown that this principle, interwoven with conspicuous state-directed programs, often runs counter to helping the workers. It is, therefore, worthwhile to note that the Chinese government has begun pressing resident multinational companies to observe the right of local workers to set up unions. The director of the Institute for Labor Relations at People's University in Beijing in his public speeches has begun to recognize that with globalization, the conflicts between workers and employers are becoming very serious and worthy of inspection. Such acknowledgment by a government-sponsored institution sends a clear message to multinationals. Nations long criticized for human rights abuses in respect to workers' rights are turning the corner and aligning themselves with the common laborer. They may no longer be aligned with the foreign investors they once courted by looking the other way when multinationals ignored worker rights within their borders.

When the official All-China Federation of Trade Unions (ACFTU) goes so far as to announce a blacklist of multinational firms (Walmart, Dell, Eastman Kodak, McDonald's, KFC, and Samsung Group), accusing them of blocking Chinese workers from unionizing, their actions speak louder than mere statements of support for the proletariat, and global firms need to take notice of this. It is interesting, however, that such rhetoric and allegations have targeted large, international resident-alien entities as opposed to their own massive industrial contingent of domestic enterprises. However, it should be noted that such reports of support for their workers may be politically motivated to calm labor strife by directing internal animosity toward the foreign employers, thereby deflecting labor unrest from national firms and government-run manufacturing facilities.

Such self-serving declarations or propaganda are always suspect when coming from a historically communist regime. Soon after the announcements regarding these internal matters were made, the Chinese government canceled a meeting of union and business to review how MNCs should adopt standards for the rights of workers in China and revoked visas for all those poised to attend. The conference, sponsored by the Organisation for Economic Co-operation and Development (OECD), had specifically included the Chinese authorities in its planning process with an agenda to incorporate the use of their organizational guidelines for MNCs. But as the program was also to cover a wide range of labor issues, additional points might have touched on local governmental policies toward workers, with potential embarrassing consequences, necessitating perhaps the last-minute cancellation. One gets a feeling from the reactionary critical comments issued by the TUAC (the Trade Union Advisory Committee to the OECD), which said that it's the right time, not the wrong time, to discuss the rights of workers in China alongside those of other nations in the world.

Whatever the motivation, the vulnerability of the global firm as the stalking horse for unethical actions seems to continue even in the most unlikely environments. It serves as a continuing example of the need for multinational firms to remain proactively cognizant of this issue, as even the cover once supplied by countries repressive of human rights may be evaporating.

Managerial Reflections

1. Ethical conduct develops on three platforms: at the personal level, on the exposure to diversity, and at the intersection of the two. Of the three, which tends to have the greatest influence on moral behavior and ethical decision making of global managers? Where does corporate culture fit in?

2. Milton Friedman's idea of CSR directs firms to be profitable while conforming to the basic rules of society. What happens when the

basic rules of society are not universal but vary as companies find themselves operating in numerous social environments?

3. Commercial institutions are often portrayed as endowed with human characteristics, having a heart, soul, and moral conscience, while others portray them as a mere legal fiction, a mechanism, an unemotional device for accomplishing unified goals. Can a corporation blend these two opposing observations?

4. In the popular, multigenerational, long-running television and movie series *Star Trek*, the prime directive of the Federation of Planets instructs starship captains to act only as visitors as they explore new frontiers, letting the societies they engage with develop of their own accord. Should MNCs follow this direction or should firms be initiators of public social change as opposed to passive bystanders?

5. In the era of modern globalization, MNCs may find themselves in the position of not only replacing national governments as the prime provider of the economic livelihoods of citizens but also, at the other side of the spectrum, supplementing their historic role as the supplier of social programs. Is this a reasonable expectation, and if so, how should companies prepare for it?

CHAPTER 4

Ethics Unabridged

Enlarge the place of your tent, and let the curtains of your habitations be stretched out; do not hold back; lengthen your cords and strengthen your stakes.

—Isaiah 54:2

Ethics is not definable, is not implementable, because it is not conscious; it involves not only our thinking, but also our feeling.
—Valdemar W. Setzer, Brazilian anthropologist

Traditionally, ethical determinations in regard to business involved the proper treatment of limited parties, those directly involved in commercial transactions. Applied morality in this respect took its cue from two primary sources. First, the influence of human relationship principles of organized religious cults that instructed worshippers to be honest and fair in their bartering activities; in essence, not to cheat the other party. Such direction was offered in the early written records of the spiritually inclined Egyptians and other societies in the West as well as in the moral guidance of the East to followers of their respective religion inspired faiths. Second is the Greek philosophical discourses that expressed similar values within the secular world. Historically, the specter of acting ethically orbited the business world.

Over the course of recorded human events as reflected in the commercial community, the expansion via world resource exploration and later the industrial revolution caused the shadow of ethical considerations to hover more closely to the business world. In the modern era of globalization, the ethical satellite circling commercial activities has spun out of its previous trajectory while splitting into a series of new applied terminologies. The definition of ethics as a system of moral principles guiding acceptable conduct has eclipsed its narrow application within the business world. Ethics has evolved and its transition has altered the traditional place it had occupied in the managerial process. It has taken on an expanded role in managerial strategic decision making and the tactics designed to achieve them. The result—ethics unabridged.

The old adage that every human action or inaction carries an ethical consideration has, therefore, been visited upon the commercial world to a degree never before considered. The subject matter loosely identified as ethics has quickly evolved gaining the ever increasing attention of managers as its historic application has been transformed. It has become an ever more important mechanism requiring a more exhaustive integration into the managerial approaches. Historically, ethics acted as a component to the commercial endeavor. It provided principles of guardianship for doing business. What was once the mortar that held the building blocks of an organization together is today an intricate part of the strategic foundation of an enterprise. It has also become a business and an industry unto itself.

Therefore, the philosophically and religiously inspired ideal has morphed into a required consideration as reflected in its being added as a valued area of inquiry at business schools throughout the world. Ethics is being recognized, more and more, as a prime imperative not just in the planning stage, but at all levels of tactical maneuvers managers must take into consideration. Inspection into this topic was initially driven by the modern era of globalization as companies moved abroad at an ever increasing rate encountering various inacceptable conduct. Coupled with the transparencies being forced upon transnational corporations by ever vigilant reporting institutions that in turn are responding to worldwide special interest groups and universal consumers, the issue of firms acting in an ethical manner has dramatically emerged. Alongside the other disciplines in the managerial process, it is now recognized as a major contributor to the success or failure of an organization. To appreciate the unexpurgated version of the term ethics and understand its place as an influential element on the commercial stage, one must first be aware of the contemporary landscape that it rests upon. The next step is to recognize two branches of the ethical application in the business world—corporate social responsibility (CSR) and responsible leadership (RL). These terms have almost replaced the use of ethics to define the morality of commercial endeavors. The classical roots had emerged as a stable trunk that has grown branches that now dwarf the original torso.

The Modern Commercial Ethical Landscape

Know the terrain…

—Sun Tzu, Chinese general

He must also learn the nature of the terrain…
—Niccolò Machiavelli, Italian political theorist and diplomat

Ethics has always acted like a satellite orbiting the commercial world. In the modern era of globalization, two interesting phenomenon have impacted the traditional role of ethics in the business community. First, its hovering trajectory has been severely altered. At times it has hit the surface with both soft and hard landings altering the terrain that commercial enterprises operate upon. This issue will be investigated initially. Second, it has split into a series of newly defined terms that need to be appreciated and understood.

The business educational field for managers is filled with references, even more so, books devoted to the lessons to be learned from the great trailblazers in history as well as those offering advice to leaders of organizations. The list of books devoted to Sun Tzu, the Chinese general, and his treatise, *The Art of War* written between 300 BC and 500 BC, reinterpreting his writings as guidance to executives would fill the shelves of any library. Those studying to become managers would be well advised to read his classic manual on how to defeat one's enemies (commercial competitors) by developing the proper strategy. A whole chapter of Tzu's book is devoted to appreciating the terrain (he distinguishes six types) upon which the opponent is to be engaged. Knowing the environment is to be well prepared as it determines the best use of one's resources; thereby dictating the tactical moves one undertakes.

Machiavelli in the 16th century, with a desire to gain the favor of his liege lord, provided an instructional dissertation on the art of maintaining a kingdom. Like Sun Tzu, the principles outlined in *The Prince* (1532) have also been used as instructional tools for managers to achieve their objectives. Machiavelli too speaks of the importance of recognizing the terrain that one will be operating upon and as such determines the strategic decisions and again the tactical maneuvers.

Many university instructors utilize the teaching of both these extraordinary thinkers in their business courses, while working executives are encouraged to pick up editions of both works with the subtitle *for managers*. Professor John S. McCallum of the Richard Ivey School of Business utilizes both references in his capstone course for MBA students called "The Chief Executive Officer (CEO)". In an article called "In War and Business, It's the Terrain That Matters," he mentions both of them along with Carl von Clausewitz's *On War*. McCallum writes:

> For executives, substitute the expression "business conditions" for the word "terrain" and you have the concept. If you are the one calling the shots, it is critical you know and understand the world around you that everyone must take as the same given. The terrain is the playing field on which you and everyone else competes, over which no one has control, but on which outcomes often totally depend. Decision makers who do not know and understand the terrain better be lucky.[1]

Before dwelling into the complicated strategic and tactical application of ethics, and following a thorough understanding of what the term means, it is prudent to develop an appreciation of the contemporary social environment in which moral values, principles, and even codes of conduct are perceived no less employed. An inspection into the current state, the public perception of ethics as specifically practiced by commercial institutions, is therefore warranted. This is the operating terrain, the backdrop for applying ethics, that companies must first recognize as they devise how best to approach the subject.

The general public develops prejudices, their take on what is happening around them, from a variety of sources. The introduction to the behavior of commercial institutions begins with history. The past has not treated their actions well. Critics of the capitalistic system have always caused suspicion to be placed on the commercial imperative. The creation of wealth in any form has always been subjected to ridicule and scorn.

The argument for chastising the quest for the profit and the moral use of factors involved in its creation is certainly with merit. Throughout history, questionable and bad practices by unscrupulous business enterprises have impacted the social welfare of the world. The treatment of workers as slaves or freemen pressed into service without any ability to control no less influence their fate has been evident in societies around the globe. Environments have been raped and pillaged for the sake of the resources they could yield, while the establishment of production facilities has resulted in the pollution if not destruction of lands. The damaging effect on the human populations of such areas is well documented. Even the so-called beneficiaries, the consumers of commercial endeavors, have been stripped of their ability to affect the market, the so-called invisible hand, due to monopolistic practices along with industry collusion and partnering with repressive governments. All these events have contributed to the black eye of business. The result has been a blanket labeling of business practices within the framework of ethical determinations as suspect at best. The public therefore remains skeptical when companies proclaim they are acting ethically. Such is the age-old prejudicial moral terrain in which commercial enterprises find themselves operating in the 21st century. Simply put, the modern ethical landscape is a torturous environment to conduct business in. The old axiom "You are damned if you do, damned if you don't" is a most appropriate reference in characterizing how firms must navigate the ethical scene.

The damming of the commercially induced imperative portrayed as morally bankrupt due to the lack of ethics employed in its operational over centuries is an acknowledged fact. But such negative conclusion overlooks the other fact, the positive side at the core of business activities, the vital trade desire. Societies may have never progressed and civilization may not have developed toward its full potential without the commercial imperative. It is a natural human condition that people like to be rewarded for what they do. The exchange process is a system whereby two parties of a transaction receive what they each perceive as an acceptable value. Is it perfect? No. But the principle has enabled people to exchange the fruits of their labors in a mutually beneficial way.

In my book *Tracing the Roots of Globalization and Business Principles*,[2] a chronological portrait is presented to show how the commercial process, built on the trade imperative, influenced and contributed to the development of civilization. As I state in the Prologue, "The gathered material was constructed as a neutral assessment and not intended to portray the practice as good or bad." The fact, however, is that people are motivated to create, to change, to innovate when they receive something in return for their efforts. The exchange process provided a system of remuneration for mankind's determination to grow and improve. It was the onus through which people reached out and touched others beyond their bordered territories. In the process, knowledge was swapped resulting in the global spread of new ideas and beliefs. In spite of the benefits of the trading system, the practice was overshadowed by the unscrupulous behavior of its participants. Such historical stigma still plagues the modern corporations of today while providing the basis for a continuing deeper inspection of their global activities.

The Two-Way Flow of Expanded Ethical Transparency

One of the major changes in the ethical landscape has evolved from transparency. It has arrived on the commercial scene from two sources, external and internal; both acting to raise public awareness and therefore place added pressure on companies to respond to the matter. Looking at corporate ethical behavior from the outside is being examined to an extent never before seen by numerous expanded reporting venues. On the other side of the two-way ethical inspectional mirror is the self-actuation, leading to the self-referendum of corporations as they issue annual reports under the banner of sustainability and CSR. This lateral consideration is handled later in the section on CSR.

The ability of the public to peer into questionable moral practices of corporations in the modern era is an outgrowth of today's 24-hour news cycle, coupled with the addition of World Wide Web blogging and the social media. It allows for the dissemination of information relative to the prime subject matter, ethical conduct, to be revealed and come under scrutiny like never before. Periodically, scandals involving either the outright negligence of companies effecting consumers or their cynical approach to the treatment of workers in facilities directly or indirectly controlled by them, the so-called sweatshop has historically been reported on. Be it overt actions or just benign neglect, such activities have called into question whether such organizations are simply incompetent or even worse, morally bankrupt. Beyond obvious unscrupulous acts, the ever moving line of political correctness has now moved closer falling under the ethical treatment umbrella due to the heightened sensitivity of the public at large. Any indiscretion, any social faux pas, any questionable treatment especially related to minority groups involving not just employees or third party supply laborers, but customers and communities as well, is coming under advanced public scrutiny. The end result is that public trust in these institutions has eroded. Today's firms, desirous of orchestrating acceptable and sustainable ethical codes of conduct, find themselves facing a public image problem. While their ancestral history is resplendent with events of dysfunctional morality, the pattern is seemingly being repeated but with the added element of wider critical exposure. A few recent examples illustrate the continuing malfeasance of global corporations and the outrage felt by the general public.

No ethical issue has inflamed the conscience of the average world citizen more than reports of abuse of global workers as the personal harm inflicted on them seems to be felt by all. It tugs at one's emotional strings like no other ethical issue. In December 2012, a fire engulfed the eight story Tazreen Fashions factory in Ashulia, Bangladesh. Fire safety precautions had been routinely overlooked. The facility was a disaster waiting to happen, and it did. While the use of sweatshoplike facilities with substandard working conditions resulting in slaverylike conditions has been reported in the past, this incident was even more deplorable due to the inhuman results. The fire killed 112 workers and scores more bore injuries that would scare them for life. Tazreen it turns out was making clothing through a series of interwoven global supply chain operations for brands and stores in the United States and Europe. It was a segment of the third party subcontracting system that allows for such marginal factories to operate on the fringes of what was supposed to be a monitored inspection program filtering out sweatshop type operators whose safety records were deplorable. However, low cost and the quick turnaround of new styles is the production hallmark of the fashion industry. An overriding motivational drive, the *bottom line*, allowed for factors like Tazreen to slip through the system as the duel pressures, cheap and quick, has created "opaque networks of subcontracts with suppliers or local buying houses."[3] Therefore, a number of easily recognized global brands as well as major worldwide retail store groups were surprised that they indirectly utilized the Tazreen factory. It was a hidden subcontractor for the firms they had actually engaged. This activity makes it hard for firms to inspect no less police third-party suppliers. The key phrase embedded in *The New York Times* headline was "…Gap in Safety…."[4] It recognized that the firms reported in the article had taken steps to alleviate such potential harmful situations, but the holes in the safety systems they had initiated still existed. This is what makes this case so interesting. Despite valiant coordinated efforts aimed at alleviating unsafe work place environments, the horrific incident could not be avoided.

Companies in the clothing industry have formed coalitions like the Fair Labor Association to verify working conditions at the facilities of third-party manufacturers. They have also formed information-pooling associations such as the Fair Factories Clearinghouse to share compliance data to weed out unsafe third-party contractors. More and more firms have their own personnel to routinely conduct onsite reviews to confirm that the factories they use are measuring up to the standards they require in their agreements with them. Such efforts are also supplemented by independent verification auditing agencies such as Cal Safety Compliance, SGS of Switzerland, and the Bureau Veritas of France. There is no doubt that proactive efforts have been made to certify supply chain links. However, in spite of these positive steps, problems did persist resulting in the tragedy of lost lives and horrific injuries to workers. Such events continue to jeopardize the good names of well-meaning global companies while tainting the ethical environment they need to operate in. It only takes one incidence of malfeasance to call into question the ethics of transnational firms as the public is primed to hold them responsible. Such is the global terrain that companies must navigate. Two comparative proverbs seem to constantly plague them … *perfect is the enemy of good* and *no good deed goes unpunished.* Try as they may to perform in an ethical manner, the public at large remains as a cruel judge and an unforgiving jury of their actions; even if proactive measures were taken to combat possible accidents.

A similar situation involving the questionable practices of third-party supplier employees, thankfully not resulting in death or grave injury, has to do with the continuing issue of child labor—a historic issue. Again, while substantial efforts were undertaken to alleviate the hiring of underage workers, the system was flawed. Samsung the South Korean electronics giant had a strict policy aimed at preventing minors from being hired. Even though the legal working age in China was 16, Samsung determined it was too low and issued specific instructions to its suppliers not to hire employees under 18. The company routinely conducted inspections to monitor compliance. To supplement periodic on site verification, they forced all of its supplier factories to install a sophisticated facial recognition system that matched government-issued photo ID cards as proof of age. Despite such measures, China Labor Watch, a labor rights activist group, uncovered evidence of girls as young as 14 working in the Shinyang Electronics factory that makes phones for Samsung in the Chinese province of Dongguan.[5] This activist organization, like other nongovernmental organizations (NGOs), has been monitoring labor practices utilized by the supply chain networks of multinational corporations (MNCs). These underage workers were part of a *labor dispatch system*, a series of middlemen who routinely funnel laborers to factories especially during peak periods when temporaries are required. They were not paid by the factory but by the employment agency. According to reports, the girls were given false government ID cards and allowed to by-pass the facial recognition system. The factory or perhaps the intermediary agency borrowed (or forged or stole) real identification and used them to register the girls as regulations required.

This incident is again indicative of the proverb *perfect is the enemy of good*. The pressure on MNCs to act ethically and thereby institute measures to the best of their ability to monitor and control the actions of those parties they contract with is a most difficult burden. They cannot rely on host government authorities to assist, as even when regulations are in force to combat illegal activities, it falls upon MNCs to police them. Local agencies are either bribed to look the other way or no resources are available to enforce them. Try as they may, many MNCs cannot control all aspects of their far flung operations. While numerous MNCs have policies in place and back them with proactive tactics to see they are complied with, acting as a cross border enforcement bureau is an impossible task. And when incidents do arise, the blame seems to always fall on them. Such is the prejudicial terrain that companies must not just navigate but endure.

Apart from the questionable ethical practices regarding the treatment of indigenous labor, other events continue to prejudice the public as to the activities of MNCs. Another reported event involved the use of bribery by the Mexican subsidiary of the large global retailer Walmart. (The subject of bribery has been discussed in Chapter 2.) The local executive staff was accused of making routine payoffs, with the overall amount total approaching $24 million, to local authorities in order to attain building permits for new store locations. In a follow up to the initial stories that circulated in the press, additional allegations included a host of more details that supposedly dramatize not only the monetary corruption, but also show a total disrespect for ethical concerns. *The New York Times's* investigative reporters Bhasin and Lutz showed how the bribes masked (1) harm to local residents, (2) threatened environmental safety, and (3) even disrespected the valued Mexican Mayan heritage.[6] Bribed local authorities allowed a Sam's Club to be constructed in a densely populated neighborhood in Mexico City without obtaining a construction license, an environmental authorization, an urban impact assessment, and not even a simple traffic permit. It led to the draining of the existing scarce resources of the neighborhood and overwhelming its residents with severe overcrowding that was already causing undue hardship. Another bribe enabled a large refrigerated distribution center to be constructed in an environmentally fragile flood basin north of Mexico City, contributing to a potential life threatening run off during the heavy rainy season. Two other reports indicated that architectural preservation maps were altered to allow for the building of Walmart supermarkets near and perhaps over sites of nationally treasured Mayan pyramids and the ruins of ancient settlements. When public voiced its opposition to such desecration, a pronounced public relations campaign was mounted by Walmart to attack such groups, portraying them as fringe lunatics with an anticapitalistic agenda using a trumped up desecration allegation which was not true.

What makes these series of alleged events so reprehensible is not just the payment of a monetary reward to officials to ease the paper gridlock, speed up the approval process, and move matters through the jungle of red tape that many local, regional, and national administrative agencies are awash in. It was not even directed to win a governmental project over rivals. From a commercial unethical viewpoint, bribery inhibits or destroys free market competition. It allows for an unfair advantage to be granted via the bribe to one party over another. Throughout the world, the "practice of bribery is acceptable when used to lube the gears of government in order to get approval for certain business ventures."[7] The cheating practice, the rigging of the system, is not only found in emerging countries but in those labeled as developing like the BRIC four (Brazil, Russia, India, and China) as well as in industrialized nations. Despite the U.S. Foreign Corrupt Practices Act, noted earlier in the text regarding the regulatory penalties for bribing officials and really aimed at preventing firms from securing lucrative government contracts, rewards for good service from those in a position to move things forward is a tolerated necessity. Bribery is also indicative of the corrupt political culture that many MNCs encounter and hence must operate within. It is part of the landscape that business is conducted upon.

In this case, the injurious activities went beyond the competitive transactional business arena. It contained an additional reprehensible element—the total disregard for the social welfare of the neighborhoods Walmart operated in as well as the social effect of bribes on the treasured culture of a nation. The payments incentivized bureaucrats to look the other way or alter records presenting a real potential social and environmental danger to the indigenous population. The destructive consequences of their behavior went beyond the scope of the normal governmental bribe for efficiency or to gain a competitive advantage. Contributing to the destruction was the disrespect shown for country's honored historical culture is just socially destructive.

A fourth event involved an environmental disaster. It was far more alarming than the two previous ethical calamities because it impacted a much wider constituency. The Deepwater Horizon oil spill, often referred to as the BP (British Petroleum) oil spill occurred in the Gulf of Mexico on April 20, 2010. The incident eclipsed the June 3, 1979 Ixtoc I oil spill also in the Gulf attributable to an exploratory well drilled by the Mexican government-owned oil company Pemex. It also harkened public notoriety back to the earlier noted Exxon Valdez oil tanker spill off the coast of Alaska. The release of oil from the tanker was extremely harmful to the local ecological system—wildlife habitat, fish, birds, and seaside creatures with the future pollution of the ocean remaining an unmeasurable factor for decades to come. But its financial impact on people was limited. The BP fiasco was the largest and most harmful accidental marine oil spill in the history of the industry. The socio-economic impact of over 4.9 million barrels being released was felt across the southern coastline of the United States. Besides the incalculable damage to the gulf waters, the wetlands and beachhead, the financial impact on the oil, fishing, and tourist industry as well as aligned business in the region was devastating.

For BP, the costs involved due to federal penalties, state mandated grants, and enormous claims have been estimated to exceed $90 billion dollars. Beyond these monetary expenditures the evolving damage to BP due to the public's ethical reaction also needs to be considered. Investors while well aware of the drain on potential profits of the company also sold off the stock as the immoral blemish took hold. The loss of market value dropped the company from second to fourth place amongst the world's major oil companies. Even more alarming was that "During the crisis, BP gas stations in the United States reported sales off between 10 and 40 percent due to the backlash against the company."[8] Following the disaster, the company ran and continues to run a public relations and marketing campaign to gain back consumer confidence and stem the tide of resentment directed against their brand image. No precise figures have been released by the company to measure the expense of such programs. But the extensive TV advertising promoting their good citizenship in regard to the region affected and also as a provider of social welfare across the nation as a job creator coupled with conservation effectiveness is certainly an unanticipated and therefore unbudgeted costly program to maintain.

This event has also changed the way companies respond to doing the right thing after an industrial accident. In the past, the standard policy was to wait until they were sued by those affected, let the courts assess damage and hope the lengthy process would minimize their financial liability. In this case, the oil company took a decidedly different track. Being well cognizant of public opinion, and the ever watchful eyes of a critical media, the company changed its strategy and therefore its tactical response. It began to make amends before the court proceedings could begin. Apart from spending billion on the aforementioned environmental clean-up it immediately announced, it then began to compensate the economic victims taking the unprecedented step of waive liability limits putting aside over $20 billion into a compensation account. Bob Dudley, the BP chief executive commented that the objective was "to reach reasonable settlements and put this behind us. I don't regret what we did. I feel proud of us as a company."[9]

At the center of this controversy, as well as the others profiled, is the conduct of the company, the perception that its unethical practices no matter how they are defined, contributed to the resulting catastrophe. The susceptibility to such allegations whether they are malice aforethought, the outright intentional disregarding of avoidable consequences or even events attributable to a nonforeseeable accident will always bare the label of ethical malfeasance.

The stigma of political correctness is like a shadow trailing ethical determinations. Every week, incidences regarding the questionable practices of companies are noted carrying the unqualified notation that the event borders on the nonethical. A young child, a passenger on an airline making its final decent on a runway, is refused permission to use the restroom and he soils himself. The upset mother being told that regulations require all to be in their seat during such procedure afterward still posts a complaint on her Facebook account. The story is picked up by the Associated Press and the specter of unethical conduct is visited on the airline. The refusal by any establishment to service customers they deem problematic, such as asking a family with a crying child to leave, or the unintentional mishandling of disabled patron's needs, or just being rude to minorities, while all justifiable concerns are being presented with a bias against commercial entities. The events are crossing over from being unsympathetic to being socially irresponsible to a question of ethics. These considerations will plague companies like the potential of a debilitating disease.

Comparison with a Historic Era

As reports surface of foreign third-party manufacturing sites operating like sweatshops, taking advantage of the indigenous workforce in unsafe facilities while local governments look the other way, the comparison harkens back to a historical economic system. The stories that question the moral turpitude of MNCs, be they in respect to the bribery of officials, disregard for native heritage, or the compromising of the environment, all seem to remind one of past era. The rise of MNCs and their influence on the world economy has been negatively compared to the mercantile period in Europe when the accumulation of wealth by rulers and merchants allowed the exploitation of those affected by this pecuniary structure. The setting up of foreign colonies by the regimes of Spain, Portugal, France, and Britain to ensure cheap resources of raw materials and labor, and to such end allowing monopolistic commercial practices, all are characteristics portrayed as applying to modern transnational corporation. Mercantilism is also associated with the triangle trade route that brought African slaves to the Western Hemisphere.

The operational practices that filled the treasuries of Royal families and the accounts of their state charted business firms are, some would argue, being duplicated by today's MNCs in a neo-mercantilist way to enhance their bottom lines. The social and economic destructive side of mercantilism inflicted upon the local inhabitants of the colonies they constructed invites a comparison with today's global outsourcing activities and harvesting of natural resources by MNCs in less developed countries. During the mercantile period local populations were manipulated and misused. They were treated like slaves or bonded laborers, working hard for long hours under oppressive and dangerous conditions, with bare minimum subsistence wages. Environmental devastation followed in the wake of such activities while social unrest was created. Modern global commercial, some would argue, are replicating the old imperialistic national imperative. The connotation linking the 1600s commercial practices of despot regimes with the modern dominance of large transnational corporations, all to the detriment of stakeholders affected by their actions, is a most damaging comparison. Seemingly at both times the rich and influential controlled the fate of others, singularly driven by the flow of material wealth into their coffers, irrespective of the harm they inflicted. Corporations need to thwart these negative contrasts as the global socioeconomic terrain is fought with such perils. Constant vigilance, coupled with strategic and tactical maneuvers, to prevent such events or to react to their emergence, whether corporations are totally responsible or just complacent with them, is a required element in the managerial process.

Questionable ethical behavior as housed in the new lexicon of inquiries as to a firm's CSR and the RL of its management has become an enemy of corporations eclipsing the attacks of competition. The home page of the online magazine of *Business Ethics: The Magazine of Corporate Social Responsibility* well states the current situation:

A lot has changed in the more than two decades since *Business Ethics* was founded (1987). Ethics and governance have emerged as front-page news and lead agenda items in corporate board rooms.... Good corporate citizenship is now studied, advocated and sometimes practiced.[10]

While news reporting will continue to be a monitor of ethical corporate behavior the general social environment that companies find themselves operating within is also susceptible to other persuasive influential components that should not be overlooked.

The Influential Entertainment Media

Movies can and do have tremendous influence in shaping young lives in the realm of entertainment towards the ideals and objectives of normal adulthood.

—Walt Disney

Outside of the past and present reporting of the questionable behavior of commercial entities, another influential medium, the entertainment industry, has emerged as an effective instrument in the formation of public opinion directed against such institutions. Many years ago, as a young man I saw the movie *Jaws*.[11] The dramatic effect on me and the large viewing audience was to make all of us very wary of entering the ocean for fear of a shark attack. Even 40 years later as an adult, whenever I am at the beach or hear of such an incident, my anxiety is awakened and I hark back to my vivid memory of the movie.

The portrayal of commercial enterprises and their unscrupulous methodology in attaining goals has been the subject of film stories for years. Perhaps one of the earliest commentaries on the potential socially harmful efficiencies of modern industrialization and its effect on factory workers was *Modern Times*.[12] In it, the iconic Little Tramp, played by Charlie Chaplin, is subject to the problems of an efficient assembly line which causes him to suffer a nervous breakdown. Set amidst the desperate unemployment conditions brought on by the Great Depression it served as a comedic commentary on the uncaring self-absorbed company executives who put profits before all else. In the post-World War II movie *The Man in the Grey Flannel Suit*,[13] based on Sloan Wilson's best seller of the same title, the effect again on the individual when subjected to the rigid conformity of the executive suite is examined. It was again a social commentary on the corporate organization seemingly operating without a moral compass, eventually playing havoc in man's personal life.

Numerous other films in the late 1900s, based on managerial malfeasance, profit trumping acceptable behavior, as taken from the headlines of the day, created a deleterious biased view of corporations. In 1989, the documentary *Roger & Me*[14] traced the economic impact of plant closings by General Motors. The layoff of thousands of Flint, Michigan, auto workers was occasioned by the transferring of their jobs to Mexico where cheaper labor was available. The decision was made in spite of the company experiencing record profits. The film was memorable and it resonated more deeply in the public's mind as the director Michael Moore attempted a face to face confrontation with the CEO of GM, Roger Smith; hence the personalized movie title. He also delves into the emotional impact of the plant closings on his friends and narrates their individual hardships. The story portrayed the actions of the company in a most unfavorable light and served as a rallying beacon for the image of for-profit firms as unprincipled, deceitful, void of integrity—in short unethical. Another documentary, *The Corporation*[15] released in 2003 in Canada examined the modern-day corporation. The profile it offered compared the contemporary profit driven entity to that of a clinically diagnosed psychopath. The symptoms it exhibited included a callous disregard for the safety and well-being of others, a deceitful lying propensity, the incapacity to experience no less feel guilt and finally the inability to conform to social norms with outright disrespect of the law. The demonization of the corporation is dramatically shown by the picture on the cover of the CD jacket using a 1950s illustration of an executive on the run with a devil's tail waving behind him. The film applies the worst of humanistic values to corporations taking its cue from an 1886 U.S. Supreme Court decision and a statement by Chief Justice Morrison R. Waite. He declared that corporations were "legal persons" having the same rights as human beings, based on the 14th Amendment to the U.S. Constitution.[16] It should be noted that the intent of the decision was to allow corporations to enjoy a specific right as a citizen, the right to sue and be sued; hence, the result was the creation of a legal person status for such entities in court proceedings.

I have stepped into management classrooms to give a lecture on ethics only to learn that the professors have already shown the film to their students with no balanced rebuttal. While some instructors use the video as a device to promote discussion on ethical conduct for future managers, many others just offer this prejudicial commentary. Those professors might be well-versed to at least offer a qualifier. I would recommend they consider the following. It stands to reason that any organization because it is composed of individuals from society will end up with people who reflect the human culture found in it. Bad, deranged, and, perhaps, medically psychotic individuals are found in every society and therefore are reflected in the makeup of the organizations drawn from it. Pious religious organizations and well intentioned governmental organizations contain such individuals. It is not the system that is to be blamed but those placed in it. A corporation is merely an economic instrument invented thousands of years ago. The device enabled investors to combine their capital, spread the risk, venture into a commercial activity, and, if successful, divide up the reward. The devil did not create it but the free will of men to collectively operate in an organized manner did.

Following the financial crisis another movie emerged that gravitated the public toward a further distrust of the business world due to a short piece of dialog. The statement by the character Gordon Geeko in the 1987 film *Wall Street*, "The point is ladies and gentlemen that greed, for lack of a better word is good,"[17] created an impression of businessmen with a label that has since stuck in the public mind-set. The noun greed, and its adjective greedy, both carry a derogatory meaning. The term is synonymous with exhibiting an insatiable drive to acquire material things; but the connotation is expanded to achieving such ends at the expense of others. In other words, one's personal desires in the business world are realized to the detriment of all those stakeholders an enterprise touches. Many link greed with unscrupulous behavior bordering on the amoral or unethical. Some even associate the term with skirting or breaking the law.

But someone who is greedy is not necessarily an evil person. Greed is defined as an "excessive, inordinate, or rapacious desire" in the *Random House Dictionary of the English Language*. It is not an egregious act but perhaps an overzealous motivation to achieve. The fact that greed can be a motivating inspiration, and thereby produce a positive outcome, is an acceptable consideration if viewed as trying harder than normal. Displaying an *excessive* desire than the average person can be a suitable choice. If one applies an *inordinate* amount of pressure on oneself through a demanding training regimen to obtain a desired goal, would such a person be deemed to possess an evil intent? Certainly no. Entrepreneurs tend to strike out on their own, forming associations and then creating organizations that mirror their inner drive to succeed. However, in spite of this alternative take on being greedy the public persona of the driven business person is still negative.

Most recently, the movie *Wolf of Wall Street*[18] continued the destructive traditional narrative attached to commercial pursuits while strengthening the fictional portrayal of the business person and their companies as laced with immorality. The movie portrays a financial organization and its founder as void of a human conscience. With unbridled impunity, it takes advantage of the hard sell with unknowing naive customers who end up like fleeced lambs. The new found wealth as generated by the unscrupulous activities of the movies' main characters results in explicit scenes of extravagance. There is no socially redeeming quality attached to what has been garnered by the commercial venture.

Oscar Wilde harangued in an 1889 essay that "Life imitates Art far more than Art imitates Life." Syndicated columnist Richard Cohen reverses this famous quotation taking a cue from the actual admission by the French bank BNP Paribas that it was criminally complaisant when it helped Iran avoid legal sanctions. The company merely paid a fine and no executive officer was punished. He applies the lesson to the main character in the movie trilogy *The Godfather*.[19] The head of the fictional mafia family, Michael Corleone, admonishes his organization to incorporate from "Corporations [as they] don't go to jail. And neither do the people who run the corporations." They just pay a penalty "for cheating and lying and selling junk and ruining people's lives, and nobody goes to jail." This modern day godfather further proclaims as he announces his assumption of the mantle of CEO that "all we have to do is change the titles, but not who we are. We're still criminals." Cohen's article while written in a humorous spirit seems to be well reflective of how society in general views the activities of corporations—a hungry wolf devoid of morality but disguised in sheep's clothing. In all deference to Mr. Wilde's stance that life can imitate art.

Besides the prejudicial references in movies, there are numerous nonfiction books and novels whose themes explore the dark side of capitalism and its resultant players—the corporation. The list would be led by the 1957 Ayn Rand classic *Atlas Shrugged*. The book is set in a dystopian United States. The story is constructed around the revolt of society's most prominent and successful industrialists who abandon their fortunes and the nation itself, in response to aggressive new regulations, whereupon most vital industries collapse. When asked to state her goal for writing the text Ms. Rand responded that she wanted to portray how desperately the world needs prime movers but to also show how viciously society treats them. To drive home her point she depicts what happens to a world when these leaders, entrepreneurs in all fields of endeavor but most notably commerce, forsake their roles. The story is woven across two prime industries, rail and steel, as their owners resist the states' strong armed movement to create a more collective as opposed to an individualistic society. Depicted as heroes, they continually oppose those labeled as *parasites*, *looters*, and *moochers*; desirous of sharing in the benefits of the heroes' labors. Rand's philosophical approach has been described as *objective ethics*. According to objectivism as applied to ethical conduct, a person's own life and happiness is the ultimate good. To achieve happiness requires a morality of rational selfishness, a process that does not reward the undeserving nor ask in return that one benefit from the wealth created by the valued activities of others. This portrait of the mind-set of corporate executives in *Atlas Shrugged* contrasted with the religious based direction that goodness consists in serving others and acting in a charitable manner to those less fortunate. It also differed from the utilitarian philosophy prodding people to undertake actions that provide the greatest good for the largest number.

A recent nonfiction book, *Capital in the Twenty-First Century* by Thomas Piketty, examines the long-term trend of economic equality, the gap between the rich and the poor or working class. The central thesis of the book is that inequality is not an accident, but rather a feature of capitalism, and can only be reversed through state interventionism, harkening one back to the underlying theme in *Atlas Shrugged*. It argues that the world is moving back to *patrimonial capitalism* or inherited wealth but in the modern era exemplified by corporate executives as opposed to traditional landed gentry and family ownership of industries. The author maintains that unless capitalism is reformed, social democratic order will be threatened. Piketty cites novels by Honoré de Balzac, Jane Austen, and Henry James to describe the rigid class structure based on accumulated capital that existed in England and France in the early 1800s. This is an interesting aspect of academic research, the use of fictional illustrations that both reflected and influenced public opinion to form the basis for a technical examination of a theoretical application. While the book is not an ethical condemnation of the capitalistic structure, it certainly calls into question the actions of commercial enterprises in the wealth accumulation process. As such, it may be mindful to recall the quote of John H. Dunning first noted in the beginning of Chapter 2 regarding capitalism. It is "a better instrument for the creation of wealth than it is for the equitable distribution of its benefits."[20]

It is the prejudiced societal environment, as influenced by entertainment and literature, that must be appreciated by managers as they strive to engage in ethical concerns and act in a reasonably acceptable manner. In short, the deck tends to be stacked against them as public perception of the commercial imperative contains a negative connotation. Public optics has produced a deleterious prejudgment of corporate behavior. As such, global managers need to be forewarned and therefore act accordingly.

Other Contributors to the Ethical Landscape

Reacting to the increasing need to provide guidance in ethical matters pertaining to managing a business, more and more undergraduate business and MBA programs in the United States and abroad have added courses specifically labeled with an ethical delineation. A *U.S. News* article titled "Business Schools Increasingly Require Students to Study Ethics" traces the introduction of classes across the nation targeting ethical considerations based "particularly in the wake of (financial) scandals surrounding Enron, Bernard Madoff and others." However, a few schools, like the University of Chicago's Booth School of Business, do not offer a business ethics course in their course catalog. When queried on such decision a spokesperson for the Booth stated that "each professor incorporates that topic in their lectures."[22] Wecker's article cites the *Aspen Institutes 2009–2010 Global List of Business Schools* whose rating criterion includes institutions that prepare MBAs for "social, ethical and environmental stewardship." Although the inclusion of courses with titles like Professional Responsibility or Responsible Leadership is certainly a growing addition to business school curriculums a number of academic institutions have carried the topic for years. For example, the Stern School of Business at New York University claims to have been "one of the first to require an ethics course more than 30 years ago." The University of Virginia also claims to be an originator of the subject at their school with "a required standalone first year course in ethics." The University of Denver indicates it has "one of the first interdisciplinary MBA programs with a core of ethics and corporate responsibility." San Francisco State University "flaunts a 25-year-old ethics requirement." The University of North Carolina's Kenan-Flagler Business School points to having an ethical requirement "on the books for nearly five decades" while the University of California-Berkeley "goes so far to say it has focused on preparing responsible business leaders since 1898."[21] Clearly, the need to proclaim support for the subject of ethics has become a race to get their name in the game for business schools.

The importance of incorporating an ethical component into business courses seems to be traceable to "Trust—or the lack of it—in business...."[23] This conclusion seems to be based on the fact that "... only 46 percent of consumers in the United States trust business to do what is right, according to the 2011 Edelman Trust Barometer... 48 percent of French consumers and 44 percent of U.K. consumers."[24]

The public's perception of business enterprises as not trustworthy is attributable to the highly visible misconduct as reported in the first decade of the 21st century. The result is that greater attention to ethics is being paid by those who prepare future managers: the business schools. Besides the brick and mortar institutions, the web is full of online courses while free business ethics abstracts are available through the *Wall Street Journal* at http://www.professorialjournal.com.

A number of academic institutions have gone beyond curriculum considerations. They have established within the auspices of their educational networks programs designed to explore ethical issues in business. In May 2014, the *Harry Susilo Institute for Ethics in a Global Economy* (IEGE) was established at the School of Management within Boston University. This permanently endowed facility based on the contribution of a Singapore-based businessman was created to promote dialog and debate through scholarly work in global ethics and by teaching cross-cultural business practices that focus on ethics in both Western and Eastern cultures. Mr. Susilo is characterized in the press releases as one who is deeply interested in the cultural roots of ethical behavior believing that they are the chief influence guiding the moral decision making by business leaders. Other schools have launched centers to further discussion of ethical issues like the *Center for Sustainability and Responsibility* at the Monterrey Institute of Technology. Some have appointed directorships for their faculty to develop specialized programs such as the Babson College *Giving Voice to Values* (GVV) within its *Center for Responsible Management Education*. This is described as an innovative, cross disciplinary business curriculum and actions oriented pedagogical approach for developing the skills, knowledge, and commitment required to implement values-based leadership. The array of institutes and centers attached to academic bodies grows every day along with the specialized courses devoted to ethically base commercial matters with a variety of collateral subject titles.

Besides academic based programs devoted to the ethical issues, numerous private enterprises have joined the *ethics industry*. The emergence of this new commercial service segment is traceable to the 1970s and the scandals in the defense industry that were later followed by the public's outrage to the shameful practices of financial malfeasance by numerous corporations. Besides a pile of regulations to prevent such future occurrences, the need for firms to institute codes of ethical conduct, to train their personnel in its application, and require highly placed managers to oversee such programs begot the formation of independent third-party service providers as formulators. Typical of such ventures is The Institute for Global Ethics (IGE). They offer under their trademarked catch phrase *Ethical Fitness* training as well as consulting services to for-profit business, governmental groups, and other nonprofits. Their Director, Marty Taylor, commenting on the activities of IGE's Center for Corporate Ethics says

> Our position, as stated in our mission, is to promote ethical behavior and cultures of integrity. While many other service providers concentrate on helping organizations understand and comply with laws and regulations, the Institute is bit different: Our focus is individual and organizational decision-making.[25]

Adding to the march to educate potential and existing managers has been the reemergence of books, dedicated journals, research articles, and even periodicals devoted to business oriented ethical matters. *Business Ethics: The Magazine of Corporate Responsibility* (www.business-ethics.com) although founded in 1987 has gained greater readership in the last decade due to the increased interest in its subject matter and its online publishing format. Additional periodicals like *CR Magazine* (www.thecro.com/biz_eth) as well as newly devoted sections of generic business directed magazines concentrate on this growing segment of the managerial process.

Perhaps the most noticeable acclamation of the importance of ethics in business has been the emergence of yearly award lists of companies that a variety of organizations feel should receive recognition for achievements in social responsibility. Business Ethics 2014 magazine's 18th Annual Awards[26] "for leading the way in corporate responsibility excellence" was divided into four categories, with the noted recipients.

1. *Corporate Responsibility Management:* Starbucks Coffee Company
2. *Environmental Sustainability:* Patagonia
3. *General Excellence:* Hypertherm Inc.
4. *Stakeholder Accountability:* Berrett-Koehler Publishers

Adding to the celebration of the socially conscience in the business world is the emergence of the responsible CEO of the year honors being bestowed on corporate executives by the same magazine. Numerous other organizations have gotten into the ethical award game as independent assessors of companies acting ethically or in the jargon of the day being socially responsible. Outside of magazines and institutes as well as public interest groups, professional service companies are offering their own list of awards, mostly in hope of gaining the attention and favor of existing or prospective clients.

Since the 1940s, the recognized measurement of consumer value in the United States was receiving the Good Housekeeping Seal of Approval although it was first introduced in 1909.[27] The Seal was indicative of an advertiser's products being evaluated by their research institute and assessed to perform as intended. In addition, those awarded pledged to follow the Good Housekeeping policy in regard to consumer refund or replacement for defective products. Although there are implied product warranties under the law, the effect was to bestow on such companies an added value of consumer confidence. Receiving the Seal acted as a veiled reference to a firm's ethical determinations in its dealings with the public. This differentiation symbol placed on one's products and used in their advertising was perhaps the first use of ethics in the marketing schemes of companies.

In today's ethically charged business environment, companies are not waiting around for awards and recognitions from third parties. More and more public firms are routinely announcing their own strides in the social responsibility arena. As an agendum to their annual financial reports, the issuances of a self-appraisal collection of ethical conduct as well as beneficial social welfare accomplishments are being released. BNY Mellon, a global leader in investment management services released its 2013 Corporate Social Responsibility Report on June 2, 2014. This internally generated document highlighted its sustainable business practices in *market integrity*, while touting their continual effort to benefit people and communities around the world. Starbucks, the retail coffeehouse, issues an annual Global Responsibility Report, Goals & Progress.[28] The report reviews their corporate commitment to "ethical sourcing, environmental stewardship and community involvement." More and more public companies have jumped on this trend to announce their ethical sustainability but with a newly applied term, CSR.

There are additional signals of the importance to corporations of the ethical imperative beyond creating and reporting on their own standards of appropriate behavior. As previously noted, many companies are aligning themselves with the ethical driven agendas of industry associations, as in the garment manufacturing segment. More and more multinational firms are becoming signatories to general worldwide guiding principles as established by recognized bodies. As reported in an article in *The New York Times* citing the motivation of companies "to Do Good," the writer states that "In 2000, 44 businesses signed up to the United Nations' global standards on human rights, worker rights, environmental stewardship and anti-corruption policies. By last year (2013), 7,717 had signed."[29]

Corporate Social Responsibility

It is easy to dodge our responsibilities, but we cannot dodge the consequences of dodging our responsibilities.
—Josiah Charles Stamp 1880–1941, English Economist and
President of the Bank of England

CSR has been discussed in Chapter 3. It was traditionally defined as an organizational process reflected in the discretionary or nonmandated actions of a firm that benefits stakeholder groups or a larger social collective.[30] The existence of CSR, its operational reach and effect on business organizations, was explained and documented. However, to what end is CSR used in the strategic and tactical approaches to business was not an easily identifiable element. That clouded consideration has now evaporated. CSR is the new corporate mantra. It has emerged as a strong component into the managerial decision-making process and therefore placed in the reporting functions of companies. It has also begun to ingrain itself in the marketing mix as a new element, introduced to promote company image and enhance brand association. To appreciate the place of this ingredient in the modern managerial process, it is wise to start with the two dominant pragmatic theoretical approaches as presented in CSR literature—institutional and profit maximization.[31]

The socially-based institutional theory is reflective of a firm's behavioral reaction to the external environmental pressure or conditions they face. Companies are motivated to gain societal goodwill by acting in an acceptable responsible manner with the result that their activities are legitimized. Legitimacy is achieved when a firm's actions are "congruent with prevailing social norms, values and expectations of performance."[32] The institutional theory should not be confused with an altruistic philosophical motivation to do a greater good or even give something back. It simply places the presence of commercial organizations in society as a socially worthwhile and desirable entity. Those prescribing to the institutional theory would argue that companies just want to reduce uncertainty— they want to be a part of the cultural alignment or the normative composition of the relative environmental societies they operate within. Like all citizens they follow the rules and uphold the norms of conduct that the community demands. The CSR institutional initiative is therefore a process to deflect any negativity or penalties of being assessed as socially adverse, an image that could result in potentially undesirable financial implications too. But the prime consideration is to avoid critically harmful societal activities being attached to their operations; a reactive defensive positioning of the firm to the social environment around it.

The other theoretical rational approach is economics-based profit maximization. A proactive offensive positioning vis-à-vis the social environment with a direct correlation to a financial wealth benefit that comes from engaging in CSR activities. Back in the mid-1980s, Peter Drucker acquainted CSR with value creation by commenting that firms can "turn a social problem into economic opportunity and economic benefit, into productive capacity, into human competence, into well-paid jobs and into wealth."[33] Judging by the present standards 45 years later, this renowned architect of modern day management was correct. In fact, CSR is the accepted from of commercial ethics. It has become a managerial tool to increase, as opposed to protecting, the performance of companies. It has taken the traditional management use of ethics and transformed it into an essential profit induced element. It may have even replaced the word ethics as the new inspectional criteria standard for profit enterprises.

The stringing together of the words social and responsibility have made their impression upon the business world in the last decade like no other theoretically devised commercial axiom. It is not easy to define exactly what the phrase means as the perception of being communally conscientious carries a plethora of potential considerations. The philosophical application of CSR was expressed in Chapter 3 as advancing the needs of humanity at large—the institutional theoretical definition. It is a universally applied theory that all people of goodwill should aspire towards. The principle has been globally spread via the spiritually induced direction to take care of those less fortunate. The concept is imbedded in every religious text across the world. It is found in western teachings of the Judo-Christian creed setting the ground rules for human society to achieve material prosperity on earth beginning with the expressed condition to share God's provided bounty. The Bible is resplendent with instructional tales of charity and good will to fellow man. Biblical scholars also point to the story of Cain and Able in Genesis 4.9 and the utterance "Am I my brother's keeper?" to signify that each individual has a responsibility to care for others. Such spiritual direction has even been applied to the management of the global economy.[34] This tradition is part of the written proclamations of other faiths as well. It is found in the Zakat, the Islamic practice of giving and consequent self-purification. It is also being proclaimed in the Dāna, the practice of giving in both Hinduism and Buddhism. These concepts of gratuitous transfer of wealth to the less privileged strikes a common chord amongst all of the world's divine belief systems.

The intertwined definition of CSR found within theology and the applied theoretical thinking was expanded with an application to a more limited spectrum; an honorable obligation owned toward the welfare and interests of society by those in a position to offer such assistance. A recognition of a social duty sometimes referred to as *noblesse oblige.* The French phrase promotes the idea that people who have a high social rank or wealth should be helpful and generous to people of lower rank or those who are economically depressed. Practically speaking, it can be described as giving back to the public at large. It is often described as being charitable to the less fortunate, a restatement of the faith directed initiative. Corporations due to their financial resources and power have been compared to the personage upon whom the obligation of the noblesse oblige is placed.

Within the commercial arena it has come to a more definitive directional meaning built around the concept that managers should consider the social consequences of their firm's actions when making business decisions. However, the scope of looking out for the welfare of those impacted by a corporation has increased expeditiously. It has crossed the threshold of socially acceptable behavior and its label is today attached to everything from political correctness to simple indifference and impoliteness. Any error in judgment by a company can result in an ethical upstream determination as the arms of CSR now encompass a wider array of issues than ever before. Managers must recognize this phenomenon and learn to deal with it in an effective manner.

At the core of such a required determination is that those in charge of commercial organizations must acknowledge and respect the community of stakeholders that their operative activities impact. This exploration of the term was introduced in Chapter 2 using a chart wheel. This is a wider application of "love thy neighbor as thyself" taken from Mark 12:31 of the New Testament. Traditionally, as reviewed in the previous chapter and in the section on CSR the effected constituency was the stakeholder community. At the core of such considerations was the original inspectional definition of the concept—how companies manage the business processes to produce an overall positive impact on society. It is best expressed as first referenced in Chapter 3 in the paper "Making Good Business" *Sense* by Lord Holme and Richard Watts.[35] The authors implored business organizations to embrace an ethical imperative as they contributed to economic development but they added a general societal element. They should also strive to improve the quality of life, not only for their workforce and the local community, but society at large. The social welfare initiative was grafted onto the ethical requirement. Today, it would seem that the two are intertwined. Any demarcation line that existed as companies applied ethical standards and then separately acted as a socially responsible agent has disappeared. Improving the quality of life was seemingly extended to everyone, everywhere—the society at large. The burden, and therefore accountability, of commercial enterprises was dramatically increased.

CSR encompasses a vast multitude of constituencies, many of which are so distant or down the line that the impact on them is difficult to ascertain with any measurable accuracy. In today's era of modern globalization, the actions of multinational or transnational firms can be compared to the proverbial tossing of a pebble into a lake and foreseeing the ripple effect on the distant shore line no less the intermediary consequences on the entire body of water. The ability to predict no less trace the totality of a managerial decision makes the application of CSR a most difficult navigational instrument to work with. This is especially true as the traditional approach to understanding CSR have given way to a contemporary application of the concept. It has moved away from the sociology-based institutional view and much closer to the economics-based profit maximization approach. Times have changed and CSR is now a priority.

Historic CSR Approaches

Historically, financial support for charitable activities, those that benefit society in general, was channeled through the philanthropic efforts of wealthy entrepreneurs who made their fortunes by creating large successful corporations. They personally endowed foundations as opposed to having their companies contribute to these worthwhile endeavors. In the past, the names of captains of industry like Ford, Rockefeller, Carnegie, Getty, and Vanderbilt appeared on these organizations. This individual–family initiative continues today. Nine out of the 10 largest philanthropic foundations in the world today are due to the supportive altruistic efforts of prosperous personal industrialists, financiers, and inventors. While the popularity of Ford is still prevalent on the list it includes Gates, Hewlett, Hohn, MacArthur, and others who made their riches and are *giving back*. It is difficult to access with certainty what motivates such individuals to be so magnanimous. Are they driven by a pure subjective altruistic desire or is there a more objective materialistic consideration to further their personal reputation by creating an ongoing socially honorable legacy that transcends their corporate accomplishments? What can be assumed is that such notable personal endeavors are not to further the image of their companies nor promote a particular brand with the consuming public.

While prosperous individuals have long realized their responsibilities to the communities in which they operate, the large scale association of corporations in the area of philanthropy has begun to take root more recently. Since the 1990s, it has become the new modus operandi to associate commercial activities with charitable endeavors. A commitment to society and the planet, positioning the company as a good community no less global citizen, has taken on a more meaningful place in the promotion of commercial enterprises.

Outright Gift Giving

One traditional route, used by corporations, has been financial support in the form of donations to local charities: the philanthropic initiative. While not exactly promoting their products or services, such indirect public relations efforts have long been recognized as touting their brand image as concerned good citizens. The idea to ingratiate themselves with existing and potential customers by showing that they *give back* acts as a courting devise. It is intended to display their goodwill efforts. To appear as deserving of continuing and new patronage.

This altruistic endeavor has its roots in the tenants of numerous religious sects. One is asked, as earlier noted, to share their god-given bounty with others. This exercise was not intended to be a publicized event but a private covenant within their spiritually driven principles. In the modern material world, it has taken on a new inspirational direction. Many firms run full page advertisements announcing their gift giving activities. Others participate in fund raising activities at affairs run by charitable groups. They are publicly thanked as an executive presents a larger than life check with his company's logo prominently displayed on it. Firms buy a table and send their employees to an event. They take out ads in event programs. Or donate or provide services to be auctioned off at the galas.

The whole arena of fund raising by nonprofit institutions is not an adjunct to the society but an organizational mainstay. The webpage of Columbia University's degree program Master of Science in Fundraising Management opens with a rather insightful portrayal of the philanthropic landscape and its extensive phenomenon.

> Nationally, there are more than 2.3 million nonprofit institutions. Over one million of these are classified as 501(c)(3) charities, a growing sector that has kept the nonprofit field robust through the recent economic crisis. In New York City alone, nonprofit organizations employ over a half a million people.[36]*

---

* To be tax-exempt under section 501(c)(3) of the Internal Revenue Code, an organization must be organized and operated exclusively for exempt purposes as set forth in section 501(c)(3). None of its earnings may inure to any private shareholder or individual. In addition, it may not be an actionable organization—it cannot attempt to influence legislation as a substantial part of its activities nor may it not participate in any campaign activity for or against political candidates.

The need for fundraising professional managers has therefore increased dramatically over the years as charitable institutions are in essence a national business with revenues approaching $300 billion in 2011.[37] While corporations made up just 5 percent of the monies generated, that is, $14.55 billion (73 percent coming from individuals, followed by foundations at 14 percent and bequests at 8 percent), they are under ever increasing pressure from the fallout stigma of CSR to get more involved.

What the figures fail to reveal is that behind the four classes of direct gift giving is that companies utilize a number of additional indirect methods that fall within the philanthropic classification. A number of firms match their own employee annual contributions to charities up to specific amounts while still others allow their staffs to donate, with pay, a day to work in the furtherance of the activities of their chosen charity. Some even provide their employees with tools and materials for construction projects for that special day. Companies in the food service industry, be they suppliers or restaurants, routinely donate unsold inventory to the kitchens of local charitable organizations. Many firms in the manufacturing sector also contribute redundant merchandise, older models or past seasonal goods, to charitable causes.

Commercial firms have a lot in common with charitable organizations. They share the same need for professional managers as both have to produce revenue in excess of expenses to survive. In essence earn a profit. A quick search of the World Wide Web reveals a score of programs offered by The Association of Fundraising Professionals as well as universities to offer business managerial skill development. Besides Columbia University's master of science in fundraising management, Boston University, New York University, and University of California (UC) San Diego grant certificates in fundraising. Indiana University through its Lilly Family School of Philanthropy as well as a host of other higher educational institutions offer training programs in the field. Arizona State University even has a Center for Service Leadership. A review of these programs clearly indicates how basic business courses contribute to the development of managerial skill building in the gift retrieval industry.

Contemporary CSR

The historic notion of a company exhibiting good or acceptable CSR activities has been transformed in the modern era from a passive or reactive position to a proactive strategic directive. The use of CSR to promote the image of a firm has morphed into the active marketing and promotion of the brand. It is now part of the competitive advantage arsenal used to persuade potential consumers to feel good about purchasing products or utilizing the services of one company over another. In the past, a negative CSR certainly hurt a firm, but today a positive CSR program has joined with the traditional publicizing actives as an additional ingredient in the marketing mix. Beyond the conventional promoting via advertising of a company's product or service benefits, the use of a good CSR story has emerged as a new tool in building a successful enterprise. It services a dual purpose in gaining and sustaining a competitive advantage. CSR is no longer a fringe consideration but a key resource, an asset upon which corporate strategy can be devised.

The Commercialization of Ethics

The union of altruism and materialism has begun to produce many unique business models while altering the face of how business is marketed to the public consumer. Ethics has moved out of the realm of the theoretical and the theological as well as its earlier portrayed application as a judge of the acceptable behavior for commercial enterprises. Reapplied under the banner of CSR, ethics is now a full-fledged member joining the other core subject matters in the world of business.

CSR as a Corporate Base.   Modern companies have quickly learned to embrace CSR and integrate it into the creation of their new enterprises. A quote by Anita Roddick, a human rights activist, and the British founder of the retailing group The Body Shop, well illustrates this emerging concept. Her statement, "Being good is good business" not only served as the motivational onus to establish her business but as the prime strategy to create a competitive advantage in the sale of beauty products and home goods. She was able to take on giants in the industry by differencing her products by utilizing natural ingredients imported from the far reaches of the globe. The Body Shop claims its products are "inspired by nature" as well as featuring rare exotic plant extracts sourced under the Community Fair Trade program. Her supply chain network was specifically geared to buy from small suppliers in underdeveloped regions of the earth placing her activities under umbrellas of being socially responsible. This unique differential approach to promoting an enterprise would later be referred to as *greenwashing*.

Following the opening of the first outlet in 1976, The Body Shop turned increasingly toward social and environmental campaigns to promote its business in the early 1990s. Their publicized *Trade Not Aid* initiative with the objective of "creating trade to help people in the Third World utilize their resources to meet their own needs" was the inspirational objective for a number of their overseas investments. It began with a paper factory in Nepal employing 37 people producing bags, notebooks, and scented drawer liners. Such initiative was repeated in other developing countries in furtherance of the company's mission to support economically disadvantaged populations around the world. In 1997, Roddick launched a global campaign to raise self-esteem in women and against the media stereotyping of women. It focused on unreasonably skinny models in the context of rising numbers in bulimia and anorexia. The company instituted pioneering social audits in the mid-1990s supporting Community Trade, reflecting its avowed practice of trading with communities in need and giving them a fair price for natural ingredients or handcrafts they purchase from these often marginalized countries. The company literally announced to its customers "Feel good about your purchase as you are directly contributing to the furthering the development of humanity around the world." Consumers were literally invited to join the company, to become part of their social responsibility agenda. As the firm's founder proclaimed to "do good" with such consideration separating The Body Shop from all its beauty industry competitors. Not so much by product differentiation but by consumer targeted segmentation. It should be noted that negative reports about the efficacy of the company statements and other financial practices have surfaced over the years but they do not take away from the historic formation and growth of this retail group as they married CSR with traditional marketing efforts.

The combining of CSR with conventional marketing practices has been used by a number of successful companies over the last three decades. Starbucks was started back in 1971, during a decade of growing social responsibility awareness by the general population. It was also the decade that launched The Body Shop. Starbucks created a niche in the simple purchase of a cup of coffee that has propelled the company to a global leader in the café business with over 20,000 stores in 65 countries. It copied from European coffee house concept of a neighborhood gathering place for family and friends offering a premium beverage. Beyond this primary product and service combination the company grafted onto the social responsibility mantra that its core customer base, the Millennials, embraced strongly.

An environmentally friendly trademarked phrase was placed alongside a logo inspired by the oceans, a twin-tailed siren from Greek mythology—it reads *Shared Planet*. Their mission statement contains an ecological determination, "Starbucks is committed to a role of environmental leadership in all facets of our business." They declare that "Instilling environmental responsibility as a corporate value" squarely marrying CSR with the firm's measurement standards. Their conservational integration into their business model is further elaborated upon in a series of operations principles that includes their striving to buy, sell, and use environmentally friendly products while encouraging all parties they deal with to share their goal. Notwithstanding the other strategic differential elements that separated their store operations from the traditional coffee shop as well as the competition their innovative ideas spurned, the integration of a CSR initiative constructed on a eco-friendly platform certainly contributed to their success.

Building on the shared planet concept the company tracks and publically announces its annual increase of coffee purchased through its Coffee and Farmer Equity (C.A.F.E.) Practices. This comprehensive coffee-buying program was created to ensure that their worldwide supply network works to promote social, economic, and environmental standards which were initially developed in collaboration with Conservation International. By their calculation such beneficial resolve has impacted more than a million workers employed by thousands of participating farms. In short, they do good to make lives better. Starbucks also promotes its participation in the purchase of Fair Trade Certified coffee.

While it may be difficult to calculate the value of incorporating a CSR component into the fabric of a company, outside of generating competitive consumer patronage, some recent acquisitions may be indicative of the worth of a company that is primarily CSR driven. For example, the purchase of The Body Shop by L'Oreal, Green & Black's by Cadbury Schweppes, and Ben & Jerry's by Unilever certainly signals the fact that CSR-driven companies do have an appeal to potential suitors based on an assessment that they contain a core distinguishable social welfare asset.

A New Type of Corporation

While the traditional for-profit corporations have injected a social agenda into the establishment of their corporate identity and used the trappings of social responsibility as a differential marketing tool to entice customers, a new legal entity has emerged that takes CSR to a new business level. It is called a benefit corporation—a socially engineered corporation. It is not a nonprofit but an enterprise that aims to make a profit. But how such profit is used or distributed is what separates it from its original structured shareholder owned company.

It is an established law that a corporation has as its main purpose the maximization of financial gain for its shareholders. In the case of *Dodge v. Ford Motor Company*,[38] the Michigan Supreme Court held that the Chairman of Ford Motor owed a duty to the shareholders to distribute the profits to his shareholders as opposed to the community as a whole or the employees. Mr. Ford could not operate the company for charitable ends, the social welfare of outlining stakeholders. Years before Henry Ford had taken the unprecedented step of doubling the wages of his employees to five dollars a day which he explained as "building for the future.... As a low-wage business is always insecure."[39] The desire to improve the welfare of his workers, to see them as partners in the business as opposed to simple labor, brought him in conflict with his two largest shareholders, the Dodge brothers.

A benefit corporation allows publically held for-profit companies to consider the needs of the greater society and the environment in addition to profit in their decision making and hence dispersal of revenue. The intent is to allow firms to assume an additional or varied role; creating shared and durable prosperity beyond shareholder return on investment (ROI). It has the effect of neutralizing the singularly directed obligation as decided in the Ford Motor case to produce a financially distributed profit for shareholders. Incorporating as a benefit corporation legally protects an entrepreneur's social welfare goals by mandating considerations other than a profit. It allows directors of such designated companies to consider the interests of all stakeholders and not just the shareholders that elected them. The driving motivation of the benefit corporation "is to weave some social responsibility in the DNA of the company itself through its charter." And as such being required by law to create "a material, positive impact on society and the environment."[40]

Benefit corporations therefore differ from the traditional corporation in regard to prime purpose, accountability, and transparency. Although both have measured criteria financial performance, in benefit corporations it is valued alongside achieving a material positive impact on society and the environment. A benefit corporation issues an annual benefit report alongside its financial report and is judged on a duel accountability scale. Shareholders feel they are rewarded not just with the payment of a dividend but with being collectively responsible in a social context.

Back in April 2010, Maryland was the first state to pass benefit corporation authorization legislation. By January 2013, 13 additional states passed laws creating such right of specialized incorporation. It is estimated that over 1,000 companies in the United States have chosen to adopt this new public commercial format. Across a wide variety of industries, well-known companies like the outdoor clothier Patagonia, manufacturers of soaps and household cleansers and Better World Books have taken this new socially directed mission as an alternative to the traditional solely for-profit enterprise.

Cross Image Branding—The New Marketing Technique

Other companies run programs that specifically align their sales revenue with a donation. They assign a percentage of a product purchase or payment for services to be shared with a nonprofit organization. In turn, these establishments allow the use of their name be to associated, in effect used, as value-added marketing aids, to differentiate and therefore entice customers to patronize the commercial enterprise. Cross image branding has become an even more effective tool that announcing a mere onetime annual donation as the linkage at the point of sale is a more constant reminder and a stronger motivational devise than just a singular charitable gift. This is accomplished in a variety of ways.

The logo or name of a charitable institution is placed on a company's package. An in-store display unit contains a header card announcing the tie in promotion, while public advertising combines both the nonprofit and for-profit identifying labels. The pink swirling ribbon with a dot emblem of the Susan G. Komen breast cancer organization appears alongside the various identification symbols of numerous well-known business brand names.

Other sales programs also contain an underlying or contributory charitable imperative. This practice is utilized across all industries. The Men's Warehouse, a retailer men's clothing chain, has a TV advertisement announcing that if a customer brings in a used suit they will donate it to a local charity and in turn offer a 50 percent discount certificate on the purchase of a new one. Village Inn, a restaurant chain, features a label over their old menu to launch a new breakfast sandwich with a tag line that one dollar off the regular price will be sent to the local boys and girls club. In the financial service sector, Master Card utilizes a charitable connection at two ends of its customer base. A TV advertisement featuring a well-known personality admonishes credit card holders to patronize restaurants that accept *the card* and that Master Card will in turn donate money to Stand Up to Cancer. In essence, they are promoting not just the use of their services but helping generate business for their retail customers via their credit card base. In the quasi professional arena, Tax Tiger, a tax resolution firm consisting of tax attorneys, certified public accountants, and enrolled agents advertises that 10 percent of its fees are donated to charity. Target, a large retail chain, calls attention to their back to school merchandise buying drive by matching consumer's purchase of classroom supplies with an equal amount for underprivileged children. Sprint, the cell phone network, runs ads noting that they were named as Most Eco Focused Wireless Carrier referencing "Compass Intelligence (January 2014)" with the tag line "Good for the environment is good for business." Budweiser, one of the largest brewers of beer, has been running a commercial that does not specifically feature its products but instead depicts a real life account noting their participation in a town welcoming home parade for a soldier. By celebrating patriotism within a human interest story they are associating their brand name with a powerful emotional identity; helping the general public appreciate the sacrifice of servicemen. The message is powerful and it depicts Budweiser as a caring compassionate company, an image all commercial organizations wish to obtain.

Examples of advertising and public relations programs featuring a CSR initiative could fill an entire book. One thing is certain; promotional tie-ins at all aspects of a firm's marketing program have taken the more historical association between the commercial and the socially charitable away from the traditional arm's length gift giving. It is no longer an adjunct socially inspired responsible activity of a company but has been integrated into their business strategy and tactical maneuvers. Whether or not injecting a moral theme via the portrayal of a firm's social responsibility into its marketing mix results in a competitive advantage, and hence increased revenue is yet to be measured, but it is strong evidence of the ethically inspired imperative of CSR on managerial decision making. The implication is clear. Business has to treat CSR as a business.

The Charitable Courting Initiative

While companies themselves are recognizing the value of an association with benevolent organizations to their marketing mix a unique reverse initiative has been created. Charities themselves are courting corporate sponsors using recognizable business jargon. TEAM LIVESTONG, a cancer fighting charity, has a website directly devoted to enticing commercial sponsorship (sponsorship@LIVESTRONG.org). The opening line of the site promotes the valuable commercial opportunities for potential corporate sponsors. Such an association helps create worldwide brand awareness, while increasing brand loyalty and reinforcing brand image. It also mentions that the partnership drives retail traffic by showcasing community responsibility. Listed in the message are specific customized leveraging activities that LIVESTRONG can provide to meet client-specific marketing objectives, such as:

- Exclusivity within category—at all major sponsorship levels
- The ability to use the Team LIVESTRONG band image and logo in promotional campaigns
- The potential to benefit from LIVESTRONG's editorial coverage in the press—before, during, and after the event
- High visibility pre-event and onsite brand association through the events

Companies that have traditionally signed up come from a variety of industries. Nike, an initial contributor since 2004 has already contributed over $25 million while American Country Investment has donated over $9 million over the last eight years. Other sponsoring firms include Car2go, Facebook, FTD, and UMB.

The LIVESTRONG promotional website extoling the business virtues of cobranding and thereby enticing corporate sponsors to associate with them is duplicated by many charitable organizations. Not only have commercial entities noted and embraced this trend, but the beneficiaries of their endowments have also begun to treat CSR as a profit maximization device moving away from their own traditional reliance on the benevolence of those who have to those who do not.

Cobranding Danger Issues

The new idea of forming a strategic marketing alliance with a charitable organization to promote the CSR activities of corporations is not without problems. The choice of a partner, in this case which philanthropic group to support, is like all alliances prone to issues surrounding either party. Planned Parenthood, a nonprofit that administers healthcare facilities primarily devoted to women, enjoys a large legion of corporate sponsors. Over the last decade the activities of this charitable organization have come under constant attack by antiabortion advocacy groups. To aid their mounting assault against Planned Parenthood, many of these pro-life parties have organized consumer boycotts targeting the commercial sponsors that contribute to the Corporate Funding Project (CFP) of Planned Parenthood. The pressure thereby exerted on the corporate sponsors to disassociate themselves or alienate the patronage of their customers seems to be working. Life Decisions International (LDI) in releasing their 2012 revised editions of The Boycott List, which identifies corporate sponsors of Planned Parenthood, reporting that their actions have stopped "at least 282 corporations" from funding causing a loss of $40 million in contributions since CFP began.[41] The LDI Boycott List as of March 2012 includes some of the largest recognizable companies in the United States. On the list are Bank of America, AOL, Bayer, eBay, Marriott, Nike, Select Comfort, Southwest and Jet Blue Airlines, Advance Publications (magazines such as *Bon Appétit, Details, Glamour, GQ, Self, Vanity Fair,* and **Vogue**), UBS (financial services), Wyndham (hotel and eatery properties), NACCO (kitchen and home appliances), and a host of additional well-known companies. The list also includes a Dishonorable Mention section of nonprofits that associate with Planned Parenthood including AARP, American Cancer Society, Salvation Army, Susan G. Komen Breast Cancer Foundation, March of Dimes, Rotary Clubs, Sierra Club, the YMCA and YWCA, and others. Besides publishing the names of firms that should be boycotted, it seems that LDI is also sending a notice to companies as to which charitable partners they should support in an effort to control their existing as well as potential alliance partners. CSR, in terms of companies forming associations that may appeal to the social conscience of their customers and hence bring added value to their brand, can be a complicated decision. Controversial beneficiaries of their charitable relationships may have to be vetted closely; an added burden to the marriage of CSR and corporate marketing programs.

Companies must also be aware that a comarketing arrangement with a charity can also contain additional problems. If the alliance partner or their spokesperson has an embarrassing scandal or makes inappropriate remarks, it can reflect on the corporate sponsor. Charitable organizations that do not live up to their nonprofit objectives or fail to exercise the highest degree of integrity are publically scorned. And by association such negative publicity can impact the image of a corporate sponsor. Lance Armstrong a cancer survivor was the founder and chief public personality of the LIVESTRONG Foundation, which originally bore his name. He was a racing cyclist winning the prestigious Tour de France a record seven consecutive times but was disqualified from all those races and banned from competitive cycling for life, for doping offenses, by the Union Cycliste Internationale (UCI) in 2012. The sponsors of the Foundation had to react quickly to distance themselves or be tainted by their supportive bond that included the organization's disgraced public spokesperson, the face of the charity.

The modern business enterprise has begun to adopt a new strategy aided and abetted by nongovernmental officialdoms with their social engineering agendas as well as charitable organizations. Besides the prime consideration, to make money, they are being pressed to develop a caring partnership attitude that is being promoted by the very stakeholder groups who wish to benefit from the relationship. Hence, the effect of corporations on society and the environment is being recognized by the very organizations that support such initiatives. This new directional tactic will be exemplified not only by the kinds of products they make, services they offer, and the resources that are used to source them, but also by how they are merchandized. It will also include the kinds of jobs they provide.

CSR Impact on Human Resources

Attracting and retaining good employees has always been an important component to the success of the commercial endeavor. Traditionally, one looked for a job that initially offered, if not in the too distant future, the opportunity to earn a good salary with the promise of advancement. Certainly, employees also gravitated to positions featuring the skill sets they enjoyed applying and industries whose products and services that appealed to them. One of the first adjustments in the work environment was exemplified by Google. It built areas adjacent to the traditional work space that offered a relaxed atmosphere to reinvigorate stressful conditions while promoting stimulatory distractions to promote employee morale. Other changes that recognized the need to be socially responsive, and in turn recognize the welfare of their employees, have included a relaxation of the traditional working hours as well as the necessity for work to be performed at a centralized location. Flexibility, so that one's workforce can better integrate their professional duties with their family life, seems to be a response to the need for companies to show their socially responsible side. The notion that firms care about the well-being of their employees is traceable to the overall CSR initiative.

In the last few decades, a new criteria has been added to the personal conditional list of potential employees regarding the profile of the companies they wish to join. It is an element identified with corporate culture and the overall working environment. More and more college graduates desire to be employed by firms that have a sustained ethical track record and, in some cases, a social improvement agenda embedded in their mission statement. A pronounced social conscience became part of the 21st century mind-set as people looked for work. According to data released in May 2012 by Net Impact, a nonprofit that aims to help business to obtain sustainability, 65 percent of MBA's surveyed say they want to make a social or environmental difference through their jobs.

Apart from being put off by companies, no less industries, that were tainted by moral scandals, the demand for employment with firms that announced their intention to be supportive of their CSR determinations has grown. Doing something that goes beyond just providing employees with income, benefits, and position advancement possibilities has become a new mantra for workers. In June 2014, Starbucks announced a most unique initiative for its employees. Their U.S. workforce would be eligible for a free college education through Arizona State University's online program. This perhaps precedent setting project would allow employees to graduate debt free from the university with no requirement to repay or stay on with the company. Although the details of the offering slightly alters the tuition benefits ranging from full reimbursement to scholarships worth $6,500 the social investment in the future of their workers is an indication that being perceived as a socially responsible organization is an attractive inducement to retain and attract new employees. An adjunct to such consideration is that Starbucks customers also see such activity as contributing to the firm's overall image as a caring company.

Go Green—Go Paperless

The growing incentive for companies to proclaim they are going green by going paperless is an ecologically friendly refrain being echoed by more and more companies. This CSR oriented anthem promotes a firm's regard for the ecosystem portraying a good image to the public and ingratiates the administrative change to environmentally conscious consumers.

Companies are asking customers to join them in eliminating the wood-pulp paper trail through payment by e-mail. Instead they advise them to use online or on screen receipt of billing statements and then with a click make the payment direct from their checking account, via an intermediary payer or as an automatic credit card charge. The procedure allows firms to claim that they are doing their part to preserve the fragile environment by saving trees from destruction. But it also has another side to the seemingly CSR initiative. The alternative pay scheme equally produces a financial gain for companies as it shrinks processing costs. Doing away with documents and administrative handling reduces the expenses associated with such tasks. It is additionally beneficial to companies as it allows payment to more quickly and more efficiently flow into company coffers.

The end result of the go green—go paperless mantra is a CSR win-win situation for all concerned. However, the self esteem recognition garnered by companies inviting their customers to switch over to a new payment system should be tempered by appreciating the financial gains they receive. Firms need to be careful not to overly portray their benevolent actions as solely driven by altruistic values. As there is a material reward component to the seemingly positive socially responsible campaign, companies would be well advised not to push this matter too hard. The balance between CSR driven activities and the underlying profit goals of companies is a fine line that managers will need to navigate carefully; although the blending of the two produces a mutually satisfactory result.

The Difficult Sides of CSR

While business needs to treat CSR as an intricate part of their strategic determinations and as such be proactive by applying it to their operational tactics, they must also be cognizant of its negative effects. The wrong move even with good intentions can backfire on a company. Critics of capitalism have a new weapon at their disposal with which to hammer the activities of companies. Those that champion sustainability have an added component to their arsenal of corporate requirements. It may be argued that executives have been handed a new competitive advantage tool that does not require huge capital investment or diversion of already committed resources. However, this asset is a duel edged sword that can cut both ways. If handled correctly, leverage can be achieved, but if mishandled, it can harm a company.

Second Transparency

The chapter began with examples of more recent questionable ethical determinations by corporations that are being examined at a greater depth than ever before. It is not only the accounts of dubious activities as reported in traditional news channels but the inspectional introspection provided by bloggers with agendas to reveal and comment on such events. This externally driven transparency is forcing companies to be more pro-active in their response to moral sensitive issues that in the past may have gone unnoticed. On the other side of the transparent phenomenon is the simple fact that more and more companies are being compelled to provide self-examination statements of how their firms respond to the CSR initiative. Not allegations of suspected unethical or socially irresponsible behavior. This is the internal aspect of the transparency portent.

The issuance of CSR or sustainability reports is a growing trend in industry. In the 2000s, only a handful of public firms of the Fortune 500 companies issued an annual information narrative on such activities. In the present decade, a majority have offered to provide a commentary on company matters pertaining to their social responsible accomplishments. The public pressure to release an accountability of issues related to CSR activities will only mount. As such, managers have a new agenda on the table of business considerations they must address.

There are recognized guidelines via regulatory financial requisites and approved accounting principles utilized in standard annual reports as normally required by incorporated by-laws of corporations. The presentation of an annual chronicle, whether it is labeled as sustainability report or information on the ethical and social responsibility activities of a firm is a self-determined commentary. Initially, statements on such matters were contained within the introductory narrative of the Chairman of the Board or CEO of a company before the normative presentation of fiscal statistical data with notes by third-party certified public accountants. The inclusion of references to socially beneficial programs was later placed in a separate column or section as contained in the traditional annual report. These considerations have now morphed into a separate and distinct periodic description of the efforts of companies in respect to these matters.

There are no formal structures for these reports no less a measurable criteria for what they need to contain. Companies therefore have the freedom to subscribe to any narrative they wish to portray. It is therefore difficult to provide a uniform or acceptable configuration as to what these self-proclamations need encompass. Companies that utilize this new form of corporate reporting are responding to a duel imperative. First, being proactive allows them to thwart potential criticism that they ignore social responsibility issues. By presenting their agenda as well as quantifiable activities to show they care about these matters, they are prescribing to the old axiom "The best defense is a good offense." This familiar adage has been applied to many fields of competitive activity. The theory behind it is that a strong proactive action will preoccupy the opposition and ultimately hinder its ability to mount an opposing counterattack, leading to a strategic advantage. By getting out front and providing evidence of being involved in socially productive endeavors, it is harder to fault corporations for exhibiting benign neglect while it may also deflect from negative activities.

Second, these positive society oriented reports can additionally provide companies with a good public image. Being perceived as a responsible citizen ingratiates them to existing and prospective patrons of their products and services. It is a public relations initiative aimed at sustaining and improving an intangible asset. By announcing and thereby calling attention in a semiformal document to their efforts that (1) improve the welfare of corporate stakeholders, (2) provide financial assistance to worthwhile charities, and (3) in general show their respect for the environment they gain a competitive advantage over other industry participants.

Quantifying CSR

But before dwelling into this complicated issue it is advisable to revisit what CSR is. First, it is not ethics although those that push companies to become good public citizens do so under the mistaken guise that CSR is its synonym. Ethics as earlier noted is a discipline dealing with what is good and bad behavior; a simple determination even if embedded in the mind-set of the one making the choice. Ethics is a set of moral principles that governs the conduct of an individual or a group; a guiding branch of philosophy that should be applied to decision making and hence affects the actions that follow. However, it is not defined as being concerned with the general welfare of society. It is not necessarily a devise to reengineer social progression nor is it an instrument to improve the lives of others. Ethics is not about sharing one's beneficial accomplishments with others. It contains no direction to be charitable. The term does not include a stewardship to sustain nor clean-up the environment. Ethical determinations do not require a forced or even a strategic relationship with those that promote any of these aforementioned worthwhile endeavors. There is also no requirement that one should issue a periodic report on one's ethical activities and the aims be achieved via qualifying measurable criteria. While it can logically be argued that CSR is a derivative of ethics, an expansion of the roots of ethical principles or actions to materially refine its application, the words are not synonymous. A thesaurus equates ethics with ideas, morals, codes, tenets, principles, and integrities—all a set of standards but having nothing to do with social responsibility.

However, the implementation of ethics certainly does impact people and the environment. It thereby contains a societal effect. The word is not defined as containing a widely disseminating positive socially redeemable element; a singular good initiative as the word ethics is demarcated by right and wrong. Being a socially responsible organization is not an easily definable consideration. The perception of doing good by promoting the general welfare is not an exact recognizable calculable equation. Unlike reporting sales and profit that due to regulatory requirements and generally accepted accounting principles are tied to uniform measurable guidelines, recording CSR results is problematic. Being transparent when it comes to financial disclosure, although the Enron scandal and other fiscal malfeasances are duly noted, is difficult to apply to a sometimes nonquantifiable result. Unlike publishing pure numbers, the ability to show social engagement no less improvement year after year, the beat Wall Street expectation mantra, requires a new field of accountability to be inaugurated. While book-keeping principles can be applied to show the constant rise in corporate charitable donations maintaining records of other forms of related or indirect support necessitate more precise detailed accounting systems as well as exacting value assignments. For example, if a company partners with a charitable group to run an advertised cross sales promotion donating a portion of the revenue to that organization, at what point does it end as the duel motivation period can eclipse a set date? Is a portion of the expenses involved from producing a commercial to paying for on-time air exposure considered as part of the donation? Do the internal costs of the company to track the program, no less manufacturing costs and unsold inventory on packaging bearing a combined message like duel logos, qualify as part of the financial contribution? If a company donates their products or the time of their employees to perform charitable activities how is this valued?

Beyond the financial issues, as part of the CSR imperative, maintaining other records is also an added consideration. For example, Starbucks routinely reports its activities with a CSR connotation. They advise on their increase in the annual purchases of coffee (by poundage) obtained through C.A.F.E. Practices with an announced initial goal. Supplies under the Fair Trade Certified designation are also tracked. In addition, they report the amount of loans given to farmers and their communities. They also offer growers monetary incentives to combat damages to the environment or the effect their activities may have on climate change. Unlike audited financial statements, these laudable programs are not always subject to independent certification. In regard to influencing the use of land, the small plots of farmers averaging 0.5 to 5 hectares, in order to promote local ecological concerns and contest to effect global climate change, these results are very difficult to evaluate.

Outside of the additional strain on corporate resources to keep adequate records of CSR designated activities no less assigning a proper measurable value and providing periodic transparent reporting, a few other issues are connected to the subject matter.

First, it must be assumed that they all qualify in the arena of public opinion as worthwhile. As noted earlier, it is difficult to gauge the reaction, the beneficial perception of presumably socially responsible actions by a company when filtered through the cultures of varying societies. Besides differences in basic social values, the roots of CSR, the economic developmental level of countries may often dictate the relative importance placed on general welfare improvement as well as protection of the environment when people just want a job to raise them out of abject poverty. It must be appreciated that many societies are at the bottom of Abraham Maslow's proposed hierarchy of needs scale, a measurement of achievement (see Figure 4.1). This motivational chart begins with the fulfillment of basic personal needs and rises to the highest level known as self-actuation.

While it is difficult to access at what point people are concerned with the general welfare of the wider society around them, it would be safe to assume it emerges at or after the middle level, *Belonging*, where socialization and relationship needs emerge. Both below and above this middle step individual needs tend to dominate. Companies must therefore be careful in choosing the right universal CSR path to align their activities with, as what plays in one society may not be appropriate, according to the Maslow criteria, in another.

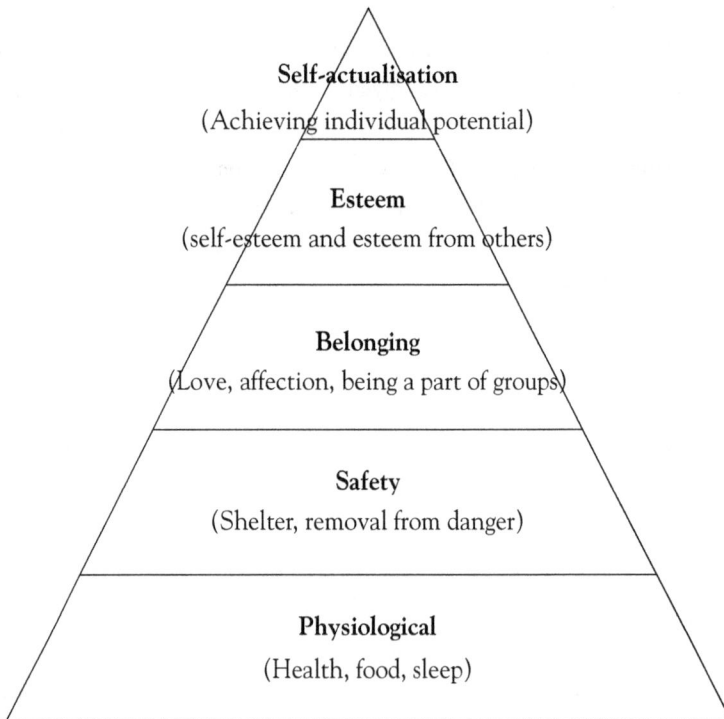

Self-actualisation
(Achieving individual potential)

Esteem
(self-esteem and esteem from others)

Belonging
(Love, affection, being a part of groups)

Safety
(Shelter, removal from danger)

Physiological
(Health, food, sleep)

Figure 4.1 Maslow's hierarchy of needs pyramid

CSR Targeting Considerations

The question is to whom or to what end is CSR directed? If the motivation is purely altruistic then the answer is those directly affected by the activity. The improvement of the life of individuals and communities as Starbucks does with indigenous supplier farmers or as Village Inn does with the local neighborhood boys and girls clubs. Who are those who might benefit by the control of diseases that are considered fatal as Master Card does with Stand Up for Cancer? However, if the intention is also to gain favor or court the patronage, of existing or potential customers of a company's products or services, the choice of which CSR path to take becomes more difficult. To be sure, firms do not want to admit that for the supportive decision to be socially responsible it should be directed by an underlying business decision, even if the aforementioned enticements of nonprofits like LIVESTRONG strongly stress this consideration. This raises the issue of CSR consumer target or, in marketing jargon, segmentation.

A recognized tool in selling to consumers is market segmentation, also known as niche or precision marketing. It is a strategy that separates a broad array of potential customers into subsets that exhibit common needs, priorities, and perceptions. They are then targeted using different marking programs that appeal best to each group taking into consideration their specific demands due to shared attributes. Segmentation uses a variety of homogeneous categories. The more recognized identities are geographic, demographic, behavioral, and psychographic; although, numerous other classification markers can be applied. The key criterion is that everyone in the targeted group responds positively to a similar stimulus.

As CSR emerges as an adjunct to the traditional marketing mix, the theory of segmentation maybe most appropriate, but with a new category identifier—segmentation by socially responsible benefits (SRB). SRB is indicative of choice as to the right strategic alliance partner to cobrand with and the proper selection of a socially recognized issue to support or align company operations that is favored by a specific target group. This new designation falls within the purview of segmentation according to the benefits sought by consumers. But unlike the traditional product benefit category, a material satisfaction characteristic to support or improve a lifestyle, the company image or that of its brands is enhanced by the consumer's emotionally charged altruistic feeling. It is a psychological appeal that simply makes the consumers feel good if what is portrayed touches their lives. Similar to the Budweiser's patriotic welcoming home of a hero, a TV commercial called the Empty Chair by another beer company, Guinness salutes the spirit of a community that honors one of their own who is out of sight but never forgotten—the troops are serving abroad and the people are awaiting their return. The ad shows a waitress in a neighborhood tavern repeatedly placing a filled glass on a vacant table. The normal activities of the establishment continue but the image of the glass left for the missing holds the attention of the viewer. The commercial ends with a returning soldier walking in and acknowledging the deed. The viewer understands that the ritual will continue as the people hopefully wait for the others. The depiction of a caring thoughtful community subliminally carries a public service message applied to the Guinness brand. As companies apply this shadowy SRB to their marketing mix to influence and entice consumers to patronize their offerings, they expect this tactic to be refined as it is constructed to operate below the threshold of consciousness but, nevertheless, stimulate a measurable result.

CSR as an International Strategy

Given the rising use of companies associating themselves with socially beneficial causes, the question as to the strategic use of such programs across all global venues is a valid inquiry. The month of October is designated as Breast Cancer Awareness Month on a worldwide basis. It is supported by the World Health Organization and a host of charitable organizations that are both international and national in design and scope. The iconic pink ribbon is used as a symbol of the program while the color pink is identified with this women's health issue globally. Ralph Lauren is one of the world's premier luxury lifestyle brands. It is universally recognized and associated with distinct design and quality. The brand's integrated approach to global advertising, marketing, merchandising, and visual presentation predominately features a polo player. However, their recent print advertisement alters the well-known player on a horse logo and depicts the symbol all in pink. It is used to announce the launching of their pink pony charitable trust. The wording indicates that 25 percent of all sales under this specific brand label will be placed within the trust and used to fund the research for the cure of cancer. The language at the bottom of the ad states that it only applies to sales in the United States. This disclaimer may address a few issues when it comes to CSR as a universal strategy.

If the company is truly global as the Polo brand is, then why the limitation? Do only customers in America respond to such a worthwhile endeavor as a motivational inducement to patronize this specially designated product line? The answer may be partly yes. The World Giving Index as published annually by the international nonprofit organization Charities Aid Foundation rates the world's most (and least) generous people. Three measurable criteria are used: monetary giving, volunteering, and helping of strangers. Over the last two years, the United States was placed 1st, and 5th while 1st again in 2013, so it would seem to follow that America would be a prime market for such a directed charitable program. Ralph Lauren has strategically utilized CSR with a tactically directed marketing or promotional tool aimed at a particular national consumer—targeting clientele in the world's most charitable country. It should be noted that the subject of market segmentation, customizing a message within the CSR arena has been discussed earlier. It is interesting that the same countries, all with a notable common culture, continue to appear in the top six positions on the list along with the United States over the last three years; Australia, Ireland, Canada, the United Kingdom, and New Zealand. Expanding the Polo pink pony CSR message via this linked CSR directed country appeal might be appropriate for the future of the program.

Notwithstanding this consideration, it is also possible that the administration and accounting of the program necessitated a more limited controllable geographical area where a system of monitoring and recording could be more efficiently applied. Allowing the activity to go worldwide would understandably involve a more complicated tracking procedure to be employed. Or perhaps this was a test to determine acceptance of this CSR initiative. But one cannot avoid the conceptual idea that the customized application of a CSR activity that resonates well, ingratiating a company's image and brand with existing and potential consumers, can be based on measurable predeterminable criteria.

A New CSR Derivative

The CSR initiative has resulted in a shift on the value companies provide customers. Companies in their desire to establish a competitive advantage have discovered a new motivator to attract and retain customers. There is a movement away from the old price and quality of the products and services they offer to a collateral focus on the character of the enterprise. The traditional economic criterion has been altered by an emotionally based element; and it has come in all sizes and shapes. Not satisfied with the mere offering of charitable contribution in numerous programed forms, firms are showing a new concern that radiates well with the consuming public.

Taking a lead from the emotionally charged patriotic stimulant is the emergence of the national preservation and heritage initiative—the cultural gift. Some have labeled this direction as "gaining nobility," the "halo association."[42] It is exemplified by companies underwriting the restoration of precious historic edifices. These physical structures are so engrained in the national conscience as to be considered sacred relics carrying an almost spiritual connotation. The Italian luxury goods manufacturer, Tod's, is funding the restoration of the Colosseum at the cost of over $32 million. Within the same industry, LVMH is devoting $3 million to upgrade the Trevi Fountain while the couture house of Versace is donating to the improvement of Milan's Galleria Vittorio Emanuele II, and Salvatore Ferragamo is doing the same with the Uffizi Gallery in Florence.

Linking one's corporate identity with such iconic structures, those associated with the art and masterpieces of venerated prized national artists, is intended to ingratiate the cultural patronage of those customers that certain firms wish to impress. As companies in the luxury business are desirous of positioning themselves as creative artisans, the association with such revered creations also sustains their crucial distinction from the mass produced widely distributed fashion brands.

Jumping on the CSR Bandwagon

There is no doubt that more and more companies are routinely making use of a programed CSR initiative to the point where it may be so commonplace as to lose any differentiation in competitive value. The desire to associate a commercial institution or even individuals with charitable endeavors to promote public favoritism and goodwill is not, however, limited to the commercial sector of a society. Take, for example, the recent activity in a criminal case in Arizona. During the penalty phase of the proceedings, when the jury had to decide between life in prison and imposing the death penalty, Jodi Arias, already convicted of first degree murder, played the social responsibility card. She placed the eye glasses she wore during the trial, a symbol of her failed coquettish defense, on an online auction. She then donated the proceeding to the food bank of greater Phoenix. Will such act of charity alter the public's hate-filled perception of her or persuade the jury to give her a more lenient sentence? Whatever the answer there is a possible lesson in this exaggerated personal social responsibility example for companies. Religious and philosophical writings encourage such acts of redemption by people so it would naturally follow that business organizations should consider similar acts. Making amends via charitable activities to garner the forgiveness of the public for illegal or even perceived unethical events is an acceptable strategy that goes beyond just the desire to ingratiate the company image or identify a brand with good social mores.

Further Valuing CSR

If the image of a corporation and its marketing efforts to entice customers is a valid consideration, then the use of CSR needs to be considered in respect to ROI just like any other expense. ROI begins with an assessment of funds to be allocated toward a project and the expected tangible revenue yield that follows. However, when it comes to utilizing ROI as a mechanism to evaluate integrating CSR into the operations of a company, the end results and the parties involved mandate a different assessment vehicle. First, the end result produces a benefit to a company that is best defined as an intangible asset—creating goodwill. Stephen B. Young, global executive director of the Caux Round Table notes that the most profitable companies have one thing in common; they focus on maximizing the value of their intangible assets. He cites a study of Brand Finances indicating that 80 percent of the value of S&P companies comes from this key source.[43]

Second, the process of CSR often means partnering or creating a strategic alliance with outside entities, a variety of stakeholders and in many cases a nonprofit charitable institution. It would be prudent therefore to construct a new term, return on social capital or RSC. The prime component in the RSC evaluation procedure is what social benefit to champion that would best comply with a company's target customer base and would fit into a corporation's operations. For a company like Starbucks with a young audience exhibiting a combined global environmental conscience as well as desire to support citizens of developing countries, its CSR program aimed at working with small farmers around the world to promote ecological concerns and improve their lives is the perfect match. For a local franchise restaurant chain like Village Inn, whose customers skew to an older age with strong ties to the community, the support of the hometown boys and girls club is a good fit. Budweiser is the beer of choice of the working class, of small town middle America, where patriotism runs deep. The company's welcoming home a local military hero with a parade plays perfectly to their patronizing constituency.

Many argue that the corporate marriage of social altruism and capitalistic materialism is a shame even if the end result is beneficial to all. CSR if approached in the form of RSC allows for a mutual reward. But one of the biggest criticisms leveled against companies utilizing the CSR initiative is that it is essentially a reaction to consumer demand just like an advanced technology or improved product characteristics that help to sell a firm's offerings. Others point out that the motivational intent is to merely enhance their marketing programs. Being socially responsible is an advertising buzzword. However, a survey by Landor Associates, a branding company, reports that 77 percent of consumers say that it is an important element in deciding to buy from companies they consider to be socially responsible. Robert Grosshandler, CEO of iGive.com, which assists consumers interested in directing a percentage of their online purchases to support charities, offers a simple conciliatory summary of the matter. "There's a heightened awareness of the need to be, and be seen as, a good corporate citizen." He goes on to state that

> In the Information Age, customers have more access to information. They're more educated. They're no longer hidden from how their food is produced or how their iPods are made. And because

of things like social media, like-minded people more easily find each other, have their say and effect change. There's a level of transparency that wasn't there before.[44]

CSR is not a fad. It is here to stay. It is an intricate part of the business environment even if the skeptics of the motivational intent are correct. Keep in mind that outside of the RSC evaluation of specific programs, including the aforementioned marketing mix SRB, companies have been formed from inception with CSR in their DNA.

The co-writers of *Firms of Endearment* believe that "Today's greatest companies are fueled by passion and purpose not cash. They earn large profits by helping all their stakeholders thrive; customers, investors, employees, partners, communities and society."[45] The authors advocate the application of a clear *stakeholder relationship management* (SRM) as the driving strategy for all corporations. They purpose that organizations in all industry sectors that recognize that doing good is good business are becoming the ultimate value creators. If they change their culture and embrace CSR, the main stay of a new profitable business model, they will be on the path to a long-term competitive advantage. To build a firm of endearment, radical new rules need to be adopted. The website touting the book lists them as follows:

- Build a high-performance business on love (It can be done. We'll prove it.)
- Help people find the self-actuation they're so desperately seeking
- Join capitalism's radical social transformation—or fall by the wayside
- Don't just talk about creating a happy productive workplace: do it
- Honor the unspoken emotional contract you share with your stakeholders
- Crate partner relationships that really are mutually beneficial
- Build a company that communities welcome enthusiastically
- Help your stakeholders win, including your investors

It is interesting that the word ethics does not appear in the list of new rules. All the noted directions seem to be positioned around promoting responsible social behavior as directed toward a wide stakeholder network.

The CSR Debate

The debate between the legally mandated fiduciary responsibility to maximize the ROI for shareholders of publicly traded companies verses CSR and doing good deeds benefiting stakeholders in places where a company does business is certainly not new. However, as CSR can be shown as a contributor to the success of corporations, the argument to distinguish between the two goals, treat them as separate ambitions, would seem to render the debate as moot. Both aspirations are congruent. They can be harmoniously applied to the strategic and tactical approaches within the managerial process.

There has always been the danger of *extreme economics*. This occurs when the simple principle of business, the only litmus test for determining the value of people, priorities, and initiatives, is risk–reward and profit–loss. These traditionally accepted memes of commercial activities is today being tempered, if not changed, to include a wider more meaningful social imperative. This explains the appeal of CSR as a counter balancing agent to the historically narrowly defined end result of business institutions.

Ethics Verses CSR

It is important to differentiate ethics and CSR. Ethics is a set of decisional making guidelines. It is a system of moral principles, values relating to human conduct, in respect to right and wrong. As such, it is laced with subjective motivational inspirations. It is not a strategy unto itself but it can be applied to strategic decision, making moral determinations to assist in its construction and implementation, the tactics employed.

On the other hand, CSR is a definitive strategy. It can be objectively utilized with measured proactive tactical maneuvers into a commercial organization. As depicted in earlier sections CSR can be the strategy behind the formation of a corporation. It can be a strategy exploited to ingratiate a corporate image to the public or integrated into the marketing mix to entice consumers to patronize a particular brand. CSR can also be an effective strategic instrument to retain and attract employees.

However, the terms ethics and social responsibility are being used interchangeably in everyday life by the media and business itself. While they technically mean very different things, they do share mutual linkages. They are both:

- Part theoretical—ties to moral philosophy with elements of religious principles;
- Part measurable—determinable results of action or inaction;
- Part of strategic motivation—can instigate or cause refrain;
- Part of tactical maneuvering—to achieve recognition or fend off accusations of misconduct; and
- Share commonly applied words to describe them—morals, beliefs, code, principles, values, integrity, conscience, and doing the right thing.

Responsible Leadership

It is a commonplace executive observation that businesses exist to make money, and the observation is usually allowed to go unchallenged. It is, however, a very limited statement about the purpose of business.
—Niel Katz and Robert L. Kahn in *The Social Psychology of Organizations* (1966)

If ethics are poor at the top, that behavior is copied down through the organization.
—Robert Noyce, inventor of the silicon chip

The traditional inspectional realm of ethical conduct has morphed in the last 10 years into the notion of being responsible. It has produced a new term to define leadership morality in the commercial world with the emergence of RL. Academic courses using such language have been introduced in business schools although it would seem any scholastic area of study that results in one joining an organization should contain a similarly offered guidance.

There has been a reawakening of the perhaps dormant term RL. This designation was originally a catch phrase to describe how people in controlling and therefore influential positions should behave. As such it came with a rather wide generic application. However, the expression as used in the modern business environment carries a more distinctive connotation. It clearly refers to a social conscience, paying attention to the requirements of stakeholders within and without an organization. This directed designation has been brought about by the recent surge of interest in the general role of commercial entities in society. More specifically the term has reemerged as the focus on the ethical conduct of managers as they devise strategy and conduct operations to achieve a successful outcome in their leadership capacity. Beyond equating RL with stakeholder engagement and the use of social capital with the context of an interconnected multicultural global society Thomas Maak harkens the term back to a basic consideration:

> Another demanding challenge is inherent in the art of leading as such: responsible leadership in business needs *leadership ethics*. This might seem to be stating the obvious. However, if we look at the many scandals and examples of "bad leadership" (Kellerman 2004) and ethical failures *in* leadership (Price 2005) in recent years, and the lack of theories on responsible leadership, then it is not surprising to see leaders struggling with questions that make up the very core of leadership. Ethics is at "the heart of leadership" (Ciulla 1998) but a theory of responsible leadership has yet to be developed.[46]

This quote well states the prime problem in approaching the issue of RL. It is a term made up of numerous changing components thereby making it difficult to apply a theoretical reference.

However, progressive business schools are integrating into their traditional curriculum courses devoted to executive guidance to foster and produce responsible leaders. In this endeavor, scholastic institutions have been supported by a host of public and private organizations devoted to promoting conscientious accountability for those individuals placed in a position to direct the actions of corporations at numerous levels.

The *Financial Times* offers a commentary on this growing phenomenon stating that "Increasingly, business schools are developing their MBA curricula to address the societal challenges, dilemmas and questions arising in governance, sustainability and ethics courses."[47] Due note is made of the fact that this movement is being promoted via an alliance of the world's leading universities and companies as organized by the Globally Responsible Leadership Initiative (GRLI) "with the aim of 'reframing the purpose of management education.'" The GRLI working in conjunction with other educational groups has created a steering committee to develop and publish a set of Principles for Responsible Management Education (PRME).

PRME—Six Guiding Principles

Principle 1 | Purpose: We will develop the capabilities of students to be future generators of sustainable value for business and society at large and to work for an inclusive and sustainable global economy.

Principle 2 | Values: We will incorporate into our academic activities and curricula the values of global social responsibility as portrayed in international initiatives such as the United Nations Global Compact.

Principle 3 | Method: We will create educational frameworks, materials, processes, and environments that enable effective learning experiences for RL.

Principle 4 | Research: We will engage in conceptual and empirical research that advances our understanding about the role, dynamics, and impact of corporations in the creation of sustainable social, environmental, and economic value.

Principle 5 | Partnership: We will interact with managers of business corporations to extend our knowledge of their challenges in meeting social and environmental responsibilities and to explore jointly effective approaches to meeting these challenges.

Principle 6 | Dialogue: We will facilitate and support dialog and debate among educators, students, business, government, consumers, media, civil society organizations, and other interested groups and stakeholders on critical issues related to global social responsibility and sustainability.

Interestingly the term RL is not specifically defined in these guiding principles. Just a framework of engaging the subject area is provided. It is also noteworthy that the word ethics does not appear in the stirring language offered.

The term RL is made up of two distinct words; the adjective responsible to describe the noun leadership. The generic definition of leadership is the process "to show the way… to guide in direction, course, action and opinion" and thereby influence others. Within an organizational structure, it is defined as "the ability of an individual to influence, motivate and enable others to contribute to the effectiveness and success of organizations of which they are a member."[48]

The generally accepted meaning of responsible carries with it an "answerable or accountable" component when one does "something within their power" as per the *Random House Dictionary of the English Language*. The definition also includes a reference to the fact that one who is responsible has the capacity for moral decision making; hence the connection to ethics. Beyond the dictionary description of these two combined words to form the phrase responsible leadership is the actionable result of the union. Maak and Pless build their definition around the stakeholder relationship prospective. Upon this base they see RL as "a relational and ethical phenomenon which occurs in social processes of interaction with those who affect or are affected by leadership and have a stake in the purpose and vision of the leadership relationship."[49] Other commentators on RL view it as containing a strong moral imperative "to behave ethically and effectively."[50]

It would seem that at this juncture the criteria for defining RL remains fluid with many questions as to its exact content remaining to be resolved. This is because RL is an emerging concept, "a multilevel phenomenon involving individuals, groups and organizations that emphasizes leadership effectiveness, ethical behavior, respect for stakeholders and economically, socially and environmentally sustainable practices."[51] It would seem that RL is moving through a transitional period. An interesting progression has emerged that is built around changes in popular attitudes regarding leadership.[52]

The traditional characteristics of a business leader placed emphasis on producing profits and thereby maximizing shareholder ROI along with legal compliance as well as minimizing harm. In the modern era, the traits of executives has been widened to include, beyond the aforementioned historic considerations, the addition of value creation across all stakeholder relationships not just shareholders, with a deeper concentration on achieving social and environmental improvement objectives. The overall approval criteria to rate the success or failure of corporate leaders, their ability to be responsible.

At this juncture the freedom to place almost anything into the RL pot and still label the mixture with the title RL perhaps best exemplifies the current identification of the term. RL has been characterized

> "as a business school subject area (that) is less about ethical theory and more about ethical practice based on case studies. The practice has a particular focus on an individual's values system and the pragmatic application of an individual's values in the real-life challenging dilemmas of business."[53]

This approach is well dramatized by a checklist of questions responsible leaders should ask themselves according to the *Financial Times*.

- Are your business activities sustainable and are not polluting the surrounding environment?
- Do you identify systemic risks that your activities might contribute to, or do you take short-term risks for quick profits that could endanger the reputation of your company?
- Do you care about the welfare of our workforce?
- Have you checked that your subcontractors do not use child labor?[54]

If one focuses on the wider globalized societal imperative to define being a responsible leader and delves deeper into the multitude of groups represented in the stakeholder alignment it would be remiss not to comment on the influence of culture as a directional guide in establishing a criteria for understanding and appreciating the term.

The Cultural Impact on RL

There are truths on this side of the Pyrenees which are falsehoods on the other.

—Michel de Montaigne 1533–1592, French essayist

In deciding on the merger of leadership and responsibility to produce a coherent relationship, a worthwhile inspectional pedagogy requires an examination of the parties or groups to whom one owes a duty to manage their affairs effectively; and hence be designated as acting responsibly. The most recognized tool to dwell into the wants and needs of people, and hence the ability to satisfy them and be declared as acting in a responsible manner is the use of culture.

Culture is a set of commonly held values that translates into group orientations and beliefs that effect one's thoughts, feelings, and perceptions. As such, it provides the guidance for all personal actions and reactions due to its influence on the mind-set. The researcher Geert Hofstede refers to culture as a software programing for the mind, a controlling mechanism that determines our reactions to others around us.[55] Culture defines the acceptable standards of social interaction amongst a particular group. It ollows that culture acts as the criteria to measure the responsible actions of leaders in a group environment as leadership itself is a universal phenomenon found in all societies. The literature abounds with numerous leadership theories on the characteristics of a leader. All agree, however, that the features of a leader in one society are not necessarily the qualities that will be considered responsible in another. Therefore, RL is a relative term—it depends on culture. The Implicit Leadership Theory (ILT), also known as the Culturally Endorsed Implicit Leadership Theory (CLT), is based on this concept. It asserts that people's underlying assumptions, stereotypes, beliefs, and schemas influence the extent to which they view someone as a good leader, and hence acting in a responsible manner. As these considerations vary across societies it is only natural that leadership trustworthy qualities will differ across cultures.[56]

Since the meaning of leadership as qualified by numerous definitions of expectation fulfillment that translates into being responsible does fluctuate; the question comes, how is RL determined? One could begin with a philosophical inquiry such as voiced by Immanuel Kant an 18th century German philosopher. He postulated that leaders are first and foremost responsible to themselves. The basic idea behind Kantian philosophy is that a person is good or bad and therefore acting responsible or irresponsible depending on the motivation of his or her actions and not on the goodness or the consequences of his or her actions. By *motivation* he meant the reason that causes one to do an action. Kant argued that one can have moral worth (i.e., be a good person and act responsible) only if one is motivated by a rationalized internal morality and not by outside influences. In other words, if a person's emotions or desires cause them to do something (i.e., please others), then that action cannot give them moral worth and they are behaving irresponsibly. The opposite philosophical view propagates that being responsible, and thereby acting in a moral manner, is determined by those to whom one is accountable—those that have entrusted the leader with the resources to accomplish the tasks they require of the person in charge. Failure to satisfy the needs of those granting one a leadership role pays a penalty—removal from the position. The difference between the two approaches to RL would seem to be embedded in internal verses an external motivation factor. The personalized and altruistic rationalized supposition echoing the sentiments of Abraham Lincoln at the beginning of Chapter 1—"When I do good, I feel good; when I do bad, I feel bad…." This would be opposed by my own quote in the beginning of Chapter 3—"The actions of men are driven more by the fear of negative consequences, and the resulting penalties, than attracted by the prospect of doing good and being rewarded."

Notwithstanding the metaphysical attempts to define ethically induced leadership, a discussion that has filled the libraries of the world, a cultural approach is warranted. But before moving into this arena it should be acknowledged that the literature on the subject does include references to generic leadership styles ranging from paternalistic to transformational and transactional. These approaches are conditional as the choice of which style to exhibit can depend on a variety of factors. However, one could reasonably argue that the major or lead impetus to adopting a particular leadership style is in response to the culture of one's followers—recognize their culturally induced mind-set so as to best appeal to the values that motivate them.

Authors Doh and Stumpf in their book on RL in a global environment devote an entire chapter to examining the effect of cultural determinants on the subject matter and weave this major contributing factor into all of the issues presented.[57] They conclude that "culture matters" and "as a consequence… responsible management… may vary… at the national, industry, organizational and group levels." The authors further note that "a cross-cultural prospective implies two aspects: culturally influenced conceptions of responsible leadership and the enactment of responsible leadership in different cultural contexts." Using a series of cultural dimensions by Trompenaars,[58] the different leadership approaches are exemplified to define being responsible in varying societies. For example, *affective* cultures value subjectivity and want their leaders to express their emotions openly, while *neutral* cultures value objectivity and want their leaders to be restraint. Being responsible is therefore positioned as being conditional on culturally induced leadership expectations, their situational behavioral actions. Interestingly, the wider social beneficial distinction that seems to accompany the term in modern definitional jargon is not specifically addressed. Doh recognizes this other aspect when he asks the question: "Do leaders consider themselves only responsible for a narrowly defined function or do they consider themselves responsible for a larger entity and a set of different stakeholders?" The answer seems to be the latter but the subject is not further addressed.

To get a handle on culture and its influence on determining RL in the context of a wider social imperative, one might look to the works of other social scientists who have devised sets of determinants or dimensional contrasts to analyze and compare societal differences. A pioneer in the field was the aforementioned Geert Hofstede.[59] He initially introduced four major dimensions, and later added a fifth, to assist in the appreciation and understanding of cross-cultural attitudes. One dimension is individualism verses collectivism. It contrasts societies that value pursuing their own individual needs as opposed to working with and contributing to the success and well-being of the larger or associated groups. Leaders in individualistic cultures may therefore exhibit a more narrow view of being responsible as they value a limited interaction with people and hence have less or few social obligations. Collective cultures tend to be more publically conscious of the needs of many groups and therefore feel their social obligations transcend a select set of individuals. They have respect for the wider good which may include the environment and the whole of society. Another Hofstede authored dimension is masculine verses feminine, also referred to as tough as opposed to tender cultures. Masculine oriented cultures are deeply task oriented achieving measurable material goals contrasting with relationship-building of feminine designated cultures. They separate work related issues from the wider welfare concerns of their employees and society in general. Feminine societies tend to be more nurturing, concerned with the quality of life and recognize the need to maintain social relationships that extend beyond the financially quantified objectives of commercial organizations. It should be noted that all societies contain elements of individualism and collectivism as well as masculine and feminine; there is just a propensity to exhibit the characteristics of one designation over the other.

Summarizing RL

RL is composed of a broad spectrum of inputs. Culture is certainly a contributor and maybe expressed as social pressures for acceptable actionable and re-actionable attributes of leaders to a variety of valued determinations. The level of socio-economic development can also affect the perceived notion of being a responsible leader when need satisfaction is introduced into the criteria mix. There is no universally recognized singular acceptable theory, although a number of pedagogies have been applied to the subject matter. Therefore, an exacting definition of what makes for a competent responsible no less an ethical trustworthy leader in today's complicated commercial world has not emerged. However, given the fact that the term is still being used throughout the academic and business world to single some type of accountability judgment relating to leaders one might propose the following summary guidelines.

Responsible leaders should:

1. Establish a universal code of conduct to guide the strategy and tactical activities of the organization that are applicable both within and without the commercial entity.

2. Create an infrastructure to implement the code and oversee its operational application with employees, contracted parties, suppliers and customers, as well as communities and their environments impacted by company decisions.
3. Issue a transparent report on issues pertaining to the code and include matters of CSR affecting the stakeholders as noted in point 2.
4. Be respectful of the varied cultural differences the company encounters as it operates in a divergent environment.
5. Remain cognizant that alternate and sometimes conflicting values will be assigned that will impact a leader's ethically inspired responsible actions.

In summary, leadership has gotten more complicated when the word responsible is the adjective used to describe the process. Maybe responsible is akin to beauty, both being *in the eyes of the beholder*. Perhaps Peter Drucker writing on the subject provided a good comparative definition of leadership by referring to responsible as a more determinable objective and not a subjective appraisal. He said "Management is doing things right; leadership is doing the right thing."[60] It would seem that the respected researcher on management and organizational principles is injecting an ethical description into the meaning of leadership. His interpretation imposes the classical question of right and wrong—the good and bad of certain actions and the results they produce. But who is to be the judge of them is left out of the equation. In the context of today's globalized social environment, the evaluating committee has accelerated at an increasing rate. Besides the historic inclusion of shareholders, employees, customers, and the CSR driven stakeholders, the media, NGOs, Wall Street analysts, and the public at large are weighing in. The judgmental criteria of leadership, no less RL, are growing as each constituency carries their own separate critical agenda into the valuation process.

Earlier, at the end of movie serials and TV programs an announcer would say "come back" or "tune in next week to see how this ends." This closing salutation is apropos to describe the state of RL. It still remains an evolving concept at all levels of interpretation.

Managerial Reflections

1. Segments of the preceding chapter were presented in a rather practical fashion treating the subject outside of the normal emotional attachments to social welfare issues and philanthropic endeavors. Do the private considerations of managers and their own philosophical and religious beliefs enter into the equation? And if so to what degree and how should they be reflected in an organization's tactical approaches?

2. RL, while an old designation in the business community, is today laced with additional and more far reaching implications. The definition of the term is therefore undergoing a renovation. Consider your own criteria upon which judgment of RL is based.

3. As companies are pressed to respond to or get ahead of allegations of inappropriate ethical behavior, they issue statements as to their beneficial activities to promote social justice and general welfare of those their operations touch. These may take the form of corporate sustainability annual reports, news releases or even full-page ads. Are such public messages a marketing inducement to attract customers and hence subject to legal challenge if they are misleading or fraudulent just like those for product attributes that prove to be false. Are they tantamount to promoting a company's image and reputation and therefore fall within the purview of a sales solicitation? Or are companies entitled to the protection of free speech under the First Amendment and should be allowed to defend their actions in regard to human rights or make public the activities they feel that contribute to improving society? If a firm attempts to be transparent, bowing to public pressure to reveal and comment on their alleged unethical   actions, should such message be legally challengeable by the public if one feels that are being untruthful in their response?*

4. If the news and entertainment media promote a public bias towards corporations and thereby contribute to a prejudicial environment in which to conduct commercial operations, what can companies do to combat their tainted image? Or does the reporting and story line

---

* Readers might want to take a look at a real case on the matter—*Kasky v. Nike. Inc.* (2002).

messages reflect the actual state of affairs and firms need to get more proactive and address the problems they created? Or does the answer lie somewhere in between?

5. Is it proper and ethical for companies to comarket or to some degree align themselves with charitable organizations using such associations as public relation messages to ingratiate themselves and thereby keep or attract customers? Should philanthropic organizations openly court corporations and partner with them? Has altruism been replaced by business pragmatism or does the end simply justify the means?

CHAPTER 5

Time for a Change?

Time-out

Neither do men put new wine in old bottles: else the bottles break, and the wine runneth out, and the bottles perish: but they put new wine into new bottles, and both are preserved.

—Matthew 9:17

Before moving on to explore how the global issues of ethical construct are handled by public-interest groups and the philosophical approaches to the matter, it may be advisable to call a time-out and again raise some underlying issues and fundamental questions. How does the sometimes fickle cycle of public opinion, which needs to be periodically awakened by disclosure of questionable practices of firms, impact the need for global enterprises to embrace an ethical imperative in the strategic planning process? Firms are always trying to gauge the impact of their actions or nonactions, constantly assessing the risk and related harm cost if something goes wrong. Is it worthwhile not only to take a proactive stance and institute a code of conduct but also to invest in the financial manpower to sustain a transparent program of constant vigil and public reporting in respect to a firm's human rights record? Would it be better to try to fly below the public radar and if incidents do arise to then handle them on an instant basis? Which strategic approach is most cost efficient given the simple fact that moral attitudes of the public ride the rails of an ethical roller coaster? Should a firm chance disclosure and then address damage control or take a proactive stance as a preventive measure? Firms need to evaluate these considerations and make a determinative decision.

Perhaps the best evaluation technique is to propose a series of questions as to the company's worldwide operations. First, ask if the global activities of a company and the products it manufactures brings the firm into constant contact with workers in emerging or developing nations where the current laws affecting labor rights are nonexistent, suspect, or reprehensible as viewed by those subject to the laws. As the resultant repercussions of being saddled with potential accusations of unethical behavior are most deeply felt at the sales level, an assessment of possible customer backlash against industry products becomes a key consideration.

The second evaluation to consider is to question if the worldwide operations of the firm require use of independent, third-party suppliers whose track record or reputation is questionable as regards their treatment of workers. Such uncontrollable contracted entities can act as hidden traps for unsuspecting firms as their actions are attributed to the companies hiring them. Inspection and investigation of third-party supplier facilities before engaging their services may red flag potential dangers. It is not enough to merely negotiate with the owners of such entities, as such surface sessions may be clouded with polite references and promises when the issue of worker treatment is raised.

A third consideration involves the obligatory partnering with repressive governments and their respective agencies. Industries that require some form of coventuring with country authorities need to be well aware of the political stance of such nations in regard to basic human rights. An assessment of the way such countries are viewed and categorized by their own home-country government should be consulted in order to better gauge the need for proactive, protective measures.

The more the aforementioned operational attributes characterize a firm's global interactions, the greater the necessity of factoring an ethical imperative into the strategic planning process.

A Starting Line

Within the confines of emerging or developing country societies, the introduction of protection for the common citizen laborers and concern with their plight is often an alien consideration. New approaches to such situations must be housed in the confines of altered systems to ensure that they are handled correctly. Pronouncements of desired intentions, as noble as they may be, cannot be placed in old institutions or they will surely fail to be achieved. Professor Lynn Sharp Paine states that there is a "compelling case that modern corporations can no longer be regarded as amoral actors operating in an 'ethics-free' zone." They "are increasingly being regarded as humanistic rather than purely economic entities."[1] Global commercial institutions may be the vehicle of the future to promote such new systems.

In almost all developed nations, laws and regulations have been drawn up to provide for specific guidelines and violation penalties in the workplace. A maze of both federal and provisional statutes, backed by governmental agency involvement, prohibits or at least minimizes worker exposure to hazardous factory conditions. Rules have been set down defining the minimum age for child labor and the hours children can work. Discrimination in the workplace and hiring and firing policies are all subject to a legal framework. A dual administrative and court system to redress labor-based grievances also exists. The U.S. Occupational Safety and Health Administration (OSHA) is charged with inspecting violations of federal safety standards in the workplace. The agency, which utilizes civil fines and criminal penalties (maximum six months in jail) as enforcement tools, came under fire to get more stringent as per a March 14, 2003, editorial in *The New York Times*.

The point is that even the home legal framework of most transnational companies does not always provide a perfect example upon which a global code can rest, as it too continues to be critically evaluated and is subject to change. It may be best therefore for a universal code to be constructed with no underlying assumed conditions or imported frames of reference. Importing standards that are subject to potential alterations into a moral vacuum can set a dangerous precedent and leave room for criticism. As such, it might be best for such provisions to be self-contained, more definitive, and able to stand on their own, encompassing an entire process in order to be effective as no external supportive structure may exist to complement their existence or adjudicate their noncompliance. Simply put, codes of conduct that are based on home-country environmental conditions by their very nature may turn out to be statements of national policy wrapped in commercial, organizational culture. When they are taken out into the world for universal application, they can become a foreign policy as opposed to a workable solution for local embedded conditions. Most corporate codes fail to recognize that a world exists beyond their borders and that a new set of encountered circumstances demanding more precise direction and defined terminology needs to be constructed. Construction of an all-encompassing global code of conduct is a daunting task, as it must blend varying points of view from different levels of socioeconomic development and therefore ethical agendas. A well-defined and administered code must not contain sweeping generalities but needs to be constructed with specific statements that expressly guide employees worldwide in their daily managerial duties.

The Initial Effort

In embracing change, entrepreneurs ensure social and economic stability.
—George Gilder, American writer and
techno-utopian intellectual

In an effort to ward off allegations of unethical practices, international firms have attempted to construct corporate codes of conduct or graft onto charters created by venerable institutions as the first line of public relations defense against accusations of improper behavior associated with their foreign operations. By at least pointing toward a publicly disseminated document, they feel they can placate or repel critics of their activities from whatever venue they emerge.

When carefully examined, many corporate codes of conduct, taking the lead from the ethical structures of the societies that such entities call home, are well-intentioned extensions of nationally felt behavior and therefore biased expressions of bordered or territorial moral behavior. They are constructed on the preexisting conditions of the national culture anchoring them, utilizing terms, and wording that at home invoke automatic definition and reaction. They are akin to national policy declarations that are not relevant to circumstances found outside a specific country's border. But when placed abroad, they are like a saltwater fish dropped into a high mountain lake. No one knows how they got there, perhaps they are an environmental oddity, a moral madness, but they cannot independently sustain themselves. They need to be transported to waters with self-contained operational sustaining apparatus that allows them to succeed.

Many codes are well-dressed declarations of promise, looking good on the outside but lacking interior substance. They are all fluff, full of social direction that plays to the population in their home market but does not have the remotest chance of creating change in foreign markets because they remain embroiled in transparent worded cloth. There seems to be a funny paradox about pronouncements of intended ethical behavior: The loftier the language, the lower the eventual deed. They are composed of well-meaning but broad and ambiguous language that does not contain a clear material definition of the terms used. Upon closer inspection, the desire for unequivocal direction seems to be missing.

Ever watchful of the public eye, companies have taken to making sweeping, general statements incorporating well-intentioned rhetoric into their codes, which sounds righteous but is so vague and purposely unclear as to be pie-in-the-sky declarations. These codes contain statements like *we should not initiate associations where there are pervasive violations of basic human rights*. Such wording fails to define what rights are seen as *basic* or what *pervasive* means. Such pronouncements rely on the ethnocentric, culturally biased interpretations of the specific society proclaiming them but have less relevance outside, where the struggle to announce them, define them, or provide actionable credence to enact them exists.

Many generic corporate codes of conduct further state that they will not expose employees to *unreasonable risk* but again fail to attach categorical criteria of which risks are acceptable and which are not. In many countries, definitive and measurable standards exist, and an entire national or federal bureau as supported by local, state, or provincial agencies exists to enforce them. In many underdeveloped nations, no such rules exist, while in other emerging countries that have moved to quantify and qualify such comprehensive criteria, little or no meaningful authoritative enforcement bureau is in place, much less adequate judicial redress for violations. Even some of the models developed by concerned groups of domestic companies acting in unison to construct a global, uniform industry ethical guide use incorporate phrases like *protect employees with adequate health and safety standards*, making sure not to define *adequate* or to develop a meaningful measurement agenda to determine the boundaries of universal safety levels.

Such wording, with a placating national slant directed perhaps at their home-market consumers and local activist groups, assumes and relies on rules and regulations that are in place in their own countries. They are, however, hollow statements as there are no collateral standardized gauges or global barometers to define them. No universally accepted red light indicators warning of danger to be heeded worldwide are in place. Many proposed codes make note of a well-intentioned promise to *actively protect the environment* but conveniently do not provide standards to measure if an environment is clean or dirty. Nor does it provide for proactive measures against which actions to maintain or improve can be qualified and quantified. The problem of whose criteria should be employed, who inspects, and who punishes for errors is rarely addressed. There are no universally accepted criteria to measure environmental safety, with the exception of the debated provisions as led by the United States of the Kato Convention on certain emissions in the air, and world governments themselves cannot agree on its value or accept its direction. Can private firms be expected to police themselves and instruct those they associate with to follow suit, when many times the prime imperative to go abroad may be to escape environmentally restrictive policies and penalties imposed by the home country?

Attempts at Universal Codes of Conduct

Chance favors the prepared mind.
—Louis Pasteur, French chemist and microbiologist

Notwithstanding the various doctrines of Western theocratic belief systems, the life-code practices offered by quasi-religious Eastern teachings as practiced by their followers around the world, and the secular declarations by individual nation-states (e.g., the U.S. Declaration of Independence), as well as the philosophical writings of numerous scholars on the subject, a historic United Nations (UN) declaration could be considered the prime ethical document recognizing universal human rights due to its wide global signatories. Hence its provisions, while not designed specifically for worldwide commercial activities, may be valuable in providing generic principles for ethical determination by business enterprises operating on a global scale.

UN Universal Declaration of Human Rights

The philosophical notion that we all share fundamental values is perhaps best expressed in the Universal Declaration of Human Rights as adopted and proclaimed by the UN General Assembly under resolution 217 A (111) on December 10, 1948. Although drafted from an underlying global political–economic agenda as opposed to a purely ethical imperative, it serves as a valuable codification of basic principles concerning human rights. As such it is a good template to begin referencing universally accepted ideas that impact and influence global commercial operations.

The preamble to the decree proclaims that we are "all members of the human family," equally sharing basic inalienable rights. Therefore, common standards may be established for the preservation and maintenance "for all peoples and all nations." The articles that follow are based on the principle that all have the right to life, liberty, and security of person without distinction of any kind. Even though we are separated by race, color, sex, language, religion, political or other opinion, property, birth, or status, all are entitled to basic human rights. Further, the jurisdiction of national sovereignty shall not abridge such fundamental rights, a motivation for the construction of universally applied ethical conduct.

A review of the initial general articles provides a valuable platform for identifying and addressing basic human rights. We will use these fundamental references to draw parallels to commercial considerations that multinational corporations (MNCs) may encounter. Article 4 prohibits slavery or involuntary servitude and could be an interpretive direction to *not* use such labor pools that are sometimes offered by repressive governments to firms entering their markets. Article 5 decrees that no one be subject to cruel, inhuman, or degrading treatment, a statement that could be applied to employment conditions with respect to dangerous environments, long work hours, and other life-threatening requirements on the job. Article 7 refers to discrimination and its equal protection under the law, a bridge to equal opportunity in the hiring or dismissal process. Article 12 speaks of attacks on one's honor and reputation, which could include oral insulting or berating of employees as opposed to physical harm. Article 13 gives the right to freedom of movement and residence within the borders of each state, a provision that could be used to disarm the ability of employers to place workers in factory dormitories when not at work and keep them confined in such compounds during the duration of their employment arrangements. Articles 19 and 20 allow for freedom of opinion and expression as well a peaceful assembly and association, provisions that may impact the right to form unions and have grievances aired in a public forum without interference or penalty.

Two articles expressly address work-related matters; hence, they are presented in their entirety. They are based on the themes annunciated in some of the initially noted articles but with a more precise definition that expands and amplifies the prior generalized statements.

Universal Declaration of Human Rights

Article 23

1. Everyone has the right to work, to free choice of employment, to just and favourable conditions of work and to protection against unemployment.
2. Everyone, without any discrimination, has the right to equal pay for equal work.
3. Everyone who works has the right to just and favourable remuneration ensuring for himself and his family an existence worthy of human dignity, and supplemented, if necessary, by other means of social protection.
4. Everyone has the right to form and to join trade unions for the protection of his interests.

Article 24

Everyone has the right to rest and leisure, including reasonable limitation of working hours and periodic holidays with pay.

Source: "Universal Declaration of Human Rights," United Nations, 1948. Available online at the United Nations website, http://www.un.org/en/documents/udhr.

These articles, although more specifically addressing commercial operations, leave room for interpretation. The liberal use of the term *favourable*, inserted before conditions of work and remuneration, and *reasonable* to quantify working hours, could be construed as subject to locally acceptable customs and traditions in the workplace. However, the main intent of the declaration, to address basic human rights with a global initiative, is embedded in many of the subsequent attempts to produce universally applicable codes of conduct in the commercial sector. It can therefore serve as a good jumping-off point or touchstone for companies desirous of constructing their own ethical code or considering grafting onto those offered by other independent institutions and agencies.

The First Commercially Directed Endeavor

The first modern commercially endorsed code of conduct and the grand-father of all modern compacts was inaugurated in 1977 under the author-ship of Reverend Leon Sullivan, a Black Baptist minister, during his tenure on the board of directors of General Motors Corporation (GM). This initiative, which came to be called the Sullivan Principles, helped to focus worldwide attention on the issue of racial injustice and it was also the initial attempt to address universal labor rights. Public sentiment pressured governmental policy to impose economic sanctions on South Africa while also arguing that although foreign direct investment (FDI) helped to transform the nation into a modern country, such commercial investments supported the repressive apartheid regime and therefore pro-moted human rights abuses.

Its original narrow ethical target, to improve conditions for non-Whites in South Africa and constrain apartheid, was initially used by 12 American corporations with operations in that country. The Sullivan Principles called for fair and equal employment practices for all races within the boundaries of company control and clearly targeted the segregated racial policies of the South African government. The Sullivan Principles created a corporate island of ethical integrity in a national sea devoid of morality and awash with inhumanity, ideas still relevant when operating in countries with oppressive regimes today. Even though such announced principles were an affront to the apartheid laws and challenged repressive regulations, the local government, not wanting to lose valued foreign investment, ignored such pronouncements even though they ran counter to their national policy. It did not wish to provoke the multinationals still operating in the country to withdraw their operations. It turns out that a number of years later the Reverend Sullivan felt that the actions called for by his principles were insufficient to displace the policies of strict segregation of the races in South Africa, that the continued presence of such companies even instituting his principles should not in good conscience continue in the country. Many of the large American firms that embraced his principles, like ExxonMobil, Kodak, IBM, Xerox, and even GM, ended up leaving the market. These divestments coupled with pressure from pension funds that held stock in other firms that conducted business in South Africa may have contributed over time to changes in the country's social policies.

While it may be well argued that such initial development of a universal code of ethical conduct for global commercial enterprises was not a forcible step in alleviating human and civil rights abuses in South Africa, it was the beginning of corporate involvement in the global issue of ethical conduct and social responsibility. However, it may have inadvertently sent a message to other repressive regimes that wished to open their borders for the fruits of foreign investment that is still valid over 30 years later in today's even more globally commercialized world.

Modified since initial publication by a committee headed by the Reverend Sullivan, the Sullivan Principles now encompass a wider criteria targeting the prevention of unacceptable worker treatment, such as exploitation of child labor, involuntary servitude, and other forms of worker abuse, to include a safe and healthy workplace. Today its eight points (six originally), called the Global Sullivan Principles (GSP), while still providing well-intentioned fundamental moral direction on global-labor treatment, are not specific enough. The annunciated points fail to emphatically define terminology as the rhetoric used is housed in generic ethical scripture as previously alluded to, leaving a well-intentioned document open for variances in interpretation.

Inherent, however, in its current contracts of endorsable declarations are two distinguishable factors that many modern constructed compacts fail to include a pledge to develop and implement company policies, procedures, training, and internal reporting structures to ensure compliance; and the periodic reporting on the implementation of such principles, clearly demonstrating the ongoing open commitment of firms that prescribe them.

Such key elements as execution and exposure separate this code from others that simply are touchstones of intended behavior. The only drawback is that the GSP organization is merely a repository for self-conducted internal monitoring by the signatories themselves of their actions and expectations. The GSP foundation-supplied questionnaire is used as a guide. It is prepared by the signatory companies themselves and the questions are to be answered to the best of *their* ability. It serves as a self-regulating, self-diagnostic internal instrument. The companies themselves are also asked to evaluate their progress on a rating scale moving from no action to full implementation of the principles. As transparent as the report may be, as it potentially allows for others to verify measures, asking a company to be judge and jury of its own actions may be a faith based initiative requiring the patients to heal themselves.

The GSP, currently chaired by one of the daughters of Reverend Sullivan since his death, went through a period of hiatus, so the historic endorsers' reporting process and the ongoing public dissemination of the principles, as well as the good work the organization has done, was marginalized beginning in 2002. The emergence of other declarations tended to place this honored, grandfathered proclamation in the rear. Today, however, the foundation has been rejuvenated and is again taking its rightful historic leadership position as a strong voice in the global ethical arena.

The principles themselves are preceded by a preamble that places commercial institutions in the role of responsible members of society in general and therefore encourages the use of such principles as a legitimate approach toward their activities. The first principle announces support for universal human rights (the term is not, however, defined) beyond just employees to encompass the communities firms operate within as well as all parties they associate with.

The second principle asks that signatories not only recognize but also promote equal opportunities for all employees regardless of their skin color, race, gender, age, ethnicity, and religious affiliation. It further requires companies not to engage in unacceptable worker treatment such as the exploitation of children, physical punishment, female abuse (not specifically defined but interpreted as sexual in nature due to the gender classification), and the use of involuntary servitude. The third principle asks that an employee's voluntary freedom of association be respected, a veiled reference to their right to organize into a collective body. The fourth principle refers to compensating employees in order to meet their basic needs (but basic needs are not specifically defined and tend to vary around the world) and to allow them to improve job performance in order to raise their socioeconomic standing. The fifth principle restates the provision to provide a safe and healthy workplace (no evaluation guidelines nor criteria are stated) for employees while noting a general desire to protect (again no specific standards are noted) the environment. The sixth principle asks companies to promote fair competition by respecting property, including intellectual property, respecting the rights of others, and not paying or accepting bribes (although the exact definition of a bribe is not indicated). The seventh principle directs firms to assist in the improvement of the quality of life in the communities in which they do business by working with local governments. The final principle involves applying all the prior principles to those with whom the company does business. Companies signing on to the Sullivan Principles are asked to be transparent in their application of its ideals, but this is not a requirement. They are further directed to see that its application permeates their entire organization and that some type of internal reporting system be employed to insure its use. In spite of some definitional drawbacks in the specification of prohibited activities and the generalization of some of its provisions, the Sullivan Principles are valued for its inauguration of a civil rights manifesto for international business. It remains as the grandfather of global corporate social responsibility and a prime template for the ethical conduct of companies in pursuit of their foreign operations.

Many firms, rather than creating their own code of conduct, have relied on other public-interest groups to provide guidance, like the Sullivan Principles initiative. In 2002, SA8000, a product of Social Acceptability International, published a nine-area proclamation based on International Labour Organization conventions and the UN Human Rights Standards with verification linked to ISO 9000-type standards first created for ensuring quality. This touchstone labor standard with monitoring systems calls for member firms not to use child or forced labor and to provide a safe working environment but falls short in defining the precise criteria for such stipulations. The International Organization for Standardization

(ISO), the group that pioneered universally acceptable principles for qualification of manufacturing systems noted earlier, recently announced its plans to issue global guidelines for corporate social responsibility. They intend to include reasonable child labor policies, promote equal opportunity for employees, ensure safe working conditions, and cover philanthropic matters. Revised guidelines may not be released until 2015. However, unlike their prior ISO standards, these guidelines do not entail a certification process and are not voluntary on the part of companies that subscribe to them. If these projected standards of acceptable behavior follow the initial report as submitted by their Advisory Group on Social Responsibility to the ISO Technical Management Board, which approves the final version, one can expect a restatement of those principles previously issued by the UN in the creation of their Global Compact as covered later in this section. As the ISO does carry substantial influence in the global commercial community, due to their prior ISO 9000 meritorious certification, their outlining of such principles will be an important step, but it may fall short in providing specific definitions of terminology and transparent accountability.

Helen Deresky reproduces in her textbook a codification of codes established by four recognized institutions toward establishing the behavior of multinational enterprises (MNEs) as originally prepared by Getz.[2] Under the section designated as "Human Rights," MNEs are told to "respect human rights and fundamentals of freedoms in the countries in which they operate" with an offsetting provision that they "should respect the social and cultural objectives, values and traditions" of such nations. Such generalized, countervailing, and conflicting statements cause both confusion and inconsistency in the application of universal codes and result in moral dilemmas for managers in the field. What are *human rights* and *fundamental freedoms*, and when confronted with alternative or different definitions, how does one choose?

Principles of the Caux Business Round Table

The Caux Round Table was founded in 1986 under the joint efforts of Frederick Phillips, former president of Philips Electronics, and Olivier Giscard d'Estaing, former vice chairman of the French business school

INSEAD. This initial marriage of a corporate executive and an academic continues today, as the organization is affiliated with the University of Virginia's Darden School of Business, a union allowing for a center of academic excellence to be maintained that bridges the gap between the business world and B-school (business school) curriculums, promoting applied educational direction on global ethical and corporate responsibility (CR) issues. The International Code of Ethics proposed in 1994 at the Caux Round Table[3] in Switzerland published principles rooted in two basic ethical ideals: *kyosei* and human dignity. These ideals define such moral pillars as follows:

> The Japanese concept of *kyosei* means living and working for the common good enabling cooperation and mutual prosperity to coexist with healthy and fair competition. Human dignity refers to the sacredness or value of each person as an end, not simply as a means to the fulfillment of other's purposes or even majority prescription.

While the definitions of such basic moral direction cannot be challenged, they need to be questioned as to their unequivocal practical guidance. Other portions of their creed state that "business established in foreign countries… should contribute to the social advancement, human rights, education, welfare and vitalization" of the society in which they operate. Such verbiage sounds great, but what are the practical ramifications of such pronouncements when a company is conducting operations in an emerging country? How do you advance its citizens, at what rate, and what programs are employed as contributions to establishing their welfare? Would mere payment of taxes to the sovereign government qualify? Would issuance of a check to a local charity or participation in construction of a social center, community hospital, or training facility fulfill duties and obligations and bring the company under the banner of the code? In the section regarding employees, firms are obligated to "respect each employee's health and dignity" and "protect employees from avoidable injury and illness in the workplace," but what criteria are used to define such levels of safekeeping? Companies are further admonished to "avoid discriminatory practices" in respect to gender, age, race, and religion, but what if the culture and society of a nation renders a contrasting approach that local managers must deal with in hiring practices as well as interpersonal relationships to efficiently and effectively operate their facility? What specifically is "compensation that improve(s) workers living conditions?" Not all countries are uniform in their economic measurement criteria. If one has nothing, lives on the street in abject poverty, and is offered a job that pays the equivalent of five dollars a day would such remuneration qualify?

The general principles built around the Round Table's desire to champion moral capitalism for a better world are admired for their bold vision. The idea that the responsibilities of business move beyond shareholders and out to stakeholders (Principle 1) are noble premises of intent. Having respect for the environment (Principle 6) and advising business not to participate in illicit operations like bribery or other corrupt practices such as trading in arms with terrorists, drug traffic, or organized crime groups (Principle 7) is to be applauded. The problem with such well-intentioned phrasing is that "the devil is in the details" (attributed to either Gustave Flaubert or Ludwig Mies van der Rohe but made famous in modern times by Ross Perot, a candidate in an American presidential election).

What exactly is *respect for the environment*? Is removing natural resources acceptable or does it depend on the degree of such activities, and who determines the impact on the environment? Is there a universal definition for bribery? Does a tip for courteous service or a token gift count in dealing with others? When does extravagant business entertaining cross the line? Must the action involve only money or does quid pro quo, reciprocity of favors, ever enter the equation? When does a terrorist become a freedom fighter and is supporting such actions be praised, not condemned?

Companies that become signatories to these noted principles receive a rather wide latitude of operational compliance and as such leave themselves open to challenges to questionable behavior. Sometimes the venerable shields that firms use to ward off and defend against unwarranted intrusion into their affairs can be filled with holes.

The UN Global Business Initiative

Kofi Annan, secretary-general of the venerable UN, at the World Economic Forum on January 31, 1999, challenged world business leaders to "embrace and enact" a global compact of practices. Covering human rights, labor standards, and the environment, the Ten Principles (originally nine with one on corruption added in 2004 and produced on the following page) asked global enterprises to make sure their organizations follow a set of core values in these areas. Principle 2 admonishes firms, requesting that they "are not complicit in human rights abuses." In regard to labor issues, Principle 4 asks firms to support "the elimination of all forms of forced and compulsory labor," while Principle 5 asks that companies uphold "the effective abolition of child labor." Principle 10 notes that "business should work against all forms of corruption, including extortion and bribery." With over 1,700 multinational firms subscribing by 2004 to the doctrines outlined in the UN Global Compact, a positive signal is being sent to multinational firms. However, while such declarations are to be lauded in their intent, they fail to define what is meant by *forced and compulsory labor* or *bribery* and do not define a universally acceptable age criterion in regard to *child labor*. Companies that cite their affirmation of the code and prescribe such as their corporate code of social and ethical conduct have tremendous leeway in the interpretation and application of the announced principles. Commentary by Pete Engardio, senior writer for *BusinessWeek*, finds fault with the Global Compact not for its language but "because the U.N. has focused more on expanding membership than on finding ways to ensure that corporations honor their commitments." He notes that "four years later there are still no clear reporting or compliance standards."[4] An interview with UN Secretary-General Kofi Annan accompanying the commentary noted the organization's desire to "expand into governance," but this esteemed body lacks the resources to monitor or enforce their principles. Given voluntary compliance by signatories and rather ambiguous, general statements of acceptable ethical behavior, how can definitive standards be created, much less imposed? (Note author's letter to the editors of *BusinessWeek*, August 2, 2004, page 18, offering such comments and concluding that the worldwide consumer will act as judge and jury of commercial compliance to the Global Compact and not the UN, as it is always loath to take any action by itself).

Principles of the UN Global Compact

The Ten Principles

Human Rights

- *Principle 1:* Businesses should support and respect the protection of internationally proclaimed human rights; and
- *Principle 2:* Make sure that they are not complicit in human rights abuses.

Labour Standards

- *Principle 3:* Businesses should uphold the freedom of association and the effective recognition of the right to collective bargaining;
- *Principle 4:* The elimination of all forms of forced and compulsory labour;
- *Principle 5:* The effective abolition of child labour; and
- *Principle 6:* The elimination of discrimination in respect of employment and occupation.

Environment

- *Principle 7:* Businesses should support a precautionary approach to environmental challenges;
- *Principle 8:* Undertake initiatives to promote greater environmental responsibility; and
- *Principle 9:* Encourage the development and diffusion of environmentally friendly technologies.

Anti-Corruption

- *Principle 10:* Businesses should work against all forms of corruption, including extortion and bribery.

Source: Reprinted by permission of the United Nations Global Compact: http://www.unglobalcompact.org

Other Universal Conventions and Declarations

The Anti-Bribery Convention of the Organisation for Economic Co-operation and Development was constructed and initially ratified by Canada in 2000; it has since been ratified by 38 other countries. The document is an attempt to eliminate bribery in international transactions and contracted ventures and features sections mandating legal ramifications for the payment of bribes. This universal declaration of principles does not mirror the U.S. Foreign Corrupt Practices Act of 1977, which makes it illegal to influence foreign officials through personal payments or political contributions, with stringent fines and imprisonment ramifications. The convention does place the subject of bribery as a moral inquiry outside the gray area of ethical decision making. The convention regulates the matter, however, to separate national laws and local regulatory guidelines, and hence may not have to be specifically recorded in a company's code of conduct short of a general declaration that its employees shall be bound by the laws of the country in which they conduct their corporate operations and activities. If such nations are signatory to the Convention, local employees would be bound to abide by its provisions. In a draft of *Viable Ethical Standards for Business* growing out of a Wharton business–church–community dialogue, general principles simply state that "employers need to respect the dignity and well-being of their workers" and that "discrimination based on race, sex or religion should be avoided." It further notes that "business should provide a safe and healthful working environment for its employees" and that "preventive measures should be taken to minimize worker injuries or sickness."[5] All these are worthwhile statements of conduct, but what definitions of *dignity* and *well-being* should be applied, what are the criteria for the establishment of a *safe and healthful working environment*, and what *preventive measures* should be taken?

Take the case of a worker in a Macau factory. Charged $15 a month for food and lodging when paid only $22 a month, the laborer had to hand over his personal identification card and was given an expired temporary resident permit. Left with such valueless documentation he risked arrest if he ventured out of the immediate neighborhood or the factory compound where employees were locked in the walled enclosure for all

but 60 minutes a day for meals. Guards routinely punched and hit workers for talking back and imposed fines of one dollar for infractions like
taking too much time in the bathroom. While such workers, desperate
for work, voluntarily leave their far-off provinces and unlawfully journey
to in-country manufacturing centers, they are not slaves in the traditional
sense. Neither the government nor the private modern slave traders spirit
them away to a life of bondage, but the resulting effect is the same. Do
the earlier examined UN Global Compact principles apply to them, as
they are not forced into labor in the conventional sense? Are they treated
with dignity and valued as sacred human beings? Are they discriminated?
Do they work in a safe environment? When all about them are subject to
similar conditions, it is difficult to proclaim wrong as despicable though
it may seem so to foreign eyes and varied senses of morality.

What is child labor? Is there a universally accepted age when one goes
from childhood to adulthood, or does each society, taking a cue from its
socioeconomic developmental level and cultural roots, decide for itself?
While the UN Global Compact, as noted earlier, requests the abolition
of child labor, it does not quantify an age. However, in the UN's own
Convention on the Rights of the Child, ratified by 192 countries, the
protocol defines as children "all human beings under the age of 18, unless
relevant national laws recognized an earlier age of majority" (Article 1).
If an "upper benchmark in defining the child" is legislated it shall control
the minimum age. It goes on to note that "states substituting an earlier
age for specific purposes must do so in the context of… best interests of
the child (Article 3), maximum survival and development (Article 6) and
participation of children (Article 12)." The convention does state capital punishment or life imprisonment "is explicitly prohibited for those
under age 18" (Article 37) but notes that "recruitment into the armed
forces or direct participation in hostilities is expressly prohibited for those
under age 15 (Article 38)." Two Optional Protocols to the convention
on the adoption of children in armed conflict (February 12, 2002) and
another on the sale of children, child prostitution, and child pornography
(January 18, 2002) have been added to the original protocol. Only the
military addition has addressed the age issue, raising to 18 years the level
for participation in hostilities and forced recruitment. As noble as the
second optional protocol is in its desire to protect and ensure the welfare

of children, it does not include an age qualification to define a child. It would seem that countries that have ratified the original Convention still have leeway, with exception of the punishment and military qualifications, to decide for themselves the age of a child in a civilian work environment.

The farm belt and ranches of America, in its history, regularly utilized the children of families on such facilities to actively participate in agricultural and livestock operations, even forcing school schedules to comply with seasonal resource needs. Even today family farms and migrant workers continue to call upon such child labor in the United States. In many religious sects and in tribal settings around the world, manhood of male children is bestowed at the age of 13 or younger. In impoverished nations, children 10 years or younger are placed by their own relatives in revenue-generating activities for the benefit of the extended family, as without such income-producing assets all would perish from starvation. Again one must ask, who makes the rules and who enforces them? Beyond the questionable child age consideration another issue plagues the labor market in many regions of the world: the practices of unscrupulous intermediaries—the labor brokers that prey on unsuspecting and naive potential employees. Authors Griffen and Pustay offer an excerpt from *Fortune* magazine in their textbook detailing a Philippine native's labor ordeal. It begins with an initial obligation of $2,400 to her local country broker as backed by a third-party loan at 10 percent a month to secure work at a Motorola subcontractor in Taiwan. Upon arrival at the Taipei airport she is met by a second labor broker demanding an additional fee of $3,900 before delivering her to the promised new job. Though the job, which will pay her $460 per month for the privilege of working 12-hour shifts, seven days a week in the factory, was most attractive her, the debts to the two labor brokers and the interest on the first loan coupled with monthly deductions for Taiwanese income tax, room and board at the factory, and a compulsory contribution to a savings bond she will get only if she completes her three-year contract are all financial obligations that make her initial act of economic desperation seem worthless.[6]

Paying up-front fees for a job in a new foreign location is a standard practice for factory workers in the Far East. However, a similar system in the tech industry in the United States has recently been uncovered with the same unethical exploitation of foreign workers. A *Business Week* feature article in October 2009 profiled the cases of white-collar skilled technicians from India. Replying to an advertisement, as well as promised sponsorship for required visas, a group of professionals paid an agency thousands of dollars in up-front fees. Upon arriving in America, they found that no position existed. Not only were these unsuspecting aliens robbed of fees paid in advance, but also many found that the company continued to garnish their meager wages from other menial jobs for years to pay off their contractual obligations that were still outstanding. Beyond such disappointment and financial loss, their plight was compounded by the federal visa violation committed, resulting in a sentence composed of 12 to 18 months of probation, fines of $2,000, and the possibility of deportation.

These unscrupulous companies, besides collecting outrageous up-front fees and continuing to require payments from foreign workers, also hold their visa documents, threatening to revoke their papers if they complain. They told the fraudulently duped workers to find other jobs, and used the leverage of retaining their documents to extract a cut of the workers' outside wages. Even when these guest workers where between assignments, placed *on the bench*, the visa-sponsoring firms are required to continue to pay them, but they do not. These are illegal practices with the federal government prosecuting violators, but the real damage is to the prospective immigrants and it has tainted the high-tech industry with the label of a sweatshop. Many honest companies in the industry unsuspectingly contribute to the immoral and illegal treatment of employees as they simply do not bother investigating the ethics of their outsourced personnel suppliers. They are blinded by the payroll savings and labor flexibility offered to them by such programs, in addition, they have neither policies nor codes of conduct that might cause them to question their association with such outsourced partners. It is virtually the same conditions that MNCs found themselves in as they contracted with foreign manufactures and assemblers when the term *sweatshop* was first applied. Their strategic actions created a negative unethical public perception of companies in regard to such practices, taking undue and unfair advantage of alien workers. The recent exposé of the white-collar professional level in the United States has raised public awareness.

Western European companies have been accused for years for using middlemen and employment agencies to receive a steady stream of trapped and controllable employees from former communist states in the East for use in factories and low-paying service jobs. In the Middle East, alien service workers from India, Pakistan, and the surrounding territories have long been imported into Dubai, Abu Dhabi, the United Arab Emirates, and Saudi Arabia, as well as other countries in the region under similar unethical systems and forced into virtual slavery once they entered jurisdictions. Many are bound up or placed in holding cells at night to insure their prisonerlike compliance. Even if they managed to escape such conditions, they are treated by these governments as illegal aliens and are subject to criminal penalties.

The key in all such situations is that the foreign worker becomes an indentured servant. They are forced to pay up-front fees that never end and their visa documents are withheld, making them prisoners of their sponsors. Local governments have no empathy for their plight and only stand ready to fine them, place them in jail, and deport them, as they have no rights as noncitizens. It is a side of globalization that is ugly and immoral but one that could be combated by firms if their employment strategies contained a universal code of ethical conduct that was not only practiced within the company but also covered third-party associations with employment outsourcing contractors.

While many prescribed universal codes of business conduct address the human rights plight of employees, whether they be direct or contracted labor, none addresses the deplorable practices of the labor agents that ply the workforce of emerging nations as they lie outside the purview of corporate governance and empowerment. The answer may be responsible global corporate citizens, as by their very ability to cross borders they become the social and ethical police officers of the world. Their enforcement tool is the value of economic opportunity they provide, and their reward a world of uplifted righteousness and the creation of consumers that will eventually buy their products. If one believes that markets without morality cannot sustain themselves, then by their actions worldwide commercial enterprises are merely planting the seeds of their own destruction. In order for a practical code of conduct to be constructed so that it is respected and followed by those unto whom it is directed for implementation and in the end make a difference, companies should consider spelling out their intentions in very definite terms.

Most of the previously reviewed sacrosanct documents (Table 5.1) are endowed with the best of intentions, but like the great historic declarations also extolling humanity and honor toward fellow human beings, they have to be supplemented by specific bills of rights to define terminology and allow for implementation of their instructions. It should also be noted that not all countries of the world unanimously agree on the codes of conduct provided for in such documents, and the ratification process for many nations is still an ongoing process. What is important, however, is that in spite of cultural differences affecting moral values and beliefs, the need for establishing basic, common-ground principles for ethical conduct in this era of increased globalization is progressing. This is happening despite those institutions that wish to maintain a status quo or feel such proactive measures are not strategically desirable and in the best interests or purview of commercial organizations. While many global firms might choose to construct a fine balance between ethical imperialism (going overseas with one's own ethical baggage and applying it locally) and cultural relativism (accepting what they encounter abroad), they may need to eventually draw that line in the sand and be specific with exacting criteria. Getting caught in the middle is problematic and a potential ethical trap.

Table 5.1 Leading international accords affecting global ethics and social responsibility by chronological order of enactment or accord year

United Nations Universal Declaration of Human Rights	1948
European Convention on Human Rights	1950
Helsinki Accords	1975
Organization for Economic Cooperation and Development Guidelines for Multinational Enterprises	1976
International Labor Office Tripartite Declaration of Principles of Multinational Enterprises and Social Responsibility	1977
United Nations Code of Conduct on Transnational Corporations	1988
Anti-Bribery Convention of the Organization for Economic Cooperation and Development	2000
United Nations Convention of the Rights of the Child (amended)	2002
United Nations Global Compact (amended)	2004

Standards of acceptable behavior need to be tied down, not left to wander off into their cultural perceptions with interpretation left to those who have to enforce the meandering conditions. A rainbow mixture of *absolutes* and *relatives* is introduced later on in the book to take the vagueness out of the equation and provide definitive guidance for those managers who wish to take control of their global ethical encounters. Procedures are offered for inspection and verification, as they must accompany the verbiage to ensure implementation. Provisions for notification with applicable periods for correction and penalties for consistent violations are also included to complete the process.

In short, to construct a meaningful code of global conduct beyond the public relations exercise, a new all-encompassing, self-sustaining doctrine is required of global corporations.

The following declarations are not included in the Table 5.1 as they are contained in the workings of private organizations and therefore have not been accorded intergovernmental recognition vis-à-vis treaties, conventions, and membership as ascribed to by national governments:

- Sullivan Principles, published in 1977 (and later altered to the Global Sullivan Principles, 1997)
- SA800 (Social Acceptability International), 2002
- International Labor Organization Conventions, various dates
- International Code of Ethics (Caux Round Table of multinational firms), 1994

The Private Corporate Alliance Initiative

The 1990s and extending into mid 2000 was a period of increased public consciousness as driven by numerous news reports of global worker abuse. The rise in awareness and with resentment directed at governments and MNCs fueled protests at World Trade Organization (WTO) meetings and caused many young people to join cause organizations. But such notoriety and its byproduct, social motivation, began to wane in the new millennium. The call for global corporations to actively institute a dialogue about the issues, no less consider adopting codes of conduct with public transparent provisions, was replaced by one of "good-faith compliance."[7] Out of the temperament of the period the UN Global Compact was constructed in the late 90s. The main critical complaint is that the private corporate signatories to the accords are under no obligation to prove their operational observance. Neither the creating body of the document, the UN, nor any appointed group has any right to verify that the compact declarations are being practiced. The public is simply asked to trust the parties who announce their intentions to follow the Compact directives, a practical nod to the fact that the public outcries of the 90s may have lost their emotional appeal.

The same critique that might be directed at the toothless and nonfunctional transparency of the UN declarations can be made of self-appointed and self-serving special interest groups formed by companies and industry groups. As opposed to or in conjunction with issuing individual corporate codes of conduct, numerous alliances have been formed by separate parties and even competitive associates in the same industry to present a uniform ethical agenda and to announce their cooperative self-appointed policing of their activities. Many such alliances are formed because the partnering entities face common ethical dilemmas or because the industries they belong to have come under general scrutiny or attack. While the goal may be well directed, wrapping the firm in the cloak of linked ethical associations might be seen as a *safety-in-numbers* shield technique. Potential criticisms may be deflected across wider screen, and no one in the alliance can gain a competitive advantage by proclaiming that their moral standards exceed those of others in the industry. The danger of such morally directed alliances is that a misstep by one of the members resulting in an allegation of impropriety can damage all in the group. Nike, the original ethical-labor bad boy, formed its own strategic alliance, the Global Alliance for Workers and Communities. The partners, Nike, Gap Inc., and Inditex SA, are all from the apparel industry and all share a common activity, the production of their clothing lines utilizing cost-efficient labor forces around the world. They have banded together to publicize their operational transparency and devote an extensive web page to their personally appointed principles and actions. While on the surface these exercises are to be lauded, an article by Jeff Ballinger finds fault with such common programs. He states, "The nefarious nature of Nike's Global Alliance strategy was revealed in the February 2001 report about nine

Nike contractors in Indonesia… failing to mention strikes, fired workers, wage cheating" and the fact that "no Nike shoe or apparel contractor… was presently engaged in meaningful collective bargaining."[8] Many such self-serving associations of corporations are therefore tainted by false or misleading reporting by any of the individual partners, and they remain suspect in regard to their public pronouncements. Even the venerable UN Global Compact may be nothing but hollow words pledged by international firms having no intention to follow its directives but out to gain the publicity value accorded to signatories and to create a shield of plausible interest expressed in the issue to ward off any potential inquiries.

Theological and Secular Moral Philosophies

Whenever two good people argue over principles, they are both right.
—Marie Ebner Von Eschenbach, Austrian writer of
psychological novels

All that philosophers have done is interpret the world in different way.
—Karl Marx, German philosopher and political theorist

The framers of codes of conduct must themselves begin at some individual philosophy. A great deal of literature through the ages has been devoted to describing and evaluating various forms of ethical behavior. The interpretation of man's relationship with his fellow man and with the environment, whether inspired by a higher deity or as dictated by nature, is a subject of countless manuscripts devoted to the philosophy of life. Fictional works interweave morality into their stories as do other forms of entertainment. (Note the earlier reference to the underlying theme of the popular film *Avatar*.) In essence, from the day we are born we are bombarded by the notions of right and wrong from all parts of the society we live and work in. Such process continues our entire life. Each of us develops an internal system that guides our behavior and values in life toward those around us. It may be valuable therefore to explore, in limited format, some of the general moral philosophies as a basis for appreciating common and divergent concepts that global managers encounter.

Faith-Based Influences: The Golden Rule

In most cultures, the roots of morality are nourished by religious earth from which they germinate. The Ten Commandments may have been the first recorded attempt to universalize morality within the confines of direction provided by a higher deity.[9] It is concise in its policies with specific direction introduced by the words "Thou shalt not...." The rules of human engagement were later expanded and sanctified in biblical text with final judicial review of one's actions reserved until death. Final pronouncement comes in the form of eternal bliss or degrees of damnation but "a corporation is a legal fiction... it has no body, it has no soul, it can't feel the pain of punishment."[10] It is therefore up to the framers and beneficiaries of such institutions to inject humanity into them.

Beyond mankind's natural affinity to include religious beliefs in constructing moral judgments in life, business ethical literature has also determined that religiosity plays a role in predicting attitudes. According to studies[11] a respondent's level of religiosity positively correlates to their ethical approach in employing situation-specific scenarios. It is worthwhile therefore to discuss one of the most referenced tenets of ethical direction as derived from a faith-based affiliation. But just prior to considering this inspirational imperative I am reminded of a quote from the poet Ed Willock, pertaining to the paradox of mixing religious direction and commercial action:

> Mr. Business went to Mass,
>
> He never missed a Sunday;
>
> Mr. Business went to hell For
>
> what he did on Monday*

To provide a more earthly appreciation for one's everyday actions, many individuals proclaim the Golden Rule. Its direction "Do unto others as you would have had done unto yourself" sets up a simple measurement table using a standard that requires no external monitoring system. It rests on a most simple tenet: One's own internal code of receivable conduct applied to others. As one would not cause harm to be

---

* The quote is considered anonymous but it has been attributed to Ed Willock editor of the now defunct Catholic monthly *Integrity* who published it in the magazine.

inflicted upon oneself, one should apply an equal standard to others. It is a respected mantra of ethical conduct referenced in many of the world's religious codes of conduct, which admonishes one to react to others by treating them in the same way as they would like to be treated. A table of many of the world's religions and their embedded use of the Golden Rule idea appears in this section (Table 5.2).

Table 5.2 Religious and social variations on the golden rule ethical direction

Variation	Basic tenets with alternative wordings and references
Bahai Faith	"Lay not on any soul a load that you would not wish to be laid upon you, and desire not for anyone the things you would not desire for yourself." (Bahá'u'lláh, Gleanings, LXVI:8)
Buddhism	"Hurt not others with that which pains yourself" (Udanavarga, v. 18); "Treat not others in ways that you yourself would find hurtful" (Udanavarga 5.18)
Christianity	"Do unto others as you would have them do unto you" (Matthew 7:12); "Do not do what you hate" (Gospel of Thomas 6, Apocrypha); "Treat others as you would like them to treat you" (Luke 6:31, *New English Bible*)
Confucianism	"Surely it is the maxim of loving-kindness: Do not unto others that you would not have them do unto you" (*Analects* 12:2); "Tse-Kung asked, 'Is there one word that can serve as a principle of conduct for life?' Confucius replied, 'It is the word *shu*—reciprocity. Do not impose on others what you do not desire.'" (*Doctrine of the Mean* 13.3); "One should not behave towards others in a way which is disagreeable to oneself." (Mencius vii.A.4)
Hinduism	"This is the sum of duty: do naught unto others what would cause pain if done to you." (Mahabharata 5.1517)
Islam	"Not one of you is a believer until you wish for others (one's brother) what you wish for yourself." (Fourth Hadith of An-Nawawi 13/No. 13 of Imam Al-Nawawi's Forty Hadiths)
Jainism	"One should treat all creatures in the world as one would like to be treated." (Mahavira, Sutrakritanga 1.11.33); "In happiness and suffering, in joy and grief, we should regard all creatures as we regard our own self." (Lord Mahavira, 24th Tirthankara)
Judaism	"What is hateful to you, do not do to your neighbor (your fellow man). That is the law: all the rest is commentary." (Talmud. Shabbat 31a; Tobit 4:125); "Thou shall love thy neighbor as thyself" (Leviticus 19:18)

Variation	Basic tenets with alternative wordings and references
Scientology	"Try not to do things to others that you would not like them to do to you. Try to treat others as you would want them to treat you." (*The Way to Happiness* by L. Ron Hubbard)
Shintoism	"Hurt not others with that which pains yourself." (Udanavarga 5.18)
Sikhism	"I am a stranger to no one; and not one is a stranger to me. Indeed, I am a friend to all." (*Guru Granth Sahib*, page 1299)
Sufism	"The basis of Sufism is consideration of the hearts and feelings of others." (Dr. Javad Nurbakhsh, Master of the Nimatullahi Sufi Order)
Taoism	"Regard your neighbor's gain as your own gain and regard your neighbor's loss as your own loss." (Tai Shang kan Ying P'ien, 213–18)
Unitarianism	"We affirm and promote respect for the interdependent web of all existence of which we are a part." (Unitarian principle of life)
Wicca	"An it harm none, do what ye will (wilt)." (The Wiccan Rule; meaning one may do what they want as long as it harms no one, including oneself)
Zoroastrianism	"Do not do unto others whatever is injurious to yourself." (Shayast-na-Shayast 13.29)
Native American Indian	"Humankind has not woven the web of life. We are but one thread within it. Whatever we do to the web, we do to ourselves." (Chief Seattle); "Respect for all life is the foundation." (The Great Law of Peace)
Yoruba—Nigerian tribe	"One going to take a pointed stick to pinch a baby bird should first try it on himself to feel how its hurts." (old adage for the treatment of others)

Leading faith traditions have always identified and promoted an agreed set of core human values based on similar principles underlying a common treatment of man toward fellow men. Religions have always been looking for the endorsement of nonreligious allies and their institutions in the tenets they prescribe, and their guidance seems to have a universal direction, providing a touchstone for handling ethical dilemmas.

The common factor inherent in all these directional quotations is the accent on or the constant use of the words *you, yourself, himself,* or *itself.* They all ask people to process and access their actions toward others within the behavioral framework of a value system based solely on the individual. Such a singular morality guide relying on a prejudicial, personal appraisal of one's actions tends to be egotistical and looks at the world through a narrow tunnel of culturally ingrained and therefore bordered criteria of right and wrong. By logical extension the concept of the Golden Rule could drive one to apply morality worldwide via ethical imperialism. Such policy "directs people to do everywhere exactly as they do at home."[12] The theory behind ethical imperialism is a belief in a singular set of absolute truths, announced with a one-or-all set of concepts requiring the same behavior and response around the world.[13]

Beyond the shared Golden Rule imperative, the texts of all the world's great religions and their derivative sects provide ethical direction; they are in essence recorded codes of conduct of prescribed and expected behavior toward others. Another common concept repeated among such revered writings in regard to the practice of commerce is best illustrated in *The Dhammapada* by Gautama, known as Buddha. One is instructed to pursue the "Right Livelihood: avoiding making money from harmful activities."[14] Overall, the directional value provided in the Old Testament, the New Testament, *The Book of Mormon*, The Koran, *The I Ching* (the foundation of both the Confucian and the Taoist way of life), Laotzu's *The Way and Its Powers*, *Analects* by Confucius, and *The Upanishads* (paving the way for Hinduism and the three main *heresies*[15] rooted in its teachings, Jainism, Buddhism, and Sikhism) are touchstones for ethical decision making and maintenance of the social contract. It is outside the purview of this book to adequately list and examine these vaunted references, no less their interpretations, to arrive at any comprehensive summary and provide guidance to the reader. This is a private journey of ethical value awareness that we must each discover on our own and then decide how such is to be incorporated into our own lives and reflected in the role of a manager.

While the importance of religion and those spiritual philosophies identified with it is personal, a collective society strongly influenced by such doctrines can impact ethical matters. Two examples illustrate this consideration.

Western Catholicism draws a distinction between the *religious* and the *secular*, whereas Islam (*submission to God* in Arabic) is much more than "just a religion in the usual Western sense, it is a total way of life"[16] with prescribed behavioral actions that must be followed by the devoted. The governments of many Arab countries utilize the *sharia* law to achieve legitimacy and consolidate their secular regulations to conform to such directed principles of social justice. Any code of conduct constructed under an orthodox Islamic society would be more prone to echo such precise directional guidance and perhaps not be tolerant of ethical diversity. In Confucian philosophy, as many scholars consider his instructions outside of the spiritual, "less emphasis is on the individual, and much more on the individual as a unit in society."[17] Codes of conduct in such cultures are built on one's responsibility to promote the greater common good and preserve the harmony of society. This value distinction that may *not* allow for the fair and equitable treatment of minorities (the discrimination factor) as such could be unsettling to societal synchronization. As one moves around the world, varying religious or philosophical ways of life should not be ignored. They are deeply embedded roots of morality. Managers must take them into consideration as they make their ethical deliberations toward the construction of a workable universal code of acceptable conduct for their employees and stakeholders wherever they are located. While religious notions of morality and ethical guidance are important in all societies, this section would not be complete without a secular reference as voiced by Albert Einstein, who said, "I do not believe in the immorality of the individual, and I consider ethics to be an exclusively human concern without any superhuman authority behind it."

Core Human Values

The desire to assemble a universal code of conduct could also be used to arrive at a supporting parallel premise that Donaldson calls *core human values*.[18] Many who subscribe to this ethical directive would describe these as their *home values*, because we all inherently think ours is the correct universal response. Others consider such an approach as a call to adhere to a composite of the world's greatest thinking on the subject. In his article on developing a system for managers to apply when away from home, Donaldson uses this concept as the first of three principles in the building of a workable model for arriving at ethical decisions.[19] To quote Donaldson, core human values are defined as a summary of "the work of scores of theologians and philosophers around the world" to produce a composite fundamental and universally recognized standard to be applied worldwide—a "respect for human dignity."[20] When such ethical principles are placed in the context of commercial operations (money-driven activities), the affronts to human dignity and core values might be exemplified by the following repugnant situations that cross the threshold of acceptable conduct:

- Third World parents cheerfully saying good-bye to their offspring as they journey off to learn a lifelong valuable skill in a distant factory, perhaps in an alien land, not knowing that their children will merely be physical laborers in a sweatshop where conditions of life and work will be akin to commercial slavery.
- Young women, who have just crossed adolescence, follow an offer of respectable work in a strange country where their passports (real or forged) are confiscated upon arrival by those who arranged the trip, promising a better life. But in reality the destination is a prison brothel that offers no escape.
- The motivated young boy just entering manhood who arrives at a foreign worksite already in debt to third-party brokers for travel expenses and employment fees, debts accumulating outrageous interest charges. He is placed into a deeper financial abyss through excessive charges for inferior food and deplorable dormitory accommodations. The result is indentured servitude for the rest of his adult life.

One is urged by Donaldson to apply core human values to all ethical dilemmas, not just the aforementioned examples of human bondage, in any society, at any time, and in any context, and such principles would remain constant. The result is a line in the sand that will not be crossed. This is a most noble crusade, but it requires the average man to possess the skillful attributes of Solomon the wise and be acquainted with all the writings of the world's great minds—an awesome task for any person and perhaps best left to an omnipotent being. What if an individual is part of an organization and cannot be on site everywhere an ethical dilemma arises? Such a specially endowed person must possess a unique ability and communication talent to pass along magnificent judgment abilities to his embedded managerial brethren worldwide, so all think and act in perfect unison in regard to any and all moral incidents. In the absence of such a mind-melding technique, the only option would be for this man or woman of spiritual wisdom to clone himself or herself to allow for equality of applied decision making.

But what if each individual developed his own set of core human values? If used as the prime basis for conducting a universal code of conduct for multinational companies, it would require every onsite manager to apply his own standards of acceptable conduct, which by extension would result in a multitude of different decisions being applied throughout the organization. The result is ethical chaos and no universally applied principles, which is a potential nightmare for an integrated global company.

Respecting Diversity: Customs and Traditions

Out of the vestiges of cultural relativism, Donaldson builds his second principle in the construction of a workable code for executives away from home. He calls it as *respect for local tradition*.[21] This component acts as a balance to his first condition of core human values. In essence, he recognizes that basic universal standards may need to be adjusted for individual societies that might be out of sync with globally accepted principles as personified by the sanctified great thinkers, as hallowed and revered as they may be to the rest of the world. This counterbalancing weight to ethical imperialism, the application of one's own perceived core values, is known as *cultural relativism*. Such principle holds that "no culture's ethics are better than any other's; therefore there are no international rights and wrongs."[22] Respect for the ways and behavior of others, their culture, traditions, and customs, is the paramount guideline. The mantra of those embracing cultural relativism is *When in Rome, do as the Romans do.* It allows for cultural wiggle room in ethical decision making.

Using such an ethical guideline, one might propose an alternative to the Golden Rule, often cited as an expression of a core value, and call it the *Platinum Rule: Do unto others as they would have had done unto themselves.* This approach puts the operational imperative on the word *themselves* and asks the ethical judge to consider the values and beliefs of those affected by one's moral decisions, as opposed to the *self*. What would the receiver of the ethical decision consider just and fair? The idea is promoted in the writings of George Bernard Shaw in his 1903 play *Man and Superman*, where he states, "Do not do unto others as you would they should do unto you. Their tastes may not be the same."

Set in the future, the famous *Star Trek* television and movie series features a prime directive by the fictional Federation of Planets to their starship captains: visit, observe, and leave. Do not disturb other worlds. Leave them to develop as their society naturally evolves and therefore requires. A similar theme is echoed by Johns Hopkins University foreign-policy expert Michael Mandelbaum: "People do not change when we tell them they should, they change when they tell themselves they must."

Internal Diversity Discrimination

A perplexing issue for MNCs using offshore labor is not so much with local citizens but the treatment in the host country of domestic employees who are deemed alien workers. A good example of this ethical dilemma is offered by employment incidents in South Korea concerning discrimination against imported migrant workers from surrounding poor Asian countries. Reports by Amnesty International depict claims of on-the-job sexual abuse, berating of workers with racial slurs, and inadequate safety training, as well as suspension of requirements under South Korean labor laws for mandatory disclosure of employee HIV (human immunodeficiency virus) status have resulted in mental and physical workplace health risks for these alien groups. These incidents reflect public xenophobia and are found not only in South Korea but also in many areas of the world. As previously noted in the Middle East, imported workers from India, the Philippines, Southeast Asia, and the African continent have been treated as second-class citizens like the labor from Mexico and South America crossing into the United States and Canada.

These incidents pose a unique and complex ethical dilemma for MNCs as they partner with or contractually engage third-party foreign suppliers and contractors in a host country that in turn hires immigrants to supplement local labor. Most codes of conduct are written to protect all workers on the job regardless of ethnic or national identity. When the local indigenous workforce applauds such principles for themselves but stops short of extending them to resident aliens, a problem can emerge. MNCs, in the enforcement of their own codes of conduct or even applying universal codes to which they are signatory, are ethically caught in the middle. Their code language, while accepted by the local citizenry, faces an additional hurdle as it runs counter to domestic tradition, customs and even host-country laws regarding imported workers. In many cases, codes of conduct addressing employee treatment have been interpreted as only applying to legal citizens and not resident aliens even with employment papers, as technically resident aliens have no rights. The situation is exacerbated when alien workers are smuggled into a country.

While the South Korean foreign ministry supports legislation against racial, ethnic, or cultural national bias (an agenda endorsed by the UN Elimination of Racial Discrimination committee), many elements inside the country argue passage would encourage more migrant workers into the country—a situation that could force the local indigenous workforce to lose scarce jobs, thereby causing social unrest. Citizens of many industrialized nations have expressed the same concerns. Treatment of foreign workers has also come to the attention of the Organisation for Economic Co-operation and Development, with respect not only to emerging nations but also to advanced, developed countries as this ethical issue, due to globalization, only grows in importance. In many societies, lineage is what determines worth. One's linkage to ancestry is not limited to family but extends to tribal associations, religious sects, and ethnic and national origins. Distinct hierarchical patterns are therefore established, and social structures are rarely breached to allow freedom of social movement and opportunity for those labeled as outsiders to be part of the social majority. Ethnic, race-based, and national prejudice therefore becomes an accepted morality. MNCs may have to construct their codes of conduct to stress that their principles apply not just to indigenous-majority labor but to imported alien workers, especially in host countries where domestic laws exclude protecting alien workers and social prejudices support discriminatory treatment on the job.

The Contextual Interloper

Donaldson concludes the triad of ethical guidance for traveling international executives with a third axiom, the introduction of *context* into the mix—when, where, and between whom ethical situations arise.[23] He recognizes that timing, the placement of events, and the parties involved may color perceptions and influence the ethical-decision outcome. The concept recognizes that the arena in which ethical decisions are made is influenced by unique circumstances, that the state of affairs, the status and positions of the parties involved, and their relationship matrix all are relevant. This is the factual, realistic component to the two previous theoretical principles: core human values or ethical imperialism, and respect for local tradition or cultural relativism.

According to psychologists, the injection of context into the ethical-decision negates the presumption that people possess strict, permanent moral platforms as launching pads for their determinations. They will apply varying principles depending on the real-life contextual situations presented to them. Behavior does not exhibit what psychologists refer to as cross-situational stability. Everyone harbors a multiplicity of moral tendencies, with certain ones activated by the context in which ethical issues materialize. The poem in the previous section on the influence of faith-based institutions is illustrative of our moralized contextual contradictions: One is pious on Sunday but irreverent on Monday. One can be honest in one circumstance and dishonest in another. The 1965 P.F. Sloan lyric, recorded by Barry McGuire in the song "Eve of Destruction," again poetically demonstrates the hypocritical human condition when it comes to ethical behavior: "hate your next-door neighbor, but don't forget to say grace."

When questioned, most people will state that they have an internal ethical determinant and often cite a guidepost like the Golden Rule, as previously discussed. In reality, they have only vague intuitions, impulses, and instincts as garnered from cultural upbringing and exposure to some spiritually based or intellectual–philosophical principles. The internal mechanism for ethical decision making is a constantly adjusting barometer scaled with a multiplicity of tendencies representing ethical ideas. There is no constant methodology or a constant command system that is used to arrive at an ethical decision. In fact, many describe their ethical determinations as simply a feeling they have in respect to the facts presented. Context supplies the triggering mechanism for selection of the then appropriate reactive solution. As noted before, when students in a classroom are asked to emphatically state a moral conviction that can be applied anytime, anywhere, with any group of players, and in any situation, they find it difficult to offer a comprehensive reply. They ask the instructor to provide a scenario, an outline of a factual situation, upon which they can construct an answer. Context, a subjectively emotional reaction, is therefore an important element to induce objective ethical reasoning.

Putting Them All Together

Armed with these three cornerstones of foundational moralities, globe-trotting executives are encouraged to build their ethical decision making. To demonstrate the Donaldson triad, visualize the ethical-decisional process as a liquid poured into an upside-down funnel or a glass beaker in a laboratory. At the tapered top, the decision is subject to the narrow confines of core human values, universal principles that shall not be compromised. As the liquid runs down the vessel it passes through a wider opening and is exposed to numerous independent local traditions, historically accepted customs, and belief systems that begin to modify the descent. As it cascades to the bottom, it hits a situational wall, causing the decision to be dramatically affected and reflected back by context. The resulting process, made up of the three proactive combining forces represented by the shape of the funnel, drives commercial institutions to take a 360-degree reactionary track. The Donaldson model allows one to respond to the proverbial, "When you come to the fork in the road, take it," a quotation attributed to baseball player Lawrence "Yogi" Berra, who has become something of a folk laureate of the English language in America.

But questions remain, as the devil is in the details. How does one decide which actions fall below the threshold of sustaining core human values, and what are those values? Which ones are properly challenged and in the end negated because they are tethered by a social umbilical cord to the Gordian knot of local traditions? How strong an ingredient is in the context of a situation that may influence the final decision? If the first two philosophical qualifiers (core human values and influence of tradition) are adjusted by the third (actual content for each ethical dilemma), could a constant uniform decision across the varying societies encountered by an organization ever be made?

Even if commercial institutions were blessed with the services of a singular superperson who, endowed with Donaldson's triangular principles, could constantly circle and hover about the world to settle every moral dilemma, each decision would be different. If each separate manager could be replicated and thereby genetically instilled with the same mind-set so all ethical decisions were equally addressed, the matters would still be settled differently due to context. Reality, not science fiction, forces transnational firms to rely on a nationally embedded multiplicity of individual managers who will not react in the same manner despite a strong corporate culture. They will not apply a uniform moral-thinking matrix based on commonly linked guiding principles unless one exists. Simply put, managers must be tethered to the same ethical compass, a universally applied corporate code of conduct, so that their decisional reactions are in equitable unison.

It is most valuable to utilize these three venerable points of Donaldson's moral framework as a base to construct concrete codes of conduct with definitive direction, as opposed to philosophic, debatable references inherent in each human being. The use of the conceptual, ethical, imperialistic core value, the influence of cultural relativism attached to local traditions, and the recognition of contextual facts surrounding the ethical question are a trio of tools that can help construct a firm's code of conduct. Besides the Donaldson model, additional moral systems abound in the quest for ethical determination. Professor Lynn Sharp Paine in her directional book *Value Shift*[24] introduces a Managers Compass for moral analysis, consisting of purpose (worthiness), people (effect upon), principles (touchstones), and power (scope of authority to enact). Her evaluation criteria provide a worthwhile framework for worldwide projects. While she repeats the idea of Donaldson's attention to people (tradition/context) and principles (core values) as guideposts to be considered, her inclusion of a motivational purpose provides a good beginning to fuel the process while the power to act is in the end, most relevant.

Whatever process is employed for global corporate-strategic direction, in the end, the ethical decisions reached must be transformed into a practical, written, companywide document for field managers to consult in their daily tactical operations.

Global Mind-sets

A man's feet should be planted in his country, but his eyes should survey the world.

—George Santayana, Spanish philosopher and essayist
(but considered to be an American man of letters)

H.W. Perlmutter, a pioneer in global strategy application, identified three mind-sets that contribute to the determination of strategic decision making by global managers: *ethnocentric*, *polycentric*, and *geocentric*. Ethnocentrism—an attitude that views everything originating from a firm's home country as the best in the world and hence demands that all decision making be based on such centralized thinking—collates with ethical imperialism. Polycentrism, representing the opposite view, appreciates that countries (societies) have vast differences and therefore decision making, the strategic approach employed, should be decentralized, with each national operating unit managing its own affairs. Cultural relativism in the application of moral standards would flow from this type of corporate mind-set. Using a geocentric approach would equate to a world-oriented way of thinking based on shared perspectives and a balancing of required objectives between home and foreign beliefs. It could include an ethical reference to core human values coupled with Donaldson's two additional ideals, respect for local traditions and context.

Other Philosophies

Other moral philosophies such as *teleology* and *deontology* might be consulted to gain a better generic insight into questions of ethical application. *Teleology* (from the Greek word root for *end*, or *purposeful result*) is tied to a review of the desired outcome as reflecting right or wrong. One's action is right or considered acceptable if it produces the desired outcome—the realization of self-interest. Moral philosophers would define it as the resultant consequences of one's actions, the theory of consequentialism.[25]

This form of ethical reasoning is usually broken down into two segments or approaches—egoism and utilitarianism. *Egoism*, or self-interest, acts as the key determinant of one's moral behavior, a kind of

Machiavellian approach to business decision making, as the real-life result achieves the intended purpose. In its extreme form egoism is hedonism. An individualized relative defining right or acceptable behavior as that which maximizes personal pleasure. A qualified measurable objective gain or improvement in one's life. A commercial example might be expressed as follows:

> A manager decides to promote a local community development project not because of some deep-seated altruistic motive, but because the project that benefits the community in which the company resides not only could ultimately bring the manager personal prestige and social status (internal and external recognition) but also could thereby elevate his or her standing with the company; which in turn benefits his or her executive progression and financial reward.

An organization making a similar decision using the same underlying philosophy would be motivated by doing any action that brings a positive, quantitative value to the corporation—it increases revenue or reduces costs.

Utilitarianism is also a derivative of consequentialism, but its measurement gauge, rather than being placed on the individual, is a determined result focused on the production of the greatest utility for the largest number of people affected by the decision. The process toward evaluating an actionable based on a cost-benefit analysis. A decision maker would calculate the utility of the consequences of all possible alternatives, and then selects the one with the greatest objective benefit. The use of such a philosophical approach could reasonably argue that, for example, offering a bribe to obtain business would be quite acceptable if the alternative is to lose hundreds of jobs in the factory, which in turn would adversely affect the welfare of the surrounding community, no less financial injury the company. Note that although the word *benefit* signifies a positive outcome, it can also be stated in the negative; the avoidance of an injury is a benefit. If a chemical plant was erected to provide jobs for 200 workers but its byproducts, released in the air and into the groundwater, were a potential environmental health hazard for thousands in the surrounding community, the decision to build the plant would be abated.

Deontology (based on the ancient Greek word for the subject of ethics) instructs one to act from a sense of duty; respectful and obedient conduct is required at all times. It is not based on the consequences that follow from one's actions but only concerns itself with recognizing fundamental, core values of right and wrong to be applied in all cases, no matter what the outcome or effect is. There are no gray areas; all things are judged as definitive black or white matters regardless of the outcome or injury inflicted; hence social-utility maximization is not part of the equation.

Take the case of American-developed pesticides used extensively at one time in the United States to combat insect destruction of agricultural produce but later found to contain potential cancer-causing chemicals and subsequently outlawed in the United States. While many emerging nations would today take the chance and use such pesticides to ensure better crop production to feed their starving populations, no American manager in such chemical firms would authorize its sale due to its possible ramifications—killing the few users despite its questionable balanced benefit to alleviate starvation of the masses.

Such alternating principles are well illustrated in the old lifeboat case brought under English admiralty law. Sixteen survivors of a storm at sea are cast into a lifeboat that can support only 10. A seaman with a pistol orders six passengers over the side, shooting any that resist so that the vessel will not capsize and thereby preserves the lives of those left on board. After they are rescued, murder charges are brought against the sailor. His defense is that his actions were necessary to save the lives of the majority aboard the lifeboat, which in fact he did—a teleology proposition and a strong utilitarian argument. The prosecution asserts murder is murder and that such strict application of the law must be followed—a deontology proposition.

While the application of commercial ethics may not result in such hard decisions with drastic consequences to those making moral judgments, the principles behind the defense or prosecution of such actions could be arguably sustained for applying standards built on cultural relativism or ethical imperialism. Cultural relativism, based on judging each society as to its separate and individual structure and with the added factor of context, is the lifeboat dilemma in this case. Alone and struggling in the stormy ocean to survive, all moral decisions on board have to be made by the local group alone within the context of their emotional situation. Questions about their actions are not subject to outside influence. Later judgmental interpretations of right and wrong by distant parties who have never experienced their plight may not be equitable. A fundamental belief in the application of teleology may lay the basis for applying a cultural-relativism approach to ethical issues in the global-commercial sector. On the other hand, those who believe that there are universal rights and wrongs that must be practiced and followed everywhere and in any situation prescribe to deontology, the underpinning moral philosophy for applying ethical imperialism in determining a moral stance in worldwide commercial operations.

Global ethical decision making, due to variances in socioeconomic developmental models and cultural differences, is like encountering the proverbial Gordian knot. Many managers when faced with such moral application use a false and inappropriate method. As Alexander the Great supposedly did, they do not try to unravel the knot but cut it by first choosing the alternative they like best, and then search among the ethical theoretical principles to find one that comes closest to allowing for the rationalization of the result. In Alexander's case, the arguments are *I am the king* (egoism) and *I can't be here all day as I am needed elsewhere for more important matters* (utilitarianism). Managers would do well to untie the knot by first identifying alternatives, evaluating them in terms of ethical systems and frameworks as presented by either Donaldson or Paine. Such methodology would help to reach a better and more appropriate universal result that is consistently applicable in any situation, as the procedural-control mechanism is based on a normative approach integrating theoretical properties and systematic criteria, both devoid of contextual-action justification to reflect the decisional outcome.

Perhaps the shining example of man's universal relation to fellow man is reflected in the American Declaration of Independence. Although not a recognized philosophical approach to morals, it nevertheless serves as an inspiration of mankind's responsibilities to fellow man to see that the basic rights of life are recognized. In this hallowed document the founding fathers proclaimed, "We hold these Truths to be self evident, that all Men are created equal, that they are endowed by their Creator with certain unalienable Rights, that among these are Life, Liberty and the

Pursuit of Happiness." This touchstone declaring the basic rights of all men became the foundation of the United States and is a good start for the development of one's ethical compass and by extension the creation of a universal discernible code of conduct. Left alone, however, without tangible, precise definitions of terminology as to what is life, liberty, and happiness, the lofty words and lauded intent ring hollow except when applied to a society of one. Even once such terms are unequivocally defined with group consensus, workable monitoring stations and enforcement guidelines must be instituted to see that such principles are protected. Hence, the development of an evolving Bill of Rights to punctuate such rights and explain them in detail while setting the stage for procedural remedies and enforcement provisions, so the entire society can transparently be guarded against infringement or loss of such rights.

The idea of general, articulated ethical principles, backed by precise definitions of the terms used therein and further augmented by implementation methods that guarantee and verify such principles are enforced, makes for a valued evaluation template when firms either construct their own codes of conduct or look for one to subscribe to. Ethically based philosophical insights, no less generic declarations declaring respect for human rights, without a cultural and faith-based ingredient along with a heavy dose of historical context and traditionally accepted values makes for a pointless recipe from which to construct universal codes of conduct. The use of philosophical rationales for ethical conflict determination and emotional steering through dilemmas make for fine theoretical discussions, but they do not provide practical real-life resolutions in a global world where all are watching and commenting on the outcome.

Summarizing Paths of Ethical Direction

The act of acting morally is behaving as if everything we do matters.
—Gloria Steinem, American feminist and social journalist

A thinking matrix for managers as presented by the aforementioned presentation of alternating theoretical approaches might best be exhibited by Table 5.3.

Table 5.3 The ethical fork in the road

Cultural relativism	Ethical imperialism
Rooted in teleology philosophy	Rooted in deontology philosophy
"When in Rome…"	"One size fits all"
Buy clothing locally	Carry home clothing bag everywhere
Abide by all local laws, conditions, customs and traditions	Utilize and apply principles from one's own moral compass universally
Passive acceptance	Proactive change
Polycentrism practiced	Ethnocentrism practiced
No control nor method of implementation needed	Exhaustive exercise of control with implementation and verification
Allows for plausible deniability	Full-blown accountability

According to Donaldson's *Middle Ground,* an appropriate ethical approach should contain a mix of the following:

- Core human values—universally applied provisions
- Local traditions—respect for host-society norms
- Context matters—special situational matters recognizing unique consequences

This requires precise definitions for globally embedded managers to follow, thereby resulting in the need for creation of a geocentric company code of conduct to be constructed. Thus, an appropriate ethical approach should do the following:

- Provide for detailed guidelines of acceptable and unacceptable conditions and practices
- Provide for verification of announced principles via controlled inspections
- Provide for violation notices and correctional time frames for compliance
- Provide for penalties and termination of relationship

Managerial Reflections

1. A number of globally directed ethical-value documents are presented with a critical review of their terminology given by the author.

Do you feel their universal principles can be applied equally around the world as a solid, indisputable direction for solving ethical dilemmas, or is their language merely well-intentioned generic hyperbole?

2. Many MNCs, as member signatories, have grafted onto code-of-conduct conventions and compacts constructed by recognized, venerable groups noted in the chapter. What are the pluses and minuses of such a decision?

3. The idea of a Platinum Rule, not to replace the Golden Rule but to act as a companion in ethical determinations, is mentioned in the text. Does merely walking *in the shoes of another* before making a moral decision really make an empathetic difference or does one, to fully understand and appreciate an alternative course of action, require a more in-depth education?

4. The lifeboat case in the chapter is real and although presented as a criminal charge of premeditated murder in the first degree, it does illustrate an ethical dilemma, as many view the abuse of human rights as a criminal act. Do you associate any immoral commercial activities with such harsh, indefensible results?

5. Polar-opposite ethical philosophies are presented as *ethical imperialism* and *cultural relativism,* and repositioned, respectively, as reflecting *ethnocentric* and *polycentric* thinking. A third mind-set, *geocentric, is* introduced. Can this terminology be defined in terms of a universal ethical philosophy?

6. Business school graduates at both the undergraduate and master of business administration levels are educated in the numerous disciplines of management, with basic courses offered ranging from economics to finance, from marketing to accounting, from human resources to supply chain management, along with a host of specialized electives. Does the integration of the ethical imperative in commercial dealing, especially within the global arena, cause one to reflect on the required assistance of an executive cadre whose backgrounds are in law, philosophy, sociology, anthropology, political science, theology, and other supplemental disciplines? How will the managerial team of the future be impacted?

CHAPTER 6

A Universal Code Template

He that will not apply new remedies must expect new evils.
—Francis Bacon, English philosopher and statesman,
attorney general and lord chancellor of England

Code Motivation: Factors and Levels

Before a code of conduct for a corporation is established, it might be valuable to evaluate the motivational factors contributing to its intended consequences or reactionary stimulus (a guidepost proposed by Professor Lynn Sharp Paine as previously noted). An exacting blueprint does not exist to define and measure the inspiration for its creation by the organization, but it might be helpful to utilize the work of two humanistic motivational psychologists, Abraham Maslow and Frederick Herzberg. Using their theories of individual work-motivation to explain the composite attitudinal approaches of managers in commercial organizations might provide some appreciation of the thinking behind the ethical-motivational imperative.

Companies contemplating the development of a corporate code of conduct may find that their motivational positioning travels along a progressive path. Their reasoning for instituting a code tends to have a Maslow hierarchy of needs-type construction matrix to it and a two-factor Herzberg approach. Both concepts build on need fulfillment of individuals in society as expressed within a commercial organizational setting. Companies desirous of establishing some type of code of conduct for their firms are motivated to assert principles that satisfy a range of desires, from basic survival to altruistic intentions.

Initially, firms at the CYA ("cover your ass") level are motivated by fear of noncompliance with domestic territorial regulations concerning the hiring and firing of employees, their treatment on the job as to health and safety, sexual harassment, and other social equality issues in the workplace. These are all morally based issues that have been qualified and quantified into a legal risk for commercial institutions. To such a list should be added the Sarbanes–Oxley Act and the Foreign Corrupt Practices Act for American firms and foreign companies affected by such provisions.

A basic ethical-defense platform emerges with a punishment factor if such matters are not properly dealt with. The purely fundamental first level pays attention to ethical decision making matching the hygiene factors, as morally applied and represented by the Herzberg theory of work motivation, and the combined physiological and safety needs of the Maslow model of need hierarchy. Companies with such stimulus have their code language targeting internal employee behavior as acceptable or unacceptable so the company does not run afoul of the law. They may not even share such documents with the public. It is solely intended for use in the confines of the company workplace, given to new employees upon hiring and requesting acknowledgement of such receipt—a legal ploy in case of potential actionable offenses. Motivational posturing at this first level may be a combination of defensible tactics coupled with loss prevention. The next level, *show and tell*, combines the motivational elements of Maslow's social needs for affiliation and esteem, as firms may use their codes to achieve a public image of ethical conduct across a wider spectrum of stakeholders as opposed to only internal employees and their potential illegal actions. They wish to acknowledge their intended contributions to the world around them in hopes that such references will have a positive effect on consumers. With more and more focus on the unethical conduct of global firms in respect to their relationships with extended third-party suppliers, manufacturing contractors, outsourced service centers, and even repressive governments, a good form of public relations is their company's code of conduct. The inclusion in the code of a signatory to a universally recognized set of ethical principles like the United Nations (UN) Global Compact or the Global Sullivan Principles, or generalized references to acceptable moral values and beliefs can often depict the firm in a very positive light. Private-alliance compacts with other firms, plus declaratory language incorporating proclamations of a global workers' group, might be used in code construction. Such attributions act as added-value incentives for customer patronage and may differentiate the firm from industry competition. They are akin to attaching the American Good Housekeeping Seal of approval to a product, but in that case the certification is awarded as opposed to signing on as a mere supporter of published principles. The motivational initiative at this second level is a combination of an offensive tactical strategy together with a material advancement or achievement objective to increase revenue. Such actions begin to approach the motivators under the Herzberg model and his use of the subtext terminology of the need for recognition and achievement.

The top level, *true blue*, which Maslow defines as self-actuation and Herzberg refers to as motivators via self-achievement and responsibility for individuals, may in the context of a commercial entity be described as an altruistic motivation. Companies and their leaders may see their activities as having a greater social influence or perhaps a duty to the general welfare of society around them. They may view themselves as philanthropic and unselfish contributors to the betterment of life for those their operations touch. A social-justice agenda may attach itself to their code of conduct, and they are inspired to fulfill a higher-order need. This level may not always allow for exacting, measurable criteria to be established or any return on ethical investment to be calculated. Need satisfaction and achievement at this juncture may be purely personal. However, at this highest level a very definitive code of conduct is constructed, as the firm may see itself as a provocation of social change. See Table 6.1, displaying the three levels of desired intent.

While no empirical evidence presently exists for the motivational imperative behind how companies construct their codes of conduct, one might suggest that from a practical point of view the first level seems appropriate as it economically protects the firm; many companies remain

Table 6.1 Motivation degrees of code construction

Motivational level	Code language	Target audience
True blue	Specific	World communities
Show and tell	Generic/general	Stakeholders/consumers
CYA	Limited/directed	Employees/regulators

at this initial juncture. Those companies moving on to the second level may come from industries wherein public notice of their activities is more pronounced; hence, the onus is on them to put forth an ethical face to their activities, which may warrant accession to this intermediate level. Those organizations aiming to reach the top level may be motivated by a deep sense of social commitment. It may be appropriate for a non-profit entity using a commercial operation to achieve its prime goal to be an instrument of moral deliverance, jumping over the basic and interim steps and begin at the top level.

There is a strong need to be aware of the motivational thinking that precedes the construction of a code of conduct. During the process, a number of directors and managers may participate. Each may have a different agenda or idea of what company needs the document is intended to satisfy. While an overriding corporate organizational culture may provide some uniform direction in regard to the social responsibility portion, the notion of ethical decision making, as previously defined, tends to reside in the individual and may be culturally induced. When the code is constructed on the canvas of global operations and targeted to be universally applied as opposed to a singular market, not all involved in its development will exhibit the same directional objective. It therefore may be prudent for the chairman or president to clearly articulate the prime and perhaps secondary or tertiary motivational factors using the aforementioned levels of desired corporate-need attainment.

Whichever inspirational impetus directs a company to construct a workable code of conduct, and no matter what level they wish to attain, it is not an easy task in a world of varying value systems and alternative thinking. The idea, however, that businessmen should conduct their activities with some degree of ethical care is a generally accepted premise and an old concept. In the Muslim holy book the Qur'an, the Prophet Mohammed proclaims, "On the day of judgment, the honest Muslim merchant will stand side by side with the martyrs." Other religions also direct their followers to be fair and equal with each other not only in general but also in the specific context of commercial relationships as previously noted in the introductory section and commented on under religion in Chapter 3, both referencing the Buddhist recitation on right-ful livelihood.

Moral Motivation: The Idea of Connected Capitalism

Motivational intent for the creation and use of a universal code of ethical conduct may be found in the remarks by Neville Isdell, former chairman of the board of the Coca-Cola Company. Speaking before the Council on Foreign Relations at their Fifth Annual Corporate Conference in March 2009, he talked of a need to redesign how business is conducted, urging his fellow executives to embody in their strategic plans the idea of *connected capitalism*. He proposes a new business model that would foster closer working relationships "with society across four platforms—communities, institutions, social challenges and values." He offers a canvas of inspectional areas upon which firms can paint their own ethical and corporate social responsibility (CSR) designs.

Coca-Cola, begun in 1886, is an icon of American business. Today, it is probably the best-known trademarked product in the world. According to a survey by branding agency Interbrand, in conjunction with *BusinessWeek*, Coca-Cola has been rated the world's most valued brand name for nine years in a row. The company sells 400-plus branded beverages in over 200 countries, with 72 percent of its leading label, the Coke line, sold outside North America. The company, according to *Forbes* magazine's 2008 rating, is the 123rd largest public corporation in the world in market value. Its sales growth internationally is 5 percent. Its worldwide operations confirm its true multinational status.

For a firm with such wide recognition and product distribution, it follows that Coca-Cola would want to protect such a valuable financial asset from any embarrassing revelations, be they fact or fiction. Just as with individuals a corporate good name is one's calling card to the public, as our reputations precede us. They help to sustain what has been achieved while providing a continuing launching pad upon which future relationships are built. Coca-Cola Company has not been immune from questions related to its ethical conduct abroad. Two years ago, it was the subject of an American college campus call to boycott its products due to reports that its Colombian-licensed bottler-distributor used physical intimidation backed by political connections and paramilitary murderers acting as state's agents to combat union organization in its plants and even kill union leaders. A U.S. federal appeals court found no connection between Coca-Cola or its local subsidiary and any of these alleged atrocities that would fall within the purview of the Alien Tort Claims Act. The company was, however, chastised for letting its prime sugar supplier in Latin America purchase raw cane from regional farm cooperatives whose members employed child workers in the fields in the harvesting process. Notwithstanding these allegations of moral turpitude in the company's third-party sale associations and outsourced supply-chain operations, questions as to how far a firm must go in applying ethical oversight, the comments by its retiring chairman are worthy of consideration.

How business enterprises should function, their mission statement, goes to the heart of determining corporate, strategic decision making. Isdell challenges business leaders to rethink and rewire how their companies relate to societies in which they ply their trade both vertically and horizontally. He calls upon them to redesign their objectives and consider the path of connected capitalism, citing a 2009 Edelman Trust Barometer finding that 62 percent of respondents in 20 countries do not trust commercial entities. This credibility factor translates into a suspicion of the capitalistic system or, to put it simply, a mistrust of those engaged in business as they have no scruples—they lack a moral compass. Such prejudicial notions are not new, as early religious doctrines, along with ancient philosophy, seized on this premise in their teachings. Social commentators and even political aspirants have historically presented the case of suppressed labor and aggrieved consumers. The ordinary worker has always been positioned at the bottom of the social ladder, while the refrain *buyer beware* has been echoed throughout history.

The remarks by Isdell conclude with a directional blueprint ("lines of sight"), what he refers to as the "four critical connections." (*Author's explanations follow in italic*).

1. Connect your business to the communities you serve. Become part of the local fabric. *Although firms may plan and operate globally they*

need to react locally, taking into consideration the customs and traditions of the people they serve.

2. Connect your business with civil society and governments. *Partner with representatives and institutions to address environmental issues that such groups cannot handle on their own. In the end we are all stewards of the same planet.*

3. Connect your philanthropy with your core business. *Do not just donate money; construct within company structure platforms that encourage and sustain discussions of corporate policy that impact share-holders, board members, employees, and the global community at large.*

4. Connect your business with the values of your employees. *Create corporate value systems that mirror the ethics of people as a corporation is only a mechanism for organizing and instituting what a group values in their civil society.*

The chairman of Coca-Cola constructed a moral compass—four directional points to help navigate in a changing world, one in which a global social agenda must be forged with the strategic corporate initiatives and determinations of multinational firms. This is a start for making globalization good, the moral challenge of global capitalism. It has two interconnected objectives:

1. An inspired, spiritual conscious effort to better society by practicing suitable ethical standards and supporting acceptable social responsibilities.

2. A secular-driven desire to protect a firm's reputation and good name, resulting in financial stability and future growth assurance.

This is connected capitalism, a duality of subjective spiritual morality with practical secular objectives, a marriage that could well motivate a corporation's strategic intent.

A Universal Affinity for Ethical Conduct

While one recognizes that the preparation of a singular applied code is difficult to achieve given the obvious differences in cultural norms and beliefs around the world, there is ample literature indicating that the subject itself is universally acknowledged. Research has shown that managers from varying national cultures "identify similar business practices as ethically suspect."[1] This idea builds on the theoretical concept that a cultural universalism or convergence has labeled certain acts as within the context of global hypernorms and therefore worthy of moral introspection. The term *hypernorms* equates to principles recognized by all societies and organizations[2] but not necessarily given the same importance nor handled in the same manner. In essence, you then have a commonly identified starting point but not a uniform and consolidated ending. As Donaldson and Dunfree note, the idea of bribery is universally viewed as a suspect action, but the ethical reaction to the subject or the degree of tolerant acceptance of the practice is a varied, justifiable determinant that is embedded in the social contract of the society and perhaps economic material desire. Therefore, it may be argued that while morally suspect behavior is judged differently around the world, the inherent properties of potential impropriety are universal.

Recent research into the variances in cross-cultural managers' willingness to justify ethically suspect behaviors using Hofstede-type cultural determinants coupled with four social institutions concluded that indeed culturally induced mind-sets and environmental conditions impact such considerations.[3] When firms go global, they not only encounter associates with such differences but develop internal organizations made up of a vast variety of national managers and employees whose views of ethical issues are varied and often in conflict. It is therefore important in this era of modern globalization that companies recognize the need to construct a cognitive code of conduct that gives substantive direction to all their employees as well as alliance partners and third-party associates so that planned actions and proactive responses to ethical matters are universally handled and applied within a common context of decision making.

Finding a collectively shared path toward ethics in this era of globalization is not an easy task, but directional inspiration might be provided by an unlikely source that reminds us all of the universal affinity for proper conduct. Hans Kung's essay "Ethical Framework for the Global Economy" in the book edited by Dunning, includes a speech to the Papal Academy of

Social Sciences delivered by Pope John Paul II on April 27, 2001. On the subject of globalization and mankind's place in its development, he states,

> As humanity embarks upon the process of globalization, it can no longer do without a common code of ethics. This does not mean a single dominant socio-economic system or culture which would impose its values and its criteria on ethical reasoning. It is within man as such, within universal humanity sprung from the Creator's hand, that the norms of social life are to be sought. Such a search is indispensable if globalization is not just another name for the absolute relativization of values, and the homogenization of life-styles and cultures. In the variety of cultural norms, universal human values exist and they must be brought out and emphasized as the guiding force of all development and progress.[4]

This papal theme of globalization and the ethical imperative was echoed by Pope Benedict XVI in his 2009 encyclical, *Caritas in Veritate* (Charity in Truth). He writes,

> Old models are disappearing, but promising new ones are taking shape on the horizon... Efforts are needed—and it is essential to say this—not only to create "ethical" sectors or segments of the economy or the world of finance, but to insure the whole economy—is ethical.[5]

Such words remind us that beneath mankind's differences there exists a communal embrace of similar principles that guides our behavior toward one another. In the search for such principles, we must be ever mindful to ground the flowery exclamations of good intentions in strong roots that the constant winds of moral change do not disturb. To avoid the pitfalls of culturally induced, individually applied morality and to allow separate, national-contextual flexibility, global companies desirous of constructing their own codes might be best served by approaching ethical dilemmas via a two-pronged classification system.

The code should be constructed based on two pillars of principled application: *absolutes*, or those reserved for the corporation, and *relatives*, or those that remain for the local entity to determine and exercise their on-site judgment. In essence, this is a dual separation of powers. Using absolutes and relatives as the two prime pillars on which to construct a universal corporate code of conduct also pays homage to the international strategic axiom to *plan globally but act locally*.

Such methodology for the separation of responsibility and authority is taken from a venerable document, the Constitution of the United States, specifically Article X in addition to and as an amendment to said instrument. It provides that "the powers not delegated to the United States by the Constitution, nor prohibited by it to the States, are reserved to the States respectively, or to the people." While certain rights are reserved for the corporation in its conduct of its global activities, designated as *absolutes*, those not enunciated remain in the purview of the local commercial entity, host-country *relatives*. Using this systematic approach that recognizes dual-control authorization, the author proposes firms that seek to build their own code of conduct consider its constructional elements following a model called the Vitruvian Man Code of Global Ethics.

The Vitruvian Man Code of Global Ethics

No man but a blockhead ever wrote except for money.
    —Samuel Johnson, English moralist, author, and essayist

The construction of a workable code of ethics that can contain a balance of principles is well symbolized by the illustration by Leonardo da Vinci titled the Vitruvian Man.

The name is derived from a treatise by the ancient Roman architect Marcus Vitruvius. This well-recognized and celebrated drawing depicts man by placing his body in both a circle and a square. Such metaphorical adjustment in Pythagorean philosophy is an attempt to indicate geometric proof of the dual nature of the human condition[6] and has been referred to as the divine proportion symbolizing the dual microcosms of man and his world. This often-duplicated illustration has also been referred to as the model of human perfection or representative of mankind in general, hence the universal man. As such, it is well suited to symbolize man's ability to sustain a balance between moral principles by placing a primary touchstone, the square, within an all-encompassing environment, in essence squaring the circle. It allows for the physical manifestation of the widely differing moral applications of ethical imperialism, the square, with cultural relativism, the circle. The square is representative of the application of core human values, while the circle is indicative of overriding respect for local tradition and the context in which ethical decisions are made. The square, given its particular properties with lines that go so far and then must end or turn in a specific direction, therefore becomes *absolute*. Specific corners are determinable—upper right or lower left—while it contains lines of equal distance or value. The circumference of the circle, however, is never ending and contains a continuous flow. While it is hard to construct a definitive starting place on the circle, its points can be referenced by measurement of degrees. It is therefore suitable to construct *relatives* upon such a scale of moveable placements, as many moral issues are always changing.

The idea of the Vitruvian Man model is to enable firms to construct a floor, an immovable base, of anchored ethical principles—the absolutes—then allow for numerous separate ceilings of additional ethical development to be erected according to local culture, customs, and legal conditions—the relatives. The global ethical building will therefore be built on a universal foundation but will contain varying height levels. It will be uniform at the bottom but not at the top.

The conceptual model for the code is based on the American constitutional legal system, which recognized the dual sovereignty of the federal government and the individual states. The bedrock principle is that federal laws established a base or floor for the protection of individual civil liberties—absolutes; and the separate state constitutions acting in their proper local, autonomous spheres of influence retained sovereignty and could provide additional safeguards or limitations—relatives. In any event, such supplementary laws could not abridge those basic human rights—absolutes granted by the federal government.

Absolutes

The conception of worth, that each person is an end per se, is not a mere abstraction. Our interest in it is not merely academic. Every outcry against the oppression of some people by other people, or against

what is morally hideous is the affirmation of the principle that a human being as such is not to be violated. A human being is not to be handled as a tool but is to be respected and revered.
—Felix Adler, intellectual social reformer and founder of the Society for Ethical Culture, writing in *An Ethical Philosophy of Life*

You have to stand for something or you'll fall for anything.
—Anonymous; old proverb and lyric from a country western song (also title of a 1999 book by Star Jones)

Absolutes are those business practices that shall not be compromised regardless of host-country beliefs and practices, with the noted exception that the company will not violate host- or home-country laws and international treaties signed by such parties. In the case of laws that are in conflict between such nations, the company shall defer to law of the foreign territory where the code of conduct is to be implemented. Under the universally recognized principle of territoriality, every sovereign nation has the right of jurisdiction within its legal territory over both its own citizens and those citizens of other countries resident or conducting business (committing acts) in such territory. (One should note that this principle may be in conflict with the previously presented Foreign Corrupt Practices Act.) Firms operating abroad must follow the legal process of the countries they choose to operate within or the result would be imperialistic anarchy. Companies can, however, go beyond minimums provided in the host-country law as long as they do not break that law. Companies would also be well advised not to enter into situations that are punishable under the laws of their home-charted nations that reach outside such borders, such as the U.S. Foreign Corrupt Practices Act and U.S. Alien Tort Claims Act.

The company will uphold core human values encompassing all mankind and that address the physical and mental well-being of all people, founded on the principle of first do no harm. Absolutes have at their conceptual base the compelling premise that moral intervention is required when, in the words of Henry Kissinger, "suffering beyond which the human conscious can withstand" is taking or may take place.[7] As such, absolutes are blind to varying levels of socioeconomic development and are geared to the pure quality of life as opposed to quantity. They are not subject to induced cultural behavior, nor tradition. They are not definable by a national-border context but are universally rooted in fundamentally accepted rights and wrongs. They become a line drawn in the sand, unimpeachable self-evident statements of the human condition. They should not be abridged in any manner and are implemented with the intensity of an orthodox religious passion. The idea of absolutes is that such declarations observe unanimous, core human values. In describing his ethical approach, Dunning likes the idea of a pyramid of morals, or what he calls "an overlapping consensus of universally accepted moral absolutes,"[8] at the apex of which lies a limited number of commonly accepted principles of ethical behavior that varying societies interpret in a similar way.

Absolutes by this definition must be dictatorial and comprehensive enough to facilitate an unequivocal response by managers in the field and must be ingrained in the corporate culture. Points enunciated therein should contain crystal-clear direction and precisely guide the decision maker. They should be strictly adhered to and presented in the marching-order format likened to the Napoleonic civil or coded law as originally derived from Roman law. Falling within the strict purview of such definition might be five basic tenets, or a bill of global labor rights that is constructed to preserve the human condition.

1. No use of slavery or forced or coerced labor, nor the withholding of people against their will under any circumstance, except adjudicated prisoners of the state, shall be tolerated. All workers shall have the freedom of movement both within and without facilities they work or are housed in, and such rights shall never be abridged in any manner. No documents relating to a citizen's right to move freely within a territory shall be retained as a condition of employment, and any contracts of employment signed by a worker shall not be used to hold such individual against their will. Any action against workers must be via the lawful application of the host-country regulations and using the prescribed adjudication process.

2. No worker shall be prohibited nor in any way interfered with, encumbered, or prevented from lawfully assembling with fellow

workers and their organizers during nonworking hours. No worker is to be punished or in any way reprimanded for such actions. Employee regular wages and benefits and employees' eligibility for overtime and promotion in the normal course of the company's operations shall not be affected by their participation in trade unions or labor associations and their lawful activities directed at the employer.

3. No worker shall be exposed to dangerous work conditions without their prior knowledge, understanding, appreciation, and freely given approval in writing. Any attempts to force or influence such decision to tolerate such offensive work conditions shall render such signed statement null and void. A dangerous work condition is defined as worker participation in any activity that would violate the laws and standards of the host country *and* those of the charted territory (firm's home country). In case of a conflict between such enunciated criteria, the most stringent regulations, those providing the most protection, shall apply.

4. No worker may be subject to physical or mental abuse in any manner. No worker may be touched with the exception of placing such worker out of immediate physical danger. No use of verbal threats or berating of workers is to be tolerated. Any disciplinary action or warnings that are warranted against a worker shall only be in written form, and if such worker is unable to effectively read and comprehend such document of instruction, a suitable, equal coworker shall read such statement to the employee and verify such explanation has been given.

5. No worker shall be subject to excessive and exhaustive work hours that would threaten their physical and mental well-being. In the exercise of such standards, a maximum daily workday shall consist of no more than a total of 10 hours, with two of such hours being considered as overtime on the job, for which additional compensation at one and a half times the prescribed hourly rate shall be paid. Therefore, the total hours of work that may be performed over a period of one week shall never exceed 60 hours during a continuous six-day period. Every worker is entitled to one full day of rest per week and shall be prohibited to work on such day.

Companies may alter, amend, or add to such absolutes to encompass any other area they feel warrants strict universal adherence, as long as crystalline guidelines with specific performance criteria are provided. In the process, they would be well advised to consult the Donaldson triad of philosophical principles and the *managerial compass* points of Paine to construct codified language to ultimately direct actions of embedded managers. Both ethicists provide a normative approach for evaluating moral alternatives and policy formulation to be utilized in the choice and screening stages to determine what activities should be designated as absolutes and others that fall into the province of relatives. Companies might also be well advised to review the main beliefs enunciated in the Global Sullivan Principles as well as the UN Global Compact and other labor human rights accords as starting blocks to frame their objectives.

Absolutes are dictated by the corporate home office and are to be given the full weight and measure of the company board of directors. As such, they must be followed to the letter, never abridged or modified. They are direct orders that can never be countermanded or changed.

Relatives

Everything is relative.
— Popular saying perhaps attributable to laws of physics dealing with space and time

Relatives are variables that need to be configured to the existing conditions of local managerial organizations and deserving of application to the individual and separate environmental circumstances of national traditions and context. As such, they will need to vary from one society to another and by their very nature are border locked, culturally self-adjusting, and in constant flux as times change. They are more akin to the English common-law doctrine where constant societal changes may affect the way in which laws are interpreted and applied, with the most current precedent being cited for interpretation.

Relatives are part of a conceptual network connecting fact to practiced belief, wherein respect for the process is more important than the outcome and therefore best left to those whose knowledge of the local commercial condition is paramount to those taking an outside-inside view. Respect for and responsibility over issues not enunciated earlier for the parent company to enforce are delegated to the designated onsite managers of such subsidiary operations, be they company employees, joint-venture personnel, or employees of third-party contractors or alliance participants. They might therefore be related to a wide range of matters and situations.

- The minimum age for child employment shall be dependent upon the social mandate and economic developmental degree of the host country.
- Worker pay scales at all levels of employment shall be guided by national economic policy of the host country and be determined by the national average for such employment skills.
- The maintenance of the climatic conditions of all facilities shall be commensurate with the applicable standards of the host country.
- Job ability discrimination and opportunities for women and minorities, including affirmative-action practices, shall be commensurate with the applicable standards of the host country.
- Environmental matters shall be per the applicable standards of the host country or under international conventions as ratified by the host country.
- Hiring and firing practices, vacations, social benefits, daily work, and nutritional and bathroom breaks shall all be in accordance with the local-industry custom.

Relatives by their very nature are subject to change and carry a contextual overtone. Therefore they are specifically administered on a purely local host-country basis. They vary from country to country and are not subject to precedents from other nations or areas where the company operates. They are expressly limited in scope and application to individual territories, their political subdivisions, and even separate facilities of operation in the same country in recognition of national or regional economic, social, and cultural differences of a common political unit. Such considerations demand that relatives are to be applied differently from province to province, rural to cosmopolitan urban centers, and factory to factory location within national borders.

Each separate localized onsite unit of the company would erect those principles it feels are relatives, while the absolutes fall within the strict purview of the corporate home office. The key, however, is to make such specific pronouncements to provide guidance for worldwide managers as activities deemed absolutes and those considered relatives. To better appreciate the alternating terms, one should view absolutes as pertaining to firm activities that can subject humans to *fragility* in life and prove to be permanently damaging. Relatives, on the other hand, are firm actions that over time can develop *resilience* with the potential to reverse the interim damage via changes in the socioeconomic structure and alterations in legal regulations.*

Over time, rules and regulations may come into force in countries that address relative situations, whereas absolutes target immediate destructive elements of unethical behavior. Any form of slavery instantly takes a crushing toll on the mind and body of workers, and the scars that linger are never fully healed; hence, it is an absolute activity that must be avoided. Wage rates are relative and tend to self-adjust over time due to supply-and-demand conditions, often resulting in minimum-wage laws being enacted. In China, the frequently cited one dollar-a-day worker is disappearing as new manufacturing entrants to the labor market are willing to pay a premium for trained, efficient workers instead of taking the time to acquaint unskilled personnel with the job at hand. They raid existing factories and advertise for the hiring of those with the existing requisite abilities for their new facilities with increased pay scales and additional benefits, thereby causing a natural wage inflation in the marketplace. Poor pay in the past may be disheartening, but it is reversible as the natural forces of labor-market supply and demand take hold.

---

* The terms *fragility* and *resilience* are borrowed from the writing of Jared Diamond in his book *Collapse* (2005), wherein he uses such language to describe environmental damage caused by mankind that is either lasting with catastrophic destructive effects or temporary and can be fixed. I am indebted to him for his fine choice of wording, although used herein in a different but equally important context.

Beyond the selection of specific contextually worded provisions in codes of conduct providing ethical direction, the code should be constructed with a general overriding pedagogy. The following should be taken into consideration when constructing a code of conduct.

1. The contents of the code need to be worded in clear, unambiguous terms, and if possible, it should be easy to translate into a variety of major languages.
2. Verification of the code should be subject to outside independent assessors who shall have free and open access, at anytime, anyplace, and with anyone who is affected by its provisions.
3. The code needs to be equally disseminated among employees as well as agents, alliance partners, subcontractors, suppliers, and distributors of its products and services.
4. The firm adopting the code needs to demonstrate the commitment of its entire organization and devote significant resources to its implementation with the designation of a competent staff to implement its directions and monitor and report on its performance in a public, transparent manner.

Verification and Monitoring

Trust, but verify.
—Ronald Reagan, president of the United States

Even the establishment of a code built on the aforementioned principles is not enough. McDonald's, a company that has prided itself on its long-standing global code of ethics, was cited for malfeasance in the application of its own code in October 2002. When publicly admonished for failure to properly monitor activities of its associates in Hong Kong, their spokesperson mistakenly aimed to admit plausible deniability by uttering "we just didn't know"—such words allow for the initial criticism to be magnified and not muffled. The emphasis on ethical responsibility has widened to encompass constant vigilance, not just well-directed and published codes of acceptable behavior. A company should reserve in its contracts with outside parties the provisions of its code of conduct. The tenets of the code can be either incorporated into the agreement or attached as a rider document. Inherent in all such agreements should be the right to inspect at all times and without formal notice by any party it appoints that the conditions of strict absolutes and recognized relatives have been maintained by the contracted entity. The accent should be on ensuring the absolutes.

If a violation of any of these principles is found, the offending organization shall be advised in writing and be given a suitable time period to remedy the situation. A further inspection after such remedy period shall be conducted to verify compliance. If upon further inspection the violations have not been corrected, the company reserves the right itself, or via request to any intermediary parties it has contracted with, to immediately terminate employees whose positions of authority and responsibility contributed to or impacted the violation in any way or the contracted entity itself. Two uncorrected violations of absolutes or relatives in a year shall be construed as material breach of any contract entered into by the company and be considered grounds for no-fault immediate termination of the agreement. All other rights and remedies to the exclusive benefit of the company are preserved in such instance. No right to arbitration or any adjudication process is available to the party in violation, as the code shall control.

Code Drafters

The actual code language should initially be constructed by a board of directors of a special committee. Being drafted at the highest level of organizational decision making adds a critical element to the document, demanding the attention of all stakeholders in the company. Assistance to the committee should come from senior global corporate executives, as well as domestic and international lawyers. This cadre should be augmented by other knowledgeable consultants in the fields and areas the instrument is to touch on, such as cross-cultural experts, international labor authorities, global economists, and historians, as well as theological and secular philosophical scholars. When in its final draft form, it should be circulated to international territorial subsidiaries for comment. When officially adopted by the board as a corporate resolution and entered into the books and records of the company, a firm has made a permanent commitment. Company vision or mission statements should reference its mandate. Its principles should be appropriately disseminated to all the corporation's stakeholders and alliance partners, down through all association levels, and incorporated in all company contracts and agreements. Like the executive branch of federal government, the chairman of the board bears the responsibility to enforce the ethical decree. Such individual should inform the president or chief executive officer (CEO) of the company to prepare a detailed organizational plan to implement and verify its execution.

Organizational Structuring

Nobody has a more sacred obligation to obey the law than those who make the law.

—Sophocles, Greek philosopher

In practical matters, the end is not mere speculative knowledge of what is to be done, but rather the doing of it. It is not enough to know about Virtue, then, but we must endeavor to possess it and to use it, or to take any other steps that may make us good.

—Aristotle, Greek philosopher

Once the code of conduct has been established along the aforementioned guidelines, the responsibility of the company does not end; in fact, it only begins. To ensure proper implementation and proper use requires a dedicated office or department of corporate responsibility should be formed. While the actual number of personnel and the respective duties of those assigned to this department will depend upon the extent of the company's global operational and activity reach, a few basic organizational guidelines can be offered.

The department should be headed by a senior corporate officer with a significant designated title both to indicate the seriousness of the firm in instituting the code and to provide that internally the office is respected. Whether titled vice president for corporate ethical compliance or Director, Ethical Assurance, such person should report directly to the CEO or managing director (partner) of the enterprise with a dotted line association to the company's head legal counsel and key strategic-planning officer. This person and the office should be placed at corporate headquarters.

The position would be responsible for the implementation and enforcement of the corporate code of conduct, including the definitions of any terminology and its interpretation throughout the organization. Such person may also initiate position papers as to alterations or changes in the code, but his or her main duty is to act as an internal regulatory agency. All documents pertaining to the code—flowing in and out of this office—should be treated as corporate legal papers and proprietary correspondence.

If the company wishes to follow the valued tenets and criteria guidelines of the Global Sullivan Principles and file an annual report with them or an outside oversight agency, such report shall be administered and prepared by this corporate office and its staff. Collaterally the company might choose to mirror the direction of companies like Gap Inc. or IBM and issue a social responsibility report as a companion to their regular annual report; this too would fall under the duties of such corporate office.

The corporate level at which the ethical imperative, as codified in the code of conduct, is instructed is extremely important. Too many executives see such a process as insulating the firm against regulatory scrutiny and potential fines and hence tend to house the functional aspects of instituting the code within the confines of a legal compliance officer. This tunnel-vision mentality is dangerous and arises because the primary goal of the corporation is to maximize stock prices; hence, managers with such narrowly defined goals see amoral behavior as running afoul of required observance of statutes and not ethical standards of acceptable behavior. Corporate executives marginalize good moral conduct unless violations are punishable by the legal system and result in depressed earnings and falling stock prices. Rarely is a particular manager singled out for a moral wrong committed by a company, as such actions are draped in anonymity, but many managers have been replaced for failing to achieve desired shareholder return. As managers do not always carry out amoral decisions themselves and personally witness the consequences, they avoid the situations that might help assure empathy and restraint. Many of today's executives entrusted with global ethical decision making responsibilities do not have the worldwide experience necessary to neither fully understand nor appreciate the complexities of applying principles within and across diverse cultural environments. Companies would be wise to view creation and implementation of a code of conduct not as a stop-gap measure to ensure against illegal activities or as a defensive shield against potential lawsuits but as a vision statement of their character and the uncompromising principles by which they conduct their operations. Therefore, the construction and administration of the code should be one step removed from the legal department—do not treat ethics as a compliance issue but as a corporate mandate. It should not be influenced nor be encumbered solely by legal conformity, as the issues it addresses go beyond such requirements. As 20th-century writer Lucille Kallen notes, a lawyer "is on a par with a piano tuner's relationship to a concert. He neither composes the music, nor interprets it—he merely keeps the machinery running."[9] The CEO of the company is the overseer of the code and its prime spokesperson. According to studies conducted by BEYOND Communications (http://www.GreenBiz.com), letters from CEOs writing in their companies' annual reports have begun to specifically include comments on the social responsibility activities of their organizations. A marked trend has begun to appear as firms feel that the inclusion of a CSR factor in their year-end reports is also a good public relations initiative. A survey conducted in the mid-2000s showed that 42 percent of the 100 of the top S&P 500 companies' reports contained such remarks, a jump of 28 percent over previous periods. Such increase was the most significant since the review was initiated in 1990s. Some other interesting points were noted and that have set the stage for changes occurring over the last 10 years in the executive suites of MNCs. CEOs describing their firms as *global citizens* increased eightfold, while those companies explaining how they measured their social responsibility actions were amplified sixfold. General comments as to the philanthropic activities and community and volunteer services increased by 125 percent in the mid-1990s, a strong indication of the importance of CSR to corporate identities. Such data indicate that companies with global operations have increasingly recognized their duty to shareholders to report on the subject, presenting such commentary either in their annual reports or in supplemental, independent social responsibility reports. This initiative presupposes that a corporate code of ethical criteria be constructed and that an organizational office be maintained to implement its provisions and periodically collect information on its proper administration with suitable reporting to the CEO.

The staff assigned to the office would include internal department coordinators as well as field personnel. The outside cadre would be made up of experts in the cultural, social, and commercial environments within their territorially assigned areas. A possible choice for such individuals might be retired business managers whose knowledgeable sensitivity has been honed with practical experience in such regions but endowed with an appreciation for change when required. These individuals should also be well informed as to national laws and regulations pertaining to code subjects (i.e., labor rights, environmental issues). These roaming ethical monitors would be available to act as inspectors and certifiers of code compliance as well as a bridge of information flow from the corporation's worldwide network. This specialized group should be given appropriate managerial designations likened to warrant officers in the U.S. military to ensure cooperation and authority with other corporate regional and national embedded personnel. When issues of conflict arise, these specialized forces would issue investigative reports and forward them to the headquarters for final determination. The specific formation of inspection and verification methods to be employed as well as report configurations for these field representatives to use in their normal duties would be constructed by the office of the corporate executive as detailed earlier. Each company would need to determine, as guided by their operational-facility reach and perhaps industry characteristics, the exact nature of such documents and reports. While the scheduling of any required materials is left to each individual enterprise, it is recommended that periodic, perhaps quarterly reports be prepared to ensure a firm's timely ability to react to any pivotal or potentially damaging matters. During the negotiation process with prospective associates, the code should be shown to such parties and they should be made aware that its provisions are to be incorporated in any agreement reached by the parties and the company. During such time and prior to signing any agreements, a member of the corporate compliance team should do a background check on the potential associate company, which should be further augmented by an onsite inspection of their proposed use of facilities. A report should be sent to the negotiating team and a copy kept as part of a permanent record.

If the operations of the corporation are conversely far reaching or even limited in scope, some firms, like Baxter International Inc., as profiled in the next section, have created regional responsibility committees. The Baxter organizational system uses these geographical groups on a more formal basis and incorporates them into their procedure for those employees seeking ethical guidance or to report potential violations of their code. Companies could alternatively utilize such committees as informal advisors on trends in business and social conduct that might impact code terminology and application, as well as sounding boards for proposed alterations to their codes of conduct. While not endowed with any decision-making power or reporting authority, their consulting value as an additional set of eyes and ears on the world stage could be worthwhile for many firms as an adjunct to the aforementioned field staff. For organizations that cannot afford a dedicated roving cadre of regional specialists, they might even take the place of such personnel.

Beyond constructing and instituting a code of conduct in companies with proper administratively structured oversights, firms also need to identify specific employees whose tasks and responsibilities will place them in harm's way ethically. These individuals are expatriates, those assigned to foreign territories, and those whose job descriptions bring them into daily contact with such complicated issues. These embedded global managers will no longer be working in a homogeneous domestic arena but in a variety of environments. They must appreciate their own biases and assumptions while becoming aware that diversity requires greater flexibility and tolerance of differences, especially when matters of ethical decision making arise. Initially, the correct choice of prospective expatriates and the institution of additional training programs with an ethical imprint will go a long way to resolving ethical conflicts they may face. Human resource departments must work to identify the best aspirants for these overseas postings and make sure that they possess not only the technical expertise for the job but also the equally, if not more, important philosophical and personal traits to deal with foreign mind-sets and varying approaches to ethical matters. A thorough verification process should help to alleviate potentially damaging situations by unqualified individuals. Additional training with indoctrination by counsel to the company code of conduct as well as the regulations of Foreign Trade Practices Act should be included. Discussion with internal personnel who held such jobs in specific geographical venues along with outside consultants with cross-cultural understandings should also be used. Morally laced situational confrontations with interactive dress rehearsals are also recommended as elements of rigorous training. Advanced preparation is the best way to combat potential disruptive, embarrassing, and costly ethical situations. Once in place, expatriates should have an open hotline where questionable ethical issues can be discussed in an anonymous format with corporate mentors as well as outside consultants. Such a system allows for constant monitoring and support for the embedded employee and it may aid the company in amending its code of conduct.

A New Managerial Code

Beyond the construction of a code of conduct for companies, especially those involved in operating across borders, a new initiative for managers has emerged. Traditionally, a number of occupations have taken a pledge to adhere to a set of principles governing their profession (e.g., doctors, attorneys, and accountants). Angel Cabrera, president of the Thunderbird School of Global Management, is championing an *oath for global business executives*. The idea was originally developed at his institution and later proposed with revisions by the Forum of Young Global Leaders, a group to which he belongs. Positioned as a voluntary list of promises, the principles encourage its subscribers to respect and protect human rights by avoiding discrimination and exploitation, protecting the environment, avoiding bribery and corruption while representing the performance and risks of their enterprises accurately and honestly. (See full list at http://www.globalbusinessoath.org/businessoath.php.) Cabrera is hopeful that a code of conduct oath will encourage managers to promote good ethical values, allow for greater transparency, and generally raise business standards so the public will gain trust in commercial institutions. Although it may be criticized as being more symbolic than actionable, it nevertheless represents a change in the mind-sets of future commercial leaders as it was initiated by business students both at Thunderbird and Harvard.

The oath was presented at various venues for signatures by participants at the 2010 World Economic Forum in Davos, Switzerland, a conference that attracts business leaders from around the globe and that acts both as a barometer and an initiator of new concepts in business management. Perhaps the most unique aspect of this oath is that it would remain with the individual manager as he or she traveled from company to company around the world. It might act as a further stimulus for MNCs to incorporate such principles into their company's managerial culture as cadres of those prescribing to the oath might be joining their ranks. On the other hand, it might prove problematic for some managers as their professional oath might come in conflict with their own organizational principles and tactical actions. Whether this proposed oath for global business executives generates support and takes off or fails to achieve wide acceptance due to a poor reception in the international commercial arena, the idea is indicative of new direction of thinking on ethics and CSR, and therefore it is a positive consideration in the field.

As a talisman (from the Greek *telesma*, meaning *complete*) to an institutional code of conduct, such a managerial oath could be the finishing element, the capstone, of ethical practice in the global commercial world.

Cost-to-Value Benefit of Sustainable Ethical Practice: Second Look

Does everything we do in life have a measurable financial value?
—Lawrence A. Beer, global commercial ethics explorer

Does business ethics payoff? Do the costs incurred by firms in the construction, implementation, and verification of a code of conduct have measurable benefits that add to a firm's value? Such questions have been approached in the text by qualifying the issue via a negative loss factor as well as a positive assessment factor. Failure to construct, no less properly maintain, the ethical principles by which a firm performs its activities can result in legal expenses, fines, and costly settlements, as well as expenditures to repair damage to a company's public persona and image with consumers. Surveys, as previously noted, indicate that consumers maintain a positive disposition to patronizing firms with good social responsibility records and may penalize those they perceive as committing wrong acts by boycotting their products and switching to other providers. In addition, the Josephson Institute of Ethics (http://www.josephsoninstitute.org.), in their promotional pamphlet "The Hidden Costs of Unethical Behavior," cites a 2003 survey by Wirthlin Worldwide stating 80 percent of consumers partly make their decision to buy a firm's goods or services based on their perception of a firm's ethics. The same comparative percentage (79 percent) emerged in a Canadian study by the Angus Reid Group in 1997, indicating that consumers would tend to buy preferentially from companies that are good corporate citizens. The same poll revealed that 74 percent of potential shareholders consider a firm's honesty before buying their stock. The Josephson Institute's bullet points list a host of other losses experienced by firms that do not have *effective training and consulting services to help* eliminate unethical behavior in the corporate environment.

The *Kasky v. Nike* case, earlier profiled, legally equated protecting a firm's moral reputation with the public at large as tantamount to an advertising program aimed at persuading customers to buy their merchandise.[10] Scandals over corporate excess and fraud reveal the high cost of unethical behavior. While the ability to develop a very specific quantitative formula to track a dollar invested in ethics to a dollar received in return remains problematic, there is a lot of business literature and well-constructed surveys that support the contention that good ethical practice has positive rewards. Periodic research published by the UK's Institute of Business Ethics (IBE)[11] comparing companies in the FTSE (*Financial Times* 250 index—sample consisting of 41 to 86 corporations) provides compelling evidence that "those firms clearly committed to ethical behavior perform better financially over the long run than those lacking such a commitment."[12] As the criteria for quantifying ethical behavior is subjective and rooted in individual, personal assessment of a situational response, the IBE focused on comparing companies with established codes of ethics or conduct to those without them. Ethics was therefore defined not in the prejudicial evaluation of performed actions but the simple, objective factor that if a company has a code, one assumes they take ethics more seriously than those that do not; the existence of a code is an indicator of a genuine ethical commitment. The presence of a code was used as a proxy for a corporate-commitment component. The results found that companies having a code of conduct outperformed those without a code when measured by four customary quantitative determinants: market value added (MVA), economic value added (EVA), price earning ratio (P/E ratio), and return on capital employed (ROEC). A positive correlation developed between an accessible ethical code and financial achievement. Companies without a code generated significantly less EVA and MVA than those with a code and experienced more P/E volatility. Noncode firms showed a decline in average ROEC, while those maintaining a code had a marked increase. Dated data has shown that in the years evaluated, 1997 to 2001, those firms with an explicit commitment as exemplified by their corporate code of ethics produced profit or turnover ratios 18 percent higher than those without a code. These survey results, although historically referenced, are important as they were the first empirical evidence from a source outside the academic community that an ethical imperative may have a beneficial effect on a firm's financial results.

The survey would seem to sustain the comments of Margaret Flaherty, director of the Accountability and Reporting project, noting,

> Developing and implementing a code of conduct is a costly endeavor and will rarely show immediate results in any standard accounting measurement—Over the long-run, however, there are benefits for companies, especially if the code is anchored within a strategic framework linked to business objectives.[13]

Such observations mirror the similar conclusion that investments in unethical firms earn abnormally negative returns for prolonged periods.[14]

Corporations exhibiting a public commitment by announcing the importance of maintaining a sense of ethical conduct as part of their managerial philosophy tend to do better in both financial and nonfinancial terms than companies that are silent on the issue, per an evaluation conducted by Professor Curtis C. Verschoor at DePaul University's School of Accountancy.[15] Verschoor's conclusion, however, was based on a review of a specific portion of a firm's annual report pertaining to voluntary disclosures about their internal controls to ensure proper financial reporting—compliance with the law. In essence, he examined a firm's announced commitment to ethical accountability and its resultant effect on a company's MVA (value a company provides to its shareholders compared with the total amount of their investments). The survey also found that the financial performance of firms acknowledging such *internal* dedication to the ethical preparation of financial information ranked higher on traditional measurement criteria including total return, sales growth, profit, net margin, and return on equity. The key point is that Verschoor's analysis focused on a firm's limited commitment to exercising good interior principles of moral behavior by its management when it comes to financial accounting, as opposed to a firm's external and wider pledge to act ethically across all operations and activity avenues that the company comes in contact with. The Verschoor survey may today be mooted by the Sarbanes–Oxley Act regarding financial-reporting compliance. Although a prime example indicating that good internal ethical conduct is a fiscal plus, it is a step below the aforementioned UK survey using the existence of a code of ethics as the primary stimulus to achieve superior reach and competitive monetary success.

One should be able to deduce that although no exacting empirical study producing a usable, sound formula that directly equates a dollar spent on promoting ethical action to specific value received has been constructed, there are positives to be gained from practicing good, ethical decision making.

In regard to accounting for the costs associated with enforcing and monitoring a corporate code of conduct, general practice would have them housed in the general administrative expense category for most companies. Many firms may place specific responsibility for administering the program under the legal and compliance department or an extension of the human resources section and include such in their budgetary structure. While most expenses will be of a periodic recurring nature, the costs of creating a program to track ethical actions and create a reporting format could be capitalized to an extent.

Reebok International Inc., which has taken heat over factory conditions in the Far East, created a Human Rights Tracking System whose software tracks such variables as number of fire escapes, wages of workers, and pay scales. The company spun off this system into a nonprofit agency called Fair Factories Clearinghouse and is encouraging other firms to pool their data, thereby avoiding costly redundant, independent collection of such information. Although the software was donated, the nonprofit entity would charge corporate subscribers between $5,000 and $60,000 a year, according to company size, in order to keep the valuable instrument technologically updated. They are currently looking for at least 20 significant alliance partners to join in data collection to make the system a valid tracking tool. Global companies that develop such information-gathering and retrieval systems may find that their pioneering investment has value beyond their company and industry. Such research-and-development venture may set up a whole new service segment, as the financial implications of associating with ethical third parties increases for all MNCs.

Comparison of Company Codes of Conduct

There is no worse thief of morality than a poorly constructed code of conduct with good intentions.

—Lawrence A. Beer, global commercial ethics explorer
(loosely based on the proverb "The road to hell is paved with good intentions"; attributable to many in various forms)

Two corporations were selected for a closer review of their publicly stated codes of conduct, Nike Inc. and Gap Inc. They were chosen as their global operational reach in respect to number of factories and countries is sufficiently large to cover a broad spectrum of ethical encounters in respect to human rights matters. Both firms have historically been publicly scrutinized in regard to their foreign ethical activities, while having a large consumer base that easily recognizes their corporate identities as such designation also corresponds with their prime brand name. The comparison is not intended to be judgmental but to provide real-life examples of well-placed intentions to address the complex nature in the construction of a workable universal code of conduct.

Gap Inc. Background

Gap Inc. operates a chain of 4,000 clothing and accessory stores in their world network targeting a young fashion-conscious audience. Their trendy, fashionable items, with a modern upbeat look, have propelled the company to gain good market share and allowed their brand name to enjoy semidesigner status. The company contracts with third-party manufacturers utilizing a global supply chain of more than 3,000 independent operators around the globe. In early 2000, the enterprise became the target, along with other large clothing retailers, of campaigners labeling them as sweatshop instigators. Interviews conducted by public-interest groups gave strong indications that *abusive working conditions* existed in 40 factories, making Gap garments in Cambodia, Indonesia, Bangladesh, El Salvador, and Mexico. Accounts of long working hours for low pay, with workers facing health hazards and brutal working conditions were found. Reports consistently accused Gap of systematically driving down wages and that their modus operandi in overseas factories demonstrates a pattern of global exploitation as opposed to working to reduce abuses in its global supply chain. When confronted with such allegations, their European spokesperson, Anita Borzyszkowska, responded, "We share the same concerns but we are proud of the work we do in factories. We're not perfect but we believe we make a difference to workers' lives."[16]

A few months later Gap Inc. and other retailers including J.C. Penney and Target Corp. experienced a major setback when a U.S. federal judge ruled that thousands of garment assemblers on the island of Saipan in the Pacific (part of the U.S. territory of the Northern Mariana Island group) could sue a variety of American companies and their manufacturing contractors as a class. The companies involved had argued that, as labor conditions varied from factory to factory and as in Gap's case it was selective as to which factories it actually used, it was unfair and arbitrary to combine all such workers on the island into a single class of petitioners. Parallel to such proceeds and potentially damaging to their legal position and historic operational activities with third-party service providers, Gap and its other retail defendants failed to stop an $8.7 million dollar settlement by 19 other firms such as Tommy Hilfiger Corp. and Liz Claiborne Inc., which also included the setting up of a strict code of conduct and independent monitoring of labor conditions on the island.[17] With a full-blown corporate code of conduct coupled with a very transparent verification procedure and public reporting process in place, Gap Inc. made the *shock confession* that many of its 3,000 foreign factories "fail to comply with minimum labor standards."[18] As a firm that initially would not have publicly admitted such faults and felt its mere solicitation of foreign labor was beneficial to the social condition of workers exhibited a 180-degree turnaround. Gap's response of creation of a globally applied corporate code of conduct with strict verification, coupled with an open reporting system, makes it worthy of examination and comment in the search for a standard, universal code of conduct for all multinational companies as they begin to access their own considerations in this area. It should be noted that Gap Inc. was granted the top slot for social reporting in the 2004 Business Ethics Awards and has become a model for corporate governance in regard to labor human rights issues ever since.

Nike Inc. Background

Nike, whose moral conduct in respect to labor rights is reiterated throughout this text, has been one of those global companies continuously targeted by an unlinked coalition of nongovernmental organizations (NGOs) and investigative journalists and activists portraying them as an embodiment of reprehensible conduct. The company has consistently been forced into defending its actions and, as noted earlier in the text, has even been attacked for procedures used to state their case publicly against the numerous accusations. The company produces footwear, clothing, equipment, and accessory items for the sports and athletic market—both the professional and consumer segments of the industry. Selling to over 19,000 retail accounts in the United States alone and in over 140 countries around the world, it has become the world leader in the category. Almost all the products the company markets are manufactured in developing countries using independent contractors. The workers, as reported on their own Global Alliance inspection association information platform, tend to be women between 20 and 24 years old. About half have completed senior high school with few having any work-related skills before entering their supported factories. Nike works with about 700 contracted entities in China, Taiwan, Korea, Mexico, and other countries to create their products. Labor conditions in such facilities have been a source of constant debate between the firm and their human rights propagandists, ranging from issues of intolerable physical and mental abuse to health and safety hazards in the working environment, along with charges of sexual trade practices in recruitment and promotion. In her book *No Logo*, author Naomi Klein accuses Nike of abandoning countries as they developed better pay and employment rights, focusing on only one goal—the lowest cost possible—to drive corporate global strategy.[19] Such critique has been offered not only in regard to Nike but also as a general negative to all firms embracing globalization. Reminiscent of fickle lovers, multinational corporations (MNCs) easily jump from one relationship to another, leaving in their wake jilted, abandoned countries. Their economic savior-like promises are left at the border as they seek out new territories in a never-ending search for the perfect global value chain, not realizing the chaos caused by their previous actions. The Klein book was published just prior to the World Trade Organization (WTO) protests in Seattle in 1999. Like many published activist works at the end of the 90s containing accusations of unethical behavior directed toward the workers of emerging nations by MNCs, the antiglobalization movement was strengthened and the consuming public was stimulated to take notice. Klein also dramatically recounts the aforementioned photo published in 1990 of a child in Pakistan stitching a Nike soccer ball, or as referred to outside the United States as a football, as an example of their use of child labor, symbolic of Nike's continuing disregard for worker's human rights. She goes on to portray the Nike swoosh logo as changing from an athletic status symbol to a metaphor for sweatshops. Nike has been most vocal in defense of their global programs with an active public relations effort. They respond to accusations by noting that they do not abandon low labor markets, citing their continued presence in countries like Taiwan and Korea in spite of increased wages and government-sponsored regulations to improve worker rights. While admitting that the noted Pakistani subcontractor employed children as depicted in the famous photo, they call this a first-time mistake with a new supplier and reference their insistence that thereafter the nonuse of child labor can be verified. Nike has also defended the local wage rates used by their contractors in U.S. dollar equivalents, pointing out that varying cost of living standards do not allow for a direct comparison, that a PPP (purchasing power parity) contrast is more appropriate in evaluating a fair wage and that offering employment and related benefits where none existed before is a good-faith contribution to emerging undeveloped nations. Nike continuously cites their serious efforts to improve conditions in all their facilities and requests critics to compare the measures they have taken over the last few years to those of their competitors in the industry.

A comparison of the corporate codes of conduct of these two companies provides examples of how global firms have reacted to charges of unethical behavior. While the respective documents used are not specifically up to date (firms are always reworking language), they can serve as useful templates to assist the reader in defining the relative positions, definitions, and overall directive approach to such complicated issues. They serve as good illustrations for other managers to review and consider as they construct their own codes of conduct. Nike's code touches on many of the major issues as does the Gap document using similar subject headings. (Complete sets of current documents are available on the respective websites of both corporations with such dissemination a testament to their desire to promote public transparency for their respective codes of conduct.)

Cross-Code Inspection

If you give me six lines written by the most honest man, I will find something to hang him.
—Cardinal Richelieu, French religious leader and statesman

A comparison of the specifics, as to definitions and explanations of the two companies, indicates the following:

Discrimination

Nike handles the matter by noting the ability of the individual *to do the job* as the single determinant, while Gap, using the same language, includes a more definitive prohibition as to preferences or discrimination due to personal beliefs or characteristics, including race, color, creed, nationality, gender, religion, age, and maternity or marital status.

Forced Labor

Nike defines such as prison, indentured, bonded, or otherwise. Gap expands the definition by including involuntary labor to encompass any conscripted labor by governments (a key issue in the aforementioned Unocal case) and further notes that payment of recruitment commissions is the responsibility of the factory (presumably not the employee) while specifically stating that no employee can remain in employment against his or her will.

Child Labor

Both documents state specific age limits, 15 or 14 (if local laws allow), but Gap goes further, citing compliance with any local laws in respect to local child-labor provisions in regard to hours, overtime, wages, and working conditions, while asking factories to maintain official documentation records. Nike, beyond their definitive age level, would seemingly allow child workers to be treated as adults as no mention is made of other regulations affecting their employment activities.

Wages and Hours

Both documents rely on local law to define compensation but use 60 hours as the maximum *regular work week* with one day in seven off. They also allow for paid annual leave and holidays as required by local law or industry standards. Overtime under Nike can be considered mandatory if a worker is notified of such condition at time of hiring, but no allowance for any hourly rate increase for overtime pay is noted. Gap states that workers can refuse overtime without any threat of punishment or dismissal while also requiring that overtime be paid at a rate greater than the standard. It also requests a wage statement to be given to all employees detailing all wages and deductions.

Working Conditions

The Nike code asks that the factory publish health and safety guidelines that also extend to employee residences where applicable while requiring the facility to also agree to comply with Nike's own standards. Such clause fails to indicate which takes precedence. Gap's provisions are extensive, beginning with a statement on the prohibited physical and mental coercion of workers (Nike recites such prohibition in its preamble) and freedom to leave their dormitories during off hours and then provides a quasi-OSHA (Occupational Safety and Health Administration) list of acceptable conditions in the worker environment.

Freedom of Association

Gap recognizes the worker's right to participate in collective bargaining and worker-organized associations without interference, while the Nike code makes mention of the matter in the code's preamble.

Environment

This area is deliberately left out of analysis and commentary but both codes address the issue.

Monitoring and Enforcement

Nike requests the factory to keep records demonstrating compliance with its provisions and to make such available for inspection. Gap announces its intention to monitor compliance with its code and in fact has a very intensive transparent system with periodic disclosure on its corporate website[20] and details of penalties for violations.

Both firms have attempted to balance absolutes and relatives in the construction of their respective codes of conduct. Words like *adequate*, *appropriate*, *sufficiently*, and *encourage* tend to take on a local interpretation and national content, while definitive words like *only*, *does not*, and *must be* move toward a universal declaration. It is interesting to note an example where good intent to ensure uniform compliance can have varying results. Discrimination under the Nike definition entails a simple qualification: *ability of an individual to do the job*, with an emphasis on the world *ability*. In Islamic societies, women might be automatically disqualified, given theocratic principles of separation from men inherent in many societies' functional activities. In Africa, traditional tribal affiliations may not allow an outsider to be accepted or to perform tasks alongside others, while the Indian caste system presents similar problems. In China and Japan, culturally induced respect for older people may limit the ability for younger managers to take senior positions that direct older executives. The more extensive Gap criteria could cause a problem when faced with such decision-making encounters, while the more liberal Nike approach could be interpreted to allow for such practical flexibility.

Nike's response to historic allegations of ethical misconduct or simple malfeasance has been labeled as *anger and panic*. Initially, such events were treated as irritations as "executives would issue denials and lash out at critics" and fear as they rushed "someone to the offending supplier to put out the fire."[21] The continuing criticism of compliance in promoting sweatshops motivated Nike to construct the aforementioned code of conduct targeting contractors. It also inaugurated a company program of random factory inspections as conducted by the Fair Labor Association, a monitoring organization, funded along with other industry firms (Reebok and Liz Claiborne) to supplement Nike's in-house staff of 97 appointed graders of foreign plants. Nike did become a signatory to the UN Global Compact, thereby creating a formidable array of proactive ethical imperatives: a code, internal and independent inspectors, and adherence to a universal declaration. Gap, besides joining the UN Global Compact, produces a very detailed and transparent inspection and reporting system to supplement its code of conduct, called the Social Responsibility Report. As first presented in 2003 and still used, the exhaustive document begins with an executive summary, presented by the firm's president and CEO, underlining the importance the firm places on the report. The program is administered under an executive vice president, chief administrative and compliance officer, and directed by a vice president of global compliance with 90 fulltime employees—indicative of the organization's commitment to proactive involvement. Gap's approval process for foreign sourcing is depicted on a timeline of evaluation with a regional listing of action by the compliance team. Data on their constant monitoring system is offered with written and charted explanations of suspected violations of their code principles. Like the early requirements inherent in the Sullivan Principles, their supplier factories are rated using *quantifiable metrics*, while responses to the investigations of worker-rights abuses by public watchdog groups like the National Labor Committee are handled in the report. It is clear from the vision of Gap Inc. expressed throughout the documents that they are attempting to project increasing transparency with respect to the implementation and verification of their code of ethics.

Gap Inc. and Nike Inc. were specifically chosen for profiling and critical comment in the previous section because both corporations have taken the time to be introspective, committing time and energy to the development of their respective corporate codes of conduct. They should be applauded for their efforts as leaders in the field.

Lessons from an Old Survey

Study the past if you would define the future.

—Confucius

The further backward you look the further forward you see.
—Winston Churchill, British statesman

While the codes of the aforementioned two firms were chosen for more extensive examination, it might be interesting if the reader had an idea of early general approaches of other companies in respect to ethics. A look back in time might enable a base line to be developed that could be used for examining future trends and continuing development of the ethical imperative in commercial institutions. In 2000, following the Seattle riots during the WTO meetings in December the year before, the ills of globalization as practiced by multinational firms began to really be placed at the forefront of public scrutiny. The ethical conduct of global companies in respect to their treatment of labor in emerging countries was one of the prime concerns of those voicing opposition to the commercial phenomenon. Following this incident, the press continued to keep the issue in front of the public.

To gauge the level of involvement with and reaction to consumer concerns as to ethical conduct prevailing in the American corporate community in the new millennium, I had a student conduct a very informal and nonscientific survey of 45 firms engaged to some degree in the global arena. The aim of this limited nonempirical inquiry was neither to compare codes of conduct nor to investigate if the actions of such firms bore out their ethical stance but to find out if such a document existed. The concept was to test, on a narrow basis, a firm's reaction to a general inquiry that an average consumer might generate.

A letter was sent in all cases to the president or CEO asking if the company had "adopted some form of a universal code of ethics standards for their international employees and operations," and if so, asking if they could send the writer a copy. It further asked if such ethical standards were "upheld and enforced, and whether or not there was an individual, committee, or a department" that oversaw such considerations.

As the answers came back the results of how the request was handled by companies were more interesting than the contents of the supplied codes of conduct. Keeping in mind that the replies were generated in the spring of 2002, let me share some of the responses received. Only 18 of the 45 companies contacted replied, and a number of those responding directed the inquirer to their own or industry websites, skirting a direct response to the collateral question posed. Many firms, such as UPS, simply confirmed that "a hard copy of these standards" was mailed with no further comment. (Gap Inc. was not included in the survey, while Nike Inc. was on the list but never replied).

McDonald's advised that, beyond the information contained in their "Welcome to McDonald's" online brochure or other sections contained therein. Their ethics policy "is considered proprietary." A similar but more restrictive reply was received from FedEx stating, "Unfortunately, this information is included in our employee handbook and is not available to the public." The Hertz Corporation directed the inquiry to their website, further noting that "our corporate policy prohibits our participation in independent study or research projects." The Coca-Cola Company responded "Unfortunately, we do not have much information written on this subject that we share." In respect to Coca-Cola, it should be noted that just two years later (circa 2004), their website contained a 27-page code of business conduct constructed of statements and a Q&A sample guideline on the noted subjects. Also, as a note of progression (circa 2009) are the comments by the recently retired chairman of the board of Coca-Cola on connected capitalism as earlier noted in the chapter. The tone of these comments from respondents in the survey suggests that probing into the ethical stance of a number of enterprises was quasi prohibitive and that any expectation of corporate transparency was deeply diminished. The survey conducted 16 years ago was an example of the tone of the times in regard to corporate inquiries concerning their codes of conduct and ethical imperatives. At such period no firm answered the survey by directing the inquirer to any strategic missions or visions of the company. The notion that their global moral positioning was embedded in policies and programs designed only for employees' eyes seemed to exemplify not only some of the responses received but also arguably the reason that many firms failed to even reply. The reason for including what could be considered an outdated survey was to paint a picture of the historic environment that new ideas concerning ethics and CSR were born and that still may influence the subject matter today. While most of the executives of such firms contacted have by now left or retired, the legacy of their thinking may still haunt their old institutions. The survey responses are merely indicative of the fractured approach to the issue by public companies in the 1990s, but the results help to frame the matter for the future. Over the last decade, public awareness of commercial ethical issues has been fueled by many of the events previously depicted in the text, and today the matter has moved further forward in the minds and actions of MNCs. Within the answers and collateral materials provided by respondent firms are the positive sprouts of what has grown over the years into a fuller recognition of the need to address global ethical issues. It also provides further insight into some of the matters still plaguing international firms. Looking back at the survey responses, General Motors (GM) dispatched a mass of literature containing their annual report, company history, car brochures, stockholder information, and a pamphlet titled "Sustainability Report." This document contained a section called "Values, Policies and Principles," with references to GM's series of information booklets published in nine languages covering corporate integrity on a variety of ethical subjects; however, none of the booklets was in the package received. Also included in this section was notice of GM's formal endorsement of the CERES Principles on environmentally responsible business policies, as well as their announced support for the Global Sullivan Principles covering a number of human- and worker-rights issues. (Note that GM had a hand in establishing the original 1977 Sullivan Principles as the founder, the Reverend Leon H. Sullivan, was then a member of their board of directors.)

IBM Corporation, although replying without a formal letter of acknowledgment, sent a comprehensive packet with information booklets titled "Progress Report—environment and well-being" (activity review), "A Blueprint—IBM Corporate Citizenship" (public-responsibility account), "Valuing Diversity: An Ongoing Commitment" (workforce building), plus "Business Conduct Guidelines." In 1994, IBM noted that with "the current focus on corporate responsibility," they were publishing their "first consolidated corporate responsibility report—a companion to our annual report, and something to which we have devoted equal care." They also redesigned their business-ethics guidelines, a 10-page list of requirements placed on their website. Such an announcement equating social responsibility with annual report of a firm is indicative of many firms of the day reacting to the public's demand for more corporate transparency in respect to ethical decision making and company activities promoting such values. The earlier noted survey of companies reporting on their social responsibility activities would seem to indicate that many CEOs have taken the IBM lead, attaching significant value to the subject matter.

7-Eleven Inc. indicated that they have more than 22,000 7-Eleven stores around the world, but outside of the Unites States and Canada they are operated by international licensees using their trademark and such third parties are "independent contractors and are solely responsible for their own policies, procedures and practices." They concluded therefore that the company "does not have a 'universal code of ethical standards.'" This approach as to the extension of corporate ethical responsibility stopping at the arm's-length associate level, even though such entities use the company brand name and hence represent their image, may be an insight into the mind-set of many companies at such a period of time; it is also an issue that troubles firms today. On the other hand, Levi Strauss & Co. took time out in their response letter to state, "We have always held every one of our contractors around the world to the highest standards." The company makes a further point, noting, "As a matter of fact, long before working conditions in plants abroad became a public issue, LS&CO. developed a strict set of guidelines governing all of our contractors."

They further referenced their "Global Sourcing and Operating Guide-lines" on their website as well as including a copy of the "Terms of Engagement & Guidelines for Country Selection."

The difference in the response to working with independent third parties may be industry specific. In the case of 7-Eleven such entities are forward service-oriented franchisees dealing with numerous domesti-cally based customers in various countries that view the stores as local establishments; with Levi Strauss such enterprises are integrated suppliers of their core product line that offers to a more uniform worldwide con-sumer base a category of goods and an industry that has historically been associated with NGO oversight and increased public awareness. This fine line of associate-partner and collaborative members in the global supply chain versus local semi-independent ventures, and one's resulting duties and responsibilities through them, remains a problem for firms in the construction and implementation of codes of conduct.

It should be noted that the inquiries were addressed to the CEO of every firm contacted. But in every case the response signatory came from another officer or staff designee. The corporate titles included senior vice president and general counsel; manager, policy, benefits, and planning; and customer and public relations specialist. One even was signed "Web-master." The Motorola response came from the vice president and direc-tor, Office of Ethics and Compliance, while the reply from International Paper was signed "Ethics Office Coordinator;" both firms indicated that a special designated title existed in the firm's organizational structure, a rather forward-looking initiative that firms today might well be advised to consider. The appointment of some type of compliance or ethical officer will probably need to be addressed by global corporations in the near future. It may be required for internal code construction and monitoring and strategic planning as well as external contact, as firms increase their response to shareholders as well as to public inquiries as per the aforemen-tioned IBM statement.

A review of the 18 responses revealed that only 11 had a published code that they would share with the public. When the individual codes were evaluated most were well-intended brief, basic statements of general intent and vague as to specific application of usable standards. A few were mere statements of philanthropic activity and environmental concern, as opposed to acceptable standards of ethical behavior toward others. Some respondents were singled out as providing adequate language in their codes that embedded country managers could more easily follow. IBM's codes were very extensive, while ExxonMobil's codes were brief but to the point. Not only was Baxter International unique in that its "Practice Standards Manual" was available in 16 languages, but also it advised its employees to alternatively discuss issues with their immediate supervisor, local business sources, their five regional business-practice committees, and the corporate-responsibility office. Such a chain of integrated organizational responsibility to engage a variety of ethnocentric, polycentric, and geocentric viewpoints with the added polar conceptual approaches, cultural relativism versus ethical imperialism, was way ahead of its time. But the approach may provide for a very well-balanced ethical decision-making system. It may be a substantial model for other multinationals to consider as it allows for local traditions and specific context of the matter to be mixed with corporate core values. One wonders if strategic planning in the company also incorporates such an essential imperative, as their involvement in the matter is quite extensive. The only potential danger of such a widespread program is that the process is elongated, may have too many inputs, and may confuse rather than provide specific direction to the embedded manager. It is, however, a most exhaustive, all-inclusive treatment for the implementation of global ethics.

While the aforementioned simplified survey, conducted within the limited confines of an undemanding general inquiry, is certainly not a definitive investigation of the matter, a few general observations might be made. In 1992, inquiries into the codes of conduct of some major companies were often dismissed, as no repercussions would probably ensue from failure to comply with requests for information. Specific answers were not for public dissemination (note only 18 out of 45 surveyed bothered to respond). The public was just warming up to the issue and not many companies were out in front of the matter, much less were they internally prepared to respond to collateral inquiries beyond providing copies of the relevant document. One would wonder if the original request had also asked if ethics was part of their corporate strategic planning process, would any firm have responded positively, no less explained how. It should be noted that Levi Strauss & Co. would seemingly use an ethical element in the corporate selection process, as their document provides guidelines for engaging partners and selecting countries to operate in. Given that these activities are part of the corporate-planning process and form evaluation criteria for country scanning and entrance decisions, inadvertently ethical concerns have been infused into the strategic plan of this firm.

Others might have responded that as all their decisions automatically incorporate their code of conduct, the strategic planning process has an ethical imperative factored therein. As noted earlier, Gap Inc. has created not only specific criteria but also a check-and-balance system with a dedicated cadre to examine and qualify all foreign associates. It also offers a publicly disseminated periodic report on these activities.

If today a similar type of query were conducted of multinational firms, one could conceivably conclude that more firms would respond. Although this is conjecture on the part of the author, one gets the feeling that corporate codes of conduct would probably reflect a greater attention to global ethical issues as more companies explore international opportunities for sales, purchases, and outsourced assistance in support areas. The survey, as conducted in early 2000, may only be valuable in providing a baseline for the future, to gauge if meaningful progress is forthcoming not only in the operational quadrants of MNCs but also in respect to their strategic motivations and intents. The responses of the companies in the survey were used simply to get a feel for their approach to ethics in general when questioned by an outside party. As such, the replies received did not reflect the contacted companies' stance on any specific ethical or CSR issues but just the availability of materials on the subject they would share with the public.

Over the last few years the attention drawn to individual executive morality and organizational ethics has certainly increased and pressured corporations to reevaluate their responsibilities to all stakeholders. Whether or not such a trend continues is hard to judge. The driving force behind the ethical imperative being placed in commercial institutions seems to be a combination of two key factors. Public pressure stemming from notoriety of alleged wrongdoing as perceived by consumers is one major consideration, as it may affect the revenue stream. On the other hand, if firms feel that there is a competitive value to be achieved in pursuing an ethical path and incorporating a social responsibility program (cause marketing) into their activities or that to ignore such direction may place firms in financial jeopardy, they will certainly embrace such principles.

The sweatshop exposés that made headlines in late 1999 and early 2000 have seemingly hit a plateau. In the past few years, such stories tend to appear only on websites devoted to investigating these matters and raising awareness among their own following. They have fallen below the public radar. One reason for this development may in fact be that global firms have been working behind the scenes to correct the errors of their past ways. By creating codes of conduct, working on enforcing provisions within and without the organization with the assistance of independent verification groups, and signing on to universal accords like the UN Global Compact, the incidents that gave rise to such stories may be dissipating. In the concluding section of the book, a project under way in Turkey, bringing together two historic combatants on the issue—manufacturers and labor-rights groups—may provide a glimpse into the future.

Managerial Reflections

1. A template for a code of conduct is presented, consisting of absolutes and relatives, with illustrative examples of how to apply the two diverse terms to specific conditions and activities of a firm. Do you agree or disagree with the references used? How would you choose to delineate areas of ethical concern—can you make up your own list?

2. Respect for local traditions forms one of the guidelines for construction of a code of conduct. In parts of the world with culturally induced customs where women are still considered chattel with reduced rights or prohibited outright from certain positions or simply cannot as a matter of accepted practice be placed in a position to direct men, how does one respond to such conditions? Would you send one of the firm's female specialists or executives to such places, and if so, what would you tell her in advance?

3. Religion plays an important part in ethical determinations, with many spiritual and philosophical teachings embracing some form of the Golden Rule, while the author introduces the Platinum Rule as a collateral consideration to reflect the notion of cultural relativism

or respect for differences. Is such a rule valid? Can you see instances where it is appropriate?

4. A comparison of the codes of Nike and Gap is used to demonstrate good attempts at devising a universal direction for employees and commercial relationships with third parties. Are the codes too general to allow for precise guidance in the field by local managers, or is the language too specific and troublesome so that it does not allow for flexibility in some contextual situations? Did either one strike the right balance?

5. Firms tend to move through three levels of ethical initiative that prompt them to develop a firm code of conduct: CYA (regulatory response), show and tell (reputation defense), and true blue (altruistic or socially connected capitalism). Should companies jump to the top of the pyramid, trusting that a true blue approach will cover the other two steps, or should a code incorporate all three levels?

CHAPTER 7

Global Ethical Strategies and Conclusions

It does not do to leave a live dragon out of your calculations.
—J. R. R. Tolkien, *The Hobbit, or There and Back Again*

A new road for ethical leadership presented by the author proposes that the definition has expanded beyond the original responsibility of a company vis-à-vis society and the environment. It is proposed that a moral abstract, basic questions of right and wrong, deeply affect "whether a company is operating in a contest of sustainability… in shareholder value calculations."[1] By housing this element within a leadership context, it follows that executive-leadership characteristics must include an ingrained ethical imperative in order to arrive at the single measurement criteria—shareholder appreciation. As opposed to examining separate companies, proponents of this conclusion cite the fact that socially responsible investment funds like the Domini 400 Social Index and the Dow Jones Sustainability Indexes (DJSI) are outperforming the market, sustaining the premise that shareholder value remains one of the primary yardstick by which success of ethical leadership initiatives is measured. While the next decade numbers are yet to sustain this direction, it is a good working hypothesis for now.

Within the context of sustaining shareholder expectations, six ethical managerial facets are targeted: shareholders, employees, customers, business partners, local communities, and the environment. Good corporate leaders are admonished to provide shareholders with annual reporting on legal and regulatory compliance as well as on social and environmental initiatives beyond compliance and to develop an investment strategy with positive criteria for encouraging activities that involve desirable social, environmental, and business practices and avoiding negative outcomes in such areas. Both employees and customers should be educated as to the social consequences of the leaders' actions, while business partners who knowingly degrade or cause damage to these six facets of corporate responsibility should be avoided. Local communities supporting regimes that violate basic human rights should be dismissed in the strategic planning process. Not only should environmental regulations and laws be complied with, but also corporate leadership should also anticipate more stringent ones. The accent on the corporate leader brings such decision making back to the individual level where ethics are born and goes beyond mere corporate-organizational compliance with laws and regulations. It targets man's respect for his fellow men and his general welfare.

Terms of Engagement

In Greek mythology, the gods of Olympus would endow special humans on earth with the elements to ensure them protection on their journeys outside their territories and in their engagements with alien groups. Such strategic implements equate to arming a warrior going off to war with the tools necessary in a combative environment. As depicted in the 1981 movie *Clash of the Titans*, the hero is divinely endowed with a helmet, a shield, and a sword to enable him to vanquish his foes. Each armament helps increase his ability to proceed safely in alien lands in order for him to fulfill not only his goal but also his destiny. Global firms in pursuit of their agendas might be wise to consider the ethical equivalent of such strategic positioning in the era of globalization. Whether they are called by a military designation or referred to in more politically correct verbiage, such as achieving socially acceptable détente or improving relations with the public at large, the intent is clear—damage control once the ethical issue is engaged. Using the Greek armor analogy, three potential positions can be used.

Helmet Mentality: Do Nothing

Just placing a helmet on the head is acknowledgment of indoctrination into a uniformed group, which can be likened to companies changing their domestic hats for global ones. But in the arena of ethical and social responsibility, it is a neutral position. In Greek stories, the helmet was donned to offer invisible presence to the wearer. Companies that subscribe to the notion to do nothing may be looking to take an indistinguishable path. They may choose to gamble with the consuming public's mind-set, feeling that it is a trend that comes and goes with no distinct understanding of what motivates or dissuades the buying decision when tied to a moral consideration. By not taking a specific stand, firms can use plausible deniability when accusations arise and then gauge their reaction and required responses accordingly. It also allows companies to defend criticism for a poorly constructed internal code while eliminating the need for implementing its guidelines with staff and the periodic-reporting function. It is akin to symbolic rhetoric recognizing that the best consideration is to do nothing, practice benign neglect, and hence become invisible to the public at large—an decision to fly below the public radar. To place one's corporate head in the sand with the collateral thinking that if we can't see them they cannot see us is a valid concept—but we all know what part of the anatomy remains exposed.

On the other hand, this position of just donning the helmet may answer a lingering question: Does social responsibility equate to social change? As global firms encounter varying societies in transitional periods of development, both political and economic, the question of tacit acceptance or desired change arises. Can a firm act socially responsible by doing nothing? Should it wait until the changing social dust settles? It may be prudent to sit back and wait, as the future effect on acceptable ethical criteria may be influenced by the sheer size of the working populations and developing economic strength of emerging nations like China and India as they serve as models for the rest of the underdeveloped world. Westernized concepts that seemingly drive multinational enterprises (MNEs) and contribute to the principles placed in their codes of conduct in regard to labor treatment and workplace standards may be revisited this century. The idea of an 8-hour work day and 40-hour work week with paid overtime along with other beneficial norms could be replaced by more strenuous standards as global competition heats up. As a greater proportion of the earth's population enters the labor force, a natural depression of wages across all industries may emerge as supply exceeds demand. Less may be received for more and the traditional Western-defined work week may be expanded. While it may seem difficult to imagine westernized nations reverting to lower standards, new benchmarks or universal standards in respect to all areas of managing people could emerge. It might be prudent for multinational firms to stand on the sideline and just don the ethical helmet exhibiting a change in territorial exposure, remaining inert, and acknowledging conditions that must be respected but waiting to take a firm stance.

Shield Mentality: Deflect and Protect

Picking up a shield may allow firms to deflect potential criticism and defend possible allegations of misconduct. It is a preparation that allows companies to prepare for a reactive confrontation if someone strikes the first blow. Many organizations utilize shields constructed by venerable institutions or perhaps through private alliances with industry competitors to present a unified ethical image. They align or graft themselves onto recognized international codes such as the Sullivan Principles, the United Nations (UN) Global Compact, or other internationally proclaimed labor accords. By becoming a signatory and agreeing to abide by such provisions, firms use this proactive positioning to announce their good intentions and draw cover from revered organizations or those alliances they create for themselves. Using a shield prepared by another can be a comforting middle ground between doing nothing, short of acknowledging the matter by merely changing their helmet or getting proactively involved by picking up a sword. At times of challenge the use of a shield, grafting onto a recognized universal code of conduct, provides a viable wall behind which to hide and shelter one from the arrows of public discontent.

The shield constructed of such documents, however, does not require accountability, as the authoring agencies do not have any system to check and report on their members' actions or inactions. Even some of the self-appointed ethical alliances do not have an outside independent-verification agency. Firms are placed on their honor to abide by their pledged allegiances to such venerable documents and hence need do nothing more than sign up to receive the shield.

Sword Mentality: Institute Change

Placing a sword in one's hand is indicative of eventual action, a proactive desire to initiate change and alter present conditions. It is an offensive weapon to strike the first blow and thereby gain a benefit before one is attacked. A global enterprise can decide to construct a code of conduct based on the aforementioned universal declarations or devise a custom version. Taking a preemptive course of action could also produce a competitive advantage, especially in industries where allegations of acceptable ethical conduct may positively affect the consumer's decision to buy. Companies desirous of creating an image of social responsibility, especially in regard to environmental matters in the mineral, oil, and timber extraction industries, might also feel their acknowledged efforts could result in a meritorious public reward, again helping to promote their product offerings.

Such a course of proactive direction requires very careful assembly, inclusion of a monitoring system, and a requirement to issue transparent assessments. It forces the firm to be proactive and make the required changes in its strategic planning systems as well as its operational structures. As taking up the ethical sword signals an intention to influence social change and take responsibility for one's actions, it comes with a potential danger if not handled correctly. Ethical swords can strike both ways—cutting into moral problems but capable of being turned on the wielder if not masterfully handled.

Global Ethical Road Maps

You got to be careful if you don't know where you're going, because you might not get there.

—Yogi Berra, American baseball player and folk poet

While multinational corporations (MNCs) may find themselves facing ethical dilemmas requiring a responsive posturing, it would have served them well, in advance of such troubling melees, to have consulted an ethical road map before proceeding on a global journey. Vigilance exhibited beforehand may help avoid missteps on the path and provide a more secure, sustainable passage as firms navigate a world where moral conduct should always be investigated before setting forth. Consulting an ethical checklist on a parallel basis with strategic decision making allows firms to inject into the process an ethical element at the start rather than engaging such issues as a tactical problem down the line.

Ethical Decision Making

Even with the construction of a workable global code of conduct that can be used both to guide the corporate strategic planning process and to handle foreign ethical dilemmas, companies would be advised to question their overall approach to anticipated events. Multinational managers would be well advised to follow an ethical road map to access their proactive actions by reviewing answers to the following questions.

Ethical Stop Signs

- *Legal review.* *Does* the anticipated action violate host or home-country laws or international treaties? If yes, don't do it!
- *Firm policy review.* *Does* the anticipated action violate the company code of ethical conduct? If yes, don't do it!
- *Local culture review.* *Does* the anticipated action violate or strongly conflict with the host country's norms, values, traditions, customs, or long-held theological or philosophical beliefs? If yes, don't do it!
- *Personal assessment.* *Does* the anticipated action violate one's own moral compass and personal commitments to their fellow man? If yes, don't do it!

Country Scanning

While a code of conduct can serve as the guiding document for ethical decision making, it does not alleviate the responsibility of global managers to continue their vigilant scanning of potential markets and partners that their firms will engage in the process of exploring foreign developmental opportunities. Companies should be well aware of the alien environments and the parties they will encounter across borders. Two key observations and areas of investigation should always be maintained: an evaluation of the country to be entered to construct firm operations, and the partners or associates in foreign markets that the firm may engage. The following charts illustrate such conditional reviews.

Country-Entry Scanning Review

One should know the country the firm is considering to enter. What is their ethical profile, whether actual or publicly perceived, in regard to the following conditional areas?

- *Labor conditions.* How are their own citizens and resident foreign workers treated by local employers? What is the level of existing country laws, regulations, and governmental enforcement agencies in regard to protecting domestic labor; specifically child work age, hours worked and overtime, facility safety, hiring and firing practices, union rights, wage garnishment to fulfill employment and third-party obliga- tions, on-site freedom of movement, and the like?
- *Commercial atmosphere.* What is the effect of local customs and traditions on business operations? Such customs might include acceptance of minorities and women, influence of faith-based institutions, governmental oversight and red tape, and more.
- *Global signatories.* Have they signed on to international treaties and compacts, such as the UN Global Compact or OECD (Organisation for Economic Co-operation and Development), that direct and obligate their governments to respect certain ethical practices? Do they actively follow such principles?
- *World opinions.* Is the government viewed as repressive, with negative global perceptions? Do their citizens have a favorable or unfavorable perception of your own home country?

If such questions produce pessimistic answers, the firm is automatically put on notice and may need to reevaluate their strategic considerations, either postponing entry or severely limiting local relationships. And if the country is entered, it will be important to closely monitor activities to avoid potential problems and red-flagged situations as such issues will eventually arise.

Partner-Review Process

The choice of partners greatly impacts the ethical direction of a company as well as its ability to apply the terms of its code of conduct to them. Whether the anticipated local alliance is via the use of an independent import, wholesale distributor and separate sales agent, a third-party, arm's-length contractor, or any other service provider, their activities will reflect on the principal engaging them. With more complex legal structures like a licensed user of one's proprietary assets (patents, copyrights, and trademarks) or an equity joint venture, the parties are tied closer together and the actions of the local partnered entity are tethered to the foreign associate, the two seen as acting in concert. Partner selection therefore directly impacts how ethics are interpreted and applied.

Partner Selection Grid

Know well your potential strategic alliance partners and third-party contractors, suppliers, and service providers. What is their background with regard to the following?

- *Reputation and prior associations.* Have any inspections revealed allegations of human rights and labor incidents or questionable behavior? What is their history in regard to ethical matters and what are the views of local parties, as well as foreign firms that deal or have dealt with them?
- *Ethical and social responsibility outlook.* Are there initial shared values between the parties? Does the partner consider ethics an essential part of the business process? Does the partner engage in any CSR programs?
- *Reaction to firm code of conduct.* Can it be incorporated easily into legal agreements and assist in guiding the overall

relationship between the parties? Will the partner accept the principal's code of conduct and actively assist in enforcing its provisions?

- *Acceptance of verification systems and penalties.* Will the other party accept such additional conditions of the association? Will they consider its incorporation into the base arrangement as an equal duty and responsibility that is subject to consequences if not upheld, including but not limited to grounds for termination?

If such considerations uncover problem areas, the firm would be wise to consider other parties and terminate matters with potential partners as such revelations, even at the negotiating stage, may signal ethical concerns will be encountered down the road when the parties are actually joined.

Ethical Positioning Scale

Firms can also use a global ethical-positioning scale for assessment to determine the extent of the stand they wish to take. They can plan in advance their responsive tactical posturing, so if problems do arise, embedded local managers know how to react.

Relative Positioning

- *Low position.* A do-nothing, limited measured action, benign neglect leading to plausible deniability if no code of conduct is constructed. A "we knew nothing, so don't blame us" attitude. The road not taken cannot be criticized for the wrong choice. Stay below the public radar screen with no public dissemination of intent that could be attacked later.
- *Medium position.* Precautionary defensive posturing based on potentially accommodating critics. Adoption of a recognized global compact that allows a firm to deflect potential critical attack. This position is dangerous, as it may cause companies to be *caught in the middle*, in that they recognized the issue but failed to completely address it.

- *High position.* Proactive plans with construction of a strongly defined code of conduct, control and monitoring mechanisms, and goal-measurement criteria along with periodic transparent reports to the public.

Dealing with Ethical Dilemmas: The 4W Approach

Ethical dilemmas normally begin to arise when an ethical imperative in the strategic planning process is missing. It is further enhanced when no local legal structure exists and the ability to consult principles in a code of acceptable conduct, be it a universal convention or individual corporate declaration that directly speaks to the issue, does not exist. Absent these guiding elements, the application of the 4Ws (who, where, when, and why) of provenance may be helpful in approaching the matter. Acting as gates of inquiry, they allow one to navigate a matrix of components affecting decision making when an ethical dilemma is encountered. Ethics requires one to do the acceptable right thing as opposed to the unacceptable wrong thing; thus, ethical dilemmas involve making a decision between two conceivable rights. Coming from the Greek word di-lemma, meaning two propositions, the process requires one to make a choice between two equally justifiable but contrasting alternatives. A correct judgment must therefore be observant of contrary values. Without this recognition, and hence the required inspection, any resultant determination is flawed. A choice cannot be made in a theoretical or cultural vacuum. The choice is subject to conditional realities that are perpetually in flux. In order to appreciate and understand the provisional issues affecting the dilemma choice, the following 4Ws of introspection are offered to allow the decision maker to balance all relevant interests and conditions. The underlying link in the process is to gain a better appreciation of the influence of cultures: that of the host society in which the problem originated and that of the foreigners drawn into the issue. The 4Ws that allow for multicultural critical thinking.

1. List the *whos*, or those involved and affected. Know the parties or players involved and their respective culturally induced mind-sets controlling their behavior and attitudes. Is the event happening in a

collective social environment, where formal relationships are important and the harmony of the group supersedes all, verses an individualistic culture, where personal interaction is less meaningful as people have few obligations to others? Is the power distance between the parties more stringent with a hierarchical structure, where authority status and position are respected, or is society more egalitarian, with challenges to authority more common? Is the culture more masculine oriented, with gender role segregation and a separation of family and work life, or is it feminine, role liberal, relationship directed, and a culture where family and social groups transcend all life? Are they part of a society where differences are tolerated, people take risks, and there is less emotional resistance to change, or do they exhibit strict rule structuring, and avoid conflict and ambiguity?

2. Appreciate the *where,* or the place the issue has arisen: the social, political, and economic environment in which the dilemma originated. Understand and appreciate the dominant and minor cultures of the host country in which the problematic event has taken place, including historic and current religious overtones and philosophical considerations that exercise some degree of control over the matter. Keep in mind that the foreign venue does not exhibit the same moral influencing conditions found in the home or headquarters country.

3. Acknowledge the *when,* or the timing of the incident and its relation to history and the current development of the area and commercial setting in which the dilemma surfaced. What is the temporal focus of the society: Is it past, present, or future directed? Is the society rationally sequential and think that *time is money,* or are their schedules polychromic and their preferences emotionally selected? Has the issue arisen during a transitional period, or do traditional values still prevail? Is the company in its initial exposure period to the new host society and viewed as an alien intruder, or has it been integrated into community as an equal member?

4. After the first three have been reviewed, explore the underlying triggers to determine *why* the problem evolved. Aim to understand and appreciate the subjective context of the cultural differences that not only ignited the matter but also may impact how it is resolved. The core dilemma can then be determined and shared with all

participants, allowing for the inclusion of respective positions of all parties affected. Lastly, use the incident as a learning mechanism for future directional decision making.

Moving through such systematic examination of culturally induced ethical determinant portals allows for a 360-degree vortex combining various approaches resulting in innovative solutions. Culture is the subjective root of ethical dilemmas encountered in business and permeates the personal, organizational, and systemic levels of decision making. Inputting into the process different ways of thinking helps to navigate complicated dilemmas and results in choices that are more worthy and contain a higher moral quality. While the 4W approach reveals surface differences, the prime consideration is the uncovering of shared ethical determination paths and using them to uncover bridges of common understanding in order to reach workable accommodations that require value-laden trade-offs.

Conclusions

On the human chessboard, all moves are possible.
        —Miriam Schiff, researcher of the human condition

Things do not change, we change.
        —Henry David Thoreau, writer, poet, and philosopher

The reality is that changes are coming… They must come. You must share in bringing them.
        —John Hersey, Pulitzer Prize–winning writer and journalist

As commercial enterprises embark on a global journey, their international managers carry with them an implied and felt dual obligation. They need to act both in their official capacities as firm employees and serve and protect the interests of all groups they encounter based on their individual personal stance. This is their moral and social responsibility to humanity. It is imperative that a code of conduct not be left pinned to the front door of the headquarters but that it be carried by global managers into the world. It is both a shield and a sword in the globalization battle that recognizes a change in helmet choice. As such, it must be practical or "it is little more than greeting-card sentiment" and should address Machiavelli's fundamental question, "What will work in the world as it is?"[2]

The Vitruvian Man model built with square absolutes providing universally clear and precise definitional guidance, while encased in a circle of delegated relatives that provide for local, culturally flexible, self-adjusting sets of standards to be applied, may provide for a workable code of conduct. A well-constructed code, while acting as a guide to embedded international managers, is also a valuable additional tool in the global strategic planning process. Companies have three kinds of choices that a firm's ethical standards impact as they enter a foreign land.[3] They can choose between adopting a proactive stance to "strictly adhere to 'higher' global standards" (imported absolutes) or maintaining a reactive, more passive position and consider local context (relatives). A third alternative, to either avoid doing business to begin within a suspect country or to pull out of an existing market, impacts multinational selection as well as the entire integration of a firm's global value-chain network.

Ethics has emerged as a critical component of the global managerial, strategic decision-making process. As Epictetus, a Greek philosopher, noted to the people of his day, "You do the greatest service to the state if you shall raise, not the roofs of the houses, but the souls of the citizens: for it is better that great souls should dwell in small houses rather than for mean slaves to lurk in great houses." Global corporations would be well advised to consider such direction as they erect their world dwellings. They should work to ensure the laborers who are used to construct them are treated with dignity and respect, or such institutions run the risk of being destroyed by their very builders and supporters, the eventual consumers the labor produces. Commercial enterprises venturing outside their borders on a worldwide journey to mine the rich human resources of the global value chain should heed to the refrain from the popular 1970 Crosby, Stills, Nash, and Young song "Teach Your Children": "You, who are on the road, must have a code, to live by."[4]

Large multinational firms, with revenue streams eclipsing most national gross domestic products, employing thousands in varying countries and exercising global political clout, are in essence modern empires unto themselves. Like historic figures Alexander the Great and Genghis Khan, the conquerors of their then-known worlds, such massive commercial forces need to contend with the governing of those whose lives they impact and influence. The world's population is developing a dual allegiance to alternative but equally compelling institutions. As citizens of their individual countries, they will look to national governments to protect them while providing basic social services. They are, however, becoming more and more beholden to the multinational behemoths to supply job opportunities, to offer required products and services, and to generally sustain and improve not only their economic condition but also their lives.

As the era of globalization morphs into a truly new worldwide socio-economic-political system, transnational business entities may replace world governments. In the original version of the movie *Rollerball*, the story line envisions a future world where MNCs run everything. They provide all the products and services the earth's population needs and desires; national governments are redundant.

The only element they lack is an intrinsic requirement to behave with an ethical imperative. However, like governments that do not act morally and fail to look out for the welfare and rights of their citizens, the constituents of such global enterprises, the worldwide beneficiaries of their products and services, will be watching them more carefully and expecting them to act morally. To the growing group of traditional stakeholders, companies may need to add to the world at large. The very success of such enterprises may hinge on their construction and implementation of a universal code of conduct, equitable and transparent to all.

An ethical wake-up call is sounding for global enterprises and they need to heed to the message. As globalization is the result of a natural progression of world commercial development so must be the creation of universal codes of conduct that accompany such a phenomenon.

Another Time-out

Throughout the text the author has tried to present varying ideas on the development of global labor standards during the era of globalization. As new labor groups are brought into the worldwide system, and therefore different approaches surface, it is hard to codify exactly what will emerge as universally accepted criteria. A step in this direction was taken in April 2005 when Nike, Patagonia, Gap, and five other companies joined with six leading antisweatshop groups to attempt to devise a single set of workable labor standards coupled with a common factory-verification system. The effort, to be known as the Joint Initiative on Corporate Accountability and Workers' Rights, began its work by running a pilot project in several dozen Turkish facilities that produce products for the commercial partners. Its goal is to use the experiment, over a two-and-a-half-year period, to test and create a broadly acceptable range of labor standards. What is unique about this approach is that it has the joint backing of the commercial sector and activist groups like Social Accountability International (SAI), a strong advocate of corporate transparency in the treatment of labor in global factories. Today, three primary groups are involved with inspectional overseeing around the world. Besides SAI, the Fair Labor Association (FLA) and the Ethical Trading Initiative, a group made up of European unions, nonprofits, and companies like Marks & Spencer and Sainsbury's Supermarkets, are working toward transparent monitoring and reporting systems. These proactive measures, especially when they are composed of a broader array of participants in the global supply chain, acting in unison and toward common goals, is a most promising step. Such efforts, however, may reverse the pressure on multinational firms to either embrace an existing code of conduct or construct their own. It may be a signal to take a time-out, wait until the learning process crystallizes the issues, and then build commercial codes of conduct on a wide, global platform of acceptable principles.

Ethics as a Strategic Imperative

All progress is initiated by challenging current conceptions and executed by supplanting existing institutions.
>   —George Bernard Shaw, Irish playwright

Great leaders, be they in business or other fields of endeavor, don't react they anticipate. One has to know what is going to happen. Reacting to an outside stimulus often occurs too late and subjects one to another's agenda. Knowing what to do in advance means being prepared. Research the subject, learn the common mistakes, withhold premature decisions, and appreciate your standards—then go out and apply them. This book was intended to foster thinking and discussion about the issue. It attempts to offer the reader a balanced set of ideas and varying avenues of ethical pursuit.

The literature on strategy, its definition, its goal and structural intent role as well as its practical use, could fill a small library. The term *strategy* (from the Greek *strategia*, meaning *generalship*) refers to moving troops into position, deployment of resources after actual engagement tactics are used. One observation of strategy is that it is the means by which policy is effectively achieved. All books on strategy open with a discussion on strategic intent, a mission statement of proposed direction and policies to be employed in achieving them, in essence defining the agenda. A wise man once said, "Know his agenda, know the man." The author, however, could not help but interject a bit of prejudicial influence, believing that ethical behavior is part of mankind's social contract with his fellow men and the earth, his lifelong agenda. George Steiner, a pioneer in the origins and practices of strategic planning, in his book *Strategic Planning* proposes a number of definitions for strategy.[5] One reference, that strategy is composed of directional decisions as to purposes and missions, stands out as it encompasses a broad spectrum that also includes an ethical component. Kenneth Andrews presents this lengthy definition of strategy in his book *The Concept of Corporate Strategy*:

> Corporate strategy is the pattern of decisions in a company that determines and reveals its objectives, purposes, or goals, produces the principal policies and plans for achieving those goals, and defines the range of business the company is to pursue, the kind of economic and human organization it is or intends to be, and the nature of the economic and non-economic contribution it intends to make to its shareholders, employees, customers, and communities.[6]

This view of strategy encompasses the wider social environment in which business entities operate and as such demands the incorporation of ethics in the strategic planning process. Michael Porter, a scholar who writes about competitive strategy as opposed to its more generic characteristics, sees strategy as "about being different," positioning a firm to offer something unique in the marketplace[7] perhaps an ethical component that resonates as a perceived added value not just to customers but with all stakeholders in the company. Fred Nickols, under the auspices of Distance Consulting LLC, presents strategy as a "bridge between policy or high-order goals on one hand and tactics of concrete action on the other."[8] He asks companies to question what kind of company they are, what they want and must become. Without specifically mentioning a moral imperative, his use of the words "high-order goals" seems to imply a social responsibility intent with some type of ethical conduct embedded in the goal.

While sections of this book have presented tactical response, once the ethical dilemma has been engaged the primary consideration is to integrate suitable and sustainable ethical policy in the formation of corporate strategy. It is a foundation upon which the building blocks of companies are constructed. MNCs would be wise to heed this direction imperative as would their decision makers, the executives of tomorrow, leading their firms into the modern globalization era. William Lazonick writes about a new economy business model that sees the "fortunes of the rich and poor joined," as firms move their operations and activities to more and more developing nations.[9] Such wider and increased social engagement begets ethical dilemmas. As firms construct their strategic plans an ethical component needs to be introduced into them.

Final Thoughts

MNCs need to put aside the historic parochialism that had them addressing ethical issues from a tactical-reaction position. They have to take the long-term systemic view, beginning at the strategic planning stage. Firms should formulate a uniform, universal policy disseminated with an institutional code of conduct that is supported by empirical and objective data as developed from an organizational system of inspection and verification. Such direction should eclipse the traditional shallow, insulated, home-office indoctrination. It should take into account differences in economic development and socially induced traditions and customs as well as context, while maintaining basic human rights principles that transcend all other variables and fall outside the bounds of cultural diversity.

Globalization is a permanent commercial phenomenon. It therefore makes good business sense for MNCs to meld ethics and social responsibility into their global strategies. Global commercial moral clarity only emerges when the issue is engaged. That procedure begins when the matter is reflected in the intent and mission statements of companies and then placed in the strategic determination process, thereby creating tactical administrative and operational programs that support and promote ethically connected capitalism. It is hoped that construction of a code of conduct that is used in the strategic planning process will enable managers to design commercial reality rather than merely reacting to it. In the end, it is a win-win situation for all.

One final restatement remains. MNEs are one of the key components in the modern global socioeconomic-political system. The commercial intent of MNEs is to leverage their international networks to create competitive advantages over their rivals. The strategies to accomplish such a goal result in continuous geographical rationalization of their value-chain activities around the world. These transnational leviathans, larger and wealthier than about 120 nation-states (as measured in gross national product and previously noted), prowl the world in search of new physical and knowledge resources, new labor pools, and new sales markets. While maintaining a basic, singular, territorial, sovereign identity due to their countries of origin or executive headquarters affiliations, they are truly citizens of the world with little or no national allegiance. They are so big that like tsunami they create their own path, crisscrossing countries under their own economic muscle. They are virtually a new instrument born out of the globalization phenomenon. They are extraterritorial ambassadors moving around the globe creating universal relationships, far-flung partners, and commercial alliances while unifying consumers and utilizing common but dispersed workforces. In mature, capitalistic free markets, they have always been a force. But in emerging nations, they sometimes usurp the ability and responsibility of the local government to guide socioeconomic changes, while in former communist societies they are replacing state-owned and state-controlled enterprises thereby becoming a new foundation for the lives of such embedded citizens. Their world influence has begun to rival the traditional power and prestige of great nations throughout history, while their image projects across the globe to a degree only achieved by religious doctrines. No wonder, with such endowed characteristics, they are perceived and judged as any leaders are: as hopeful purveyors of good or acceptable ethical principles and appliers of social responsibility.

It is against this backdrop that global business and global managers must construct their strategies, marshal their tactical activities, and make their decisions in the 21st century. They will be watched, criticized, and praised as they carry out their missions. It has been the intent of this book to prepare managers for this added requirement: The construction and administration of their transnational duties and responsibilities as leaders of their respective global organizations.

Managerial Reflections

1. A series of tactical responses is offered when an ethical issue is encountered by global firms stated in terms of a warrior's adornments: *helmet*, do-nothing, neutral posturing; *shield,* a prereactive defensive maneuver; and *sword*, a proactive planned offensive. Such deployments would acquaint with what points on the ethical positioning scale: low, medium, and high?

2. Ethical stop signs prompting a review of potential ethical issues are noted to help a firm navigate in its global operations. At what level of the organization should such a review be conducted—headquarters, regional, or local, and who should participate—what divisions, specialized personnel, and outside consultants?

3. A country scanning model is introduced to catch potential ethical problems. Beyond the objective considerations should the opinions of NGOs and perception of consumers be part of the evaluated criteria?

4. A partnership evaluation chart is included to investigate the ethical practices of anticipated associates the firm may engage in its foreign operations. Apart from those with whom they will have a legal contractual arrangement and hence an opportunity to introduce ethical provision into the agreement and monitor them, how far down the supply chain or up the customer distribution succession should the inquiry proceed?

Notes

Preface

1. Allen (1831).
2. Liedtka (1992).
3. Shakespeare (1881), *Henry VI*, part 2, act 4, scene 2.

Chapter 1

1. Moore and Lewis (1999), p. 11.
2. Moore and Lewis (1999), p. 21.
3. Moore and Lewis (1999), p. 184.
4. Lichtheim (1976), p. 156.
5. Hill (2005), p. 102.
6. Anderson and Cavanagh (2000).

Chapter 2

1. Dunning (2003), p. 12.
2. Dunning (2003), p. 9.
3. Friedman (1999).
4. Doh (2005); Griffen and Pustay (2005); Hill (2005); Phatak, Bhagat, and Kashlak (2005)—representative of just a few of the textbooks on international business featuring a chapter or large section on the subject of ethics.
5. Doh (2005).
6. Saloner, Shepard, and Podolny (2001), p. 328.
7. The Body Shop International (1998a).
8. The Body Shop International (1998b).
9. Vickey (2002), p. 48.
10. Vickey (2002), p. 50.
11. Fredericks (2002).
12. *Kasky v. Nike Inc.* (2002); *Nike v. Kasky* (2002).
13. Porter (1980), p. 4.
14. Porter (1990), p. 71.
15. Tarr (2004).
16. *Fortune* (2003), APSI S10.
17. *BusinessWeek* (2009).

18. *BusinessWeek* (2009).

19. *BusinessWeek* (2009).

20. *BusinessWeek* (2004).

21. Welch (2009).

22. Kidder (2004).

23. Holt, Quelch, and Taylor (2004).

24. *Guide to Best Practices in Corporate Social Responsibility* (2009).

25. Diamond (2005).

26. Hodge (2000), p. 36.

Chapter 3

1. Friedman (2005).

2. England (2003), ch. 1.

3. England (2003), ch. 1.

4. England (2003), ch. 1.

5. Friedman (1970), p. 33.

6. Friedman (1970), p. 33.

7. Dunning (2003), p. 7.

8. Friedman (1970), p. 33.

9. Donaldson (1996), pp. 49–62.

10. Deresky (2006), p. 31.

11. Wild, Wild, and Han (2006), p. 111.

12. Hodgetts and Luthans (2003), p. 7.

13. Wild, Wild, and Han (2003), p. 12.

14. *Business Respect* (2004), no. 79.

15. *Business Respect* (2004), no. 76.

16. Almona (2005).

17. Schmida (2005).

18. Schmida (2005).

19. Tong and Hu (2005).

20. Tong and Hu (2005).

21. Goodwell (1994).

22. Badaracco (1997), p. 30.

23. Citigroup Annual Report (2002).

Chapter 4

1. McCallum (2007).

2. Beer (2011).

3. Yardley (2012).
4. Yardley (2012).
5. Barboza (2014).
6. Bhasin and Lutz (2012).
7. Nunnold (2012).
8. Weber (2010).
9. Nocera (2014).
10. *Business Ethics: The Magazine of Corporate Responsibility.* (n.d.)
11. *Jaws* (1975).
12. *Modern Times* (1936).
13. *The Man in the Grey Flannel Suit* (1956).
14. *Roger & Me* (1989).
15. *The Corporation* (2003).
16. *Santa Clara County v. Southern Pacific Railroad Co.* (1886).
17. *Wall Street* (1987).
18. *Wolf of Wall Street* (2013).
19. Cohen (2014).
20. Dunning (2003).
21. Wecker (2011).
22. Wecker (2011).
23. *Integrating Business Ethics in Business Courses* (2012).
24. Edelman (2011).
25. Traylor (2012).
26. *CR Magazine* (2014).
27. Goodhousekeeping (1909).
28. Starbucks (2013).
29. Porter (2014).
30. Barnett (2007).
31. Young and Makhija (2014).
32. Sethi (1975).
33. Drucker (1984).
34. Reed and Beed (2005).
35. Holme and Watts (2000).
36. *Master of Fundraising Management* (2014).
37. National Philanthropic Trust (2014).
38. *Dodge v. Ford Motor Company* (1919).
39. Porter (2014).
40. Schreckinger (2012).
41. Westen (2012).
42. Friedman (2014).
43. Geromel (2012).

44. Knowledge@Wharton (2012).
45. Sisodia, Sheth, and Wolfe (2014).
46. Maak citing Kellerman (2004), Price (2005), and Ciulla (1998) in his article "Responsible Leadership, Stakeholder Engagement, and the Emergence of Social Capital" (2007).
47. Financial Times Lexicon (2014).
48. House (1997).
49. Maak and Pless (2006).
50. Ciulla (1998).
51. Burton-Jones (2014).
52. Mirivs (2010).
53. Burton-Jones (2014).
54. Financial Times Lexicon (2014).
55. Hofstede (1980).
56. Javidan et al. (2006).
57. Doh and Stumpf (2006).
58. Trompenaars and Hampden-Turner (1998).
59. Hofstede (1980).
60. Drucker (2003).

Chapter 5

1. Graham (2003), pp. 97–105.
2. Deresky (2002), p. 41.
3. "Caux Round Table: Principles for Business" (1994).
4. Engardio (2004), pp. 86–87.
5. Holland (1999).
6. Griffen and Pustay (2005), p. 122.
7. Ballinger (2001), pp. 34–37.
8. Ballinger (2001), pp. 34–37.
9. Readers might wish to consult Abbas and Gibbs (1998).
10. Graham (2003), pp. 97–105.
11. Barnet, Bass, and Brown (1996).
12. Donaldson (1996).
13. Donaldson (1996).
14. Seymour-Smith (1998), p. 75.
15. Seymour-Smith (1998), p. 20.
16. Seymour-Smith (1998), p. 26.
17. Seymour-Smith (1998), p. 36.
18. Donaldson (1996).
19. Donaldson (1996).

20. Donaldson (1996).
21. Donaldson (1996).
22. Donaldson (1996).
23. Donaldson (1996).
24. Paine (2003).
25. Perlmutter (1969).

Chapter 6

1. Cullen, Parboteeah, and Hoegl (2004), pp. 411–21.
2. Donaldson and Dunfree (1994).
3. Cullen, Parboteeah, and Hoegl (2004), pp. 411–21.
4. Dunning (2003), p. 151. This book contains a series of essays from various scholarly disciplines; noteworthy are the variations on the theme of making globalization good from the perspective of Christian, Islamic, Jewish, and Eastern religious teachings.
5. Benedict XVI (2009), pp. 40, 45.
6. Place (2000).
7. Kissinger (2003, April 17), Hanity and Combs, Fox News cable program.
8. Dunning (2003), p. 23.
9. Nash and Zullo (1995), p. 36.
10. *Kasky v. Nike* (2002).
11. Webley and More (2003).
12. Flaherty (2005).
13. Flaherty (2005).
14. Long and Rao (1995), pp. 65–73.
15. Verschoor (1999).
16. *Business Respect* (2002), no. 44.
17. *Business Respect* (2002), no. 30.
18. *Business Respect* (2004), no. 74.
19. Klein (1999).
20. Gap Inc. (2004).
21. *BusinessWeek* (2004).

Chapter 7

1. Laszlo and Nash (2004).
2. Badaracco (1977), p. 81.
3. Morrison (2003), p. 245.
4. Nash (1977).

5. Steiner (1979).
6. Andrews (1987), pp. 18–19.
7. Porter (1980).
8. Nickols (2000).
9. Lazonick (2009).

References

Abbas, J., and M. Gibbs. 1998. "Foundation of Business Ethics in Contemporary Religious Thought: The Ten Commandment perspective." *International Journal of Social Economics* 25, no. 10, pp. 1552–64.

Allen, J. 1831. *As a Man Thinketh*. Seattle, WA: CreateSpace. http://www.books.google.com (accessed February 23, 2010)

Almona, C. 2005. The Great CSI Debate. Business in Africa, Market Intelligence, January 14. www.businessinafrica.net/market_intelligence/403853.htm (accessed June 21, 2008).

Anderson, S., and J. Cavanagh. 2000. *Top 200: The Rise of Corporate Global Power*. Washington DC: Institute for Policy Studies.

Andrews, K. 1987. *The Concept of Corporate Strategy*. 3rd ed. New York: Dow Jones Edwards.

Badaracco, J., Jr. 1997. *Defining Moments*. Boston, MA: Harvard Business Press.

Ballinger, J. Fall 2001. "Nike's Voice Looms Large." *Social Policy* 32, no. 1, pp. 34–37.

Barboza, D. 2014. "Despite a Pledge by Samsung, Child Labor Proves Resilient." *New York Times*, International Business, July 10. http://www.nytimes.com/2014/07/11/business/international/children-found-working-at-samsung-supplier-in-china.html (accessed July 11, 2014).

Barnett, M.L. 2007. "Stakeholder Influence Capacity and the Variability of Financial Returns to Corporate Social Responsibility." *Academy of Management Review* 32, no. 3, pp. 794–816.

Barnett, T., K. Bass, and G. Brown. 1996. "Religiosity, Ethical Ideology, Andintentions to Report a Peer's Wrongdoing." *Journal of Business Ethics* 15, no. 11, pg. 1161–74.

Beer, L.A. 2011. *Tracing the Roots of Globalization and Business Principles*. New York: Business Expert Press.

Benedict XVI. 2009. "Encyclical Letter." *Caritas in Veritate*. pp. 40, 45.

Bhasin, K., and A. Lutz. 2012. "7 Stunning New Details about Walmart's Mexican Bribery Scandal." *New York Times,* December 18. http://www.businessinsider.com/new-details-in-walmart-bribery-scandal-2012-12 (accessed June 18, 2014).

The Body Shop International. 1998a. Mission Statement, Annual Report, 1.

The Body Shop International. 1998b. *The Body Shop Approach to Ethical Auditing*.

Burton-Jones, A. 2014. "MBA White Paper, Responsible leadership" http://www.griffith.edu.au/__data/assets/pdf_file/0007/468565/mba-white-paper-responsible-leadership.pdf (accessed May 15, 2014).

Business Ethics: The Magazine of Corporate Responsibility. n.d. www.buisness-ethics.com

Business Respect CSR Dispatches. 2002, 2003, 2004. No. 79, December 2004; No. 76, July 2004; No. 74, May 2004; No. 52, March 2003; No. 50, February 2003; No. 44, November 2002; No. 30, May 2002. http://www.mallenbaker.net/ (accessed September 15, 2007).

BusinessWeek. 2004. "The New Nike," September 20, pp. 78–86. http://www.businessweek.com/stories/2004-09-19/the-new-nike

BusinessWeek. 2004. "The Best B-Schools," October 18, p. 81. http://www.businessweek.com/stories/2004-10-31/the-best-b-schools-of-2004-the-best-b-schools-cover-story-oct-dot-18-2004

BusinessWeek. 2009. "100 Best Global Brands," September 28, p. 38. http://www.businessweek.com/magazine/toc/09_39/B4148brands.htm

"Caux Round Table: Principles for Business." 1994. http://www.cauxroundtable.org/index.cfm/menuid=8

Citigroup Annual Report. 2002. http://www.citigroup.com/citi/corporate governance/ar.htm (accessed May 15, 2004).

Ciulla, J., ed. 1998. *Ethics, The Heart of Leadership.* Westport, CT: Praeger Press.

Cohen, R. July 8, 2014. "The Godfather: Part IV: How to Create the Perfect Crime Family." *The Arizona Republic*, Phoenix, AZ, p. A14.

The Corporation. 2003. Produced by Mark Archbar and Bart Simpson, Directed by Mark Archbar and Jennifer Abbot, Written by Joel Nalkan, Harold Crooks, and Mark Archbar. Los Angeles, CA: Big Pictures Media Corporation.

CR Magazine. 2014. Business Ethics 2014 magazine's 18th Annual Awards. http://www.thecro.com/?q=node/167

Cullen, J.B., K.P. Parboteeah, and M. Hoegl, M. 2004. "Cross-National Differences in Manager's Willingness to Justify Ethically Suspect Behaviors: A Test of Institutional Anomie Theory." *Academy of Management Journal 47*, no. 2, pp. 411–21.

Deresky, H. 2002. *Global Management*, Exhibit 2.3. Upper Saddle River, NJ: Prentice Hall, pp. 41–43.

Deresky, H. 2006. *International Management, Managing Across Borders and Cultures.* 5th ed. Upper Saddle River, NJ: Pearson Prentice Hall.

Diamond, J. 2005. *Collapse.* New York: Penguin Group.

Dodge v. Ford Motor Company, 170 N.W. 688 (Mich 1919).

Doh, J. 2005. "Review of *Making Globalization Good* (book)." *Journal of International Business Studies 36*, no. 1, pp. 119–21.

Doh, J., and S. Stumpf. 2006. *Handbook on Responsible Leadership and Governance in Global Business.* Northampton, MA: Edward Elgar Publishing.

Donaldson, T. 1996. "Values in Tensions: Ethics Away From Home." *Harvard Business Review 64*, no. 5, pp. 49–62.

Donaldson, T., and T.W. Dunfree. 1994. "Toward a Unified Conception of Business Ethics: Integrative Social Contracts Theory." *Academy of Management Review* 19, pp. 252–84.

Dunning, J.H., ed. 2003. *Making Globalization Good.* Oxford: Oxford University Press.

Drucker, P. 1984. "Converting Social Problems into Business Opportunities: The New Meaning of Corporate Social Responsibility." *California Management Review* 26, no. 2, pp. 53–63.

Drucker, P. 2003. *The Essential Drucker: The Best of Sixty Years of Peter Drucker's Essential Writings on Management.* New York: Collins Business.

Edelman. 2011. *Edelman Trust Barometer.* http:/www.edelman.com/trust/2011 (accessed April 21, 2012).

Engardio, P. July 12, 2004. "Global Compact: Little Impact, Commentary—Social Issues Globalization." *BusinessWeek,* pp.86–87.

England, L. 2003. "Chapter 1: Principles of Business Ethics." *English Language Programs.* U.S. Department of State, Online Forum. http://exchanges.state.gov./forum/journal/bus1background.htm (accessed May 18, 2007).

Flaherty, M. 2005. *World Business Council for Sustainable Development.* http://www.wbcsd.org (accessed June 15, 2006).

Financial Times Lexicon. 2014. "Definition of Responsible Leadership." Retrieved June 10, 2014 from: http:// lexicon.ft.com/term?term=responsible-leadership (accessed June 10, 2014).

Fortune. May 15, 2003. "Corporate America's Social Conscience." APSI S10 (special advertising supplement).

Fredericks, S. 2002. "Rotten to the, Hard or Soft, Core." http://Khilafah.com (accessed June 15, 2005).

Friedman, M. September 13, 1970. "The Social Responsibility of Business is to Increase Profits." *The New York Times Magazine,* pp. 33.

Friedman, T. 1999. *The Lexus and the Olive Tree.* New York: Random House.

Friedman, T. 2005. *The World is Flat.* New York: Farrar, Straus, and Giroux.

Friedman, V. 2014. "For the Wolf of Luxury A Chance to Be a Lamb." *New York Times,* Sunday Business, October 5th.

Gap Inc. 2004. Social Responsibility Report. Gapinc.com. http://www.gapinc.com/social_resp/social_resp_body.shtm (accessed June 26, 2005).

Geromel, R. 2012. "Can We Use Corporate Social Responsibility to Evaluate Companies?" *Forbes,* May 21. http://www.forbes.com/sites/ricardogeromel/2012.05/21/csr-corprate-social-responsibility/ (accessed June 14, 2012).

Goodhousekeeping. 1909. *Good Housekeeping Seal of Approval.* http://www.goodhousekeeping.com/cm/goodhousekeeping/images/mV/new-ghk-seal-logo-mdn.jpg (accessed May 2011).

Goodwell, R. 1994. *Ethics in American Business: Policies, Programs and Perceptions.* Washington, DC: Ethics Resources Center.

Graham, A. Summer 2003. Thought Leader: Business Ethicist Lynn Sharp Paine. *strategy+business 31*, pp. 97–105.

Griffen, R.W., and M.W. Pustay. 2005. *International Business*. 4th ed. Upper Saddle River, NJ: Pearson Prentice Hall.

Guide to Best Practices in Corporate Social Responsibility (Vol. 2). 2009. Rockville, MD: PR News Press.

Hill, C. 2005. *Global Business Today*. 4th ed. New York: McGraw-Hill/Irwin.

Hodge, S. 2000. *Global Smarts*. New York: John Wiley & Sons.

Hodgetts, R.M., and F. Luthans. 2003. *International Management*. 4th ed. New York: McGraw-Hill/Irwin.

Hofstede, G. 1980. *Cultures Consequences: International Differences in Work Related Values*. Beverly Hill, CA: Sage Publications.

Holland, R.C. 1999. *Viable Ethical Standards for Business: Building on the Common Ground*. Philadelphia, PA: Wharton School of the University of Pennsylvania. http://astro.temple.edu/~dialogue/Codes/wharton.htm (accessed October 20, 2005)

Holme, L., and R. Watts. January, 2000. *Making Good Business Sense*. http://www.wbcsd.org/web/publications/csr2000.pdf (accessed September 21, 2012).

House, R.J., and R.N. Aditya. 1997. "The Social Scientific Study of Leadership: Quo Vadis?" *Journal of Management* 23, no. 3, pp. 409–73.

Holt, D., Quelch, J., and Taylor, E. September, 2004. "How Global Brands Compete." *Harvard Business Review*, reprint no. R0409D, pp. 1–8.

Integrating Business Ethics in Business Courses. 2012. http://e-businessethics.com/wp-content/uploads/Integrating-Business-Ethics-in-Business-Courses.pdf (accessed July 2012).

Javidan, M., P. Dorfman, M. de Luque, and R. House. 2006. "In the Eye of the Beholder: Cross Cultural Lessons in Leadership from Project GLOBE." *The Academy of Management Perspectives* 20, no. 1, pp. 67–90.

Jaws. 1975. Producers Richard D. Zanuck and David Brown, Directed by Steven Spielberg, Written by Peter Benchley and Carl Gottlieb from novel by Peter Benchley. Los Angeles, CA: Zanuck/Brown Productions.

Kasky v. Nike Inc. 2002. 27 Cal. 4th 939, 119 Cal. Rptr. 2d 296, 45 P.3d 243, 02C.D.O.S. 3790 No. 9087859, California Supreme Court. http://www.firstamendmentcenter.org/facilbrary/case.aspx?case=Nike_v_Kasky (accessed September 2006)

Kellerman, B. 2004. *Bad Leadership: What it is, How it Happens, Why it Matters*. Boston, MA: Harvard Business School Press

Kidder, R.M. 2004. Finding an Ethical Employer: Five Questions to Ask in a Job Interview. Institute for Global Ethics. http:// www.globalethics.org (accessed August 2006).

Kissinger, H. April 17, 2003. Interview by Sean Hannity, Hannity & Colmes, Fox News.

Klein, N. 1999. *No Logo: Taking Aim at the Brand Bullies*. New York: Picador Inc.

Knowledge@Wharton. 2012. "Why Companies Can No Longer Afford to Ignore Their Social Responsibilities." *Wharton School of Business*, May 28. http://business.time.com/2012/05/28/why-companies-can-no-longer-afford-to-ignore-their-.

Laszlo, C., and Nash, J. October 23, 2004. "Six Facets of Ethical Leadership: An Executive's Guide to the New Ethics in Business." *Electronic Journal of Business Ethics and Organizational Studies* 9, no. 2. http://ejbo.jyu.fi/index.cgi?page=articles/0601_1 (accessed August 30, 2005).

Lazonick, W. 2009. "The New Economy Business Model and the Crisis of U.S. Capitalism." *Capitalism and Society* 4, no. 2, article 4.

Lichtheim, M. 1976. Vol. 9 of *Ancient Egyptian Literature: The New Kingdom*. Berkeley, CA: University of California Press.

Liedtka, J. 1992. "Exploring Ethics Issues Using Personal Interviews." *Business Ethics Quarterly* 2, no. 2.

Long, D., and S. Rao. 1995. "The Wealth Effects of Unethical Business Behavior." *Journal of Economics and Finance* 19, no. 2, pp. 65–73.

Maak, T. 2007. "Responsible Leadership, Stakeholder Engagement, and the Emergence of Social Capital." *Journal of Business Ethics* 74, pp. 329–43.

Maak, T., and N.M. Pless. 2006. "Responsible Leadership in a Stakeholder Society—A Relational Prospective." *Journal of Business Ethics* 66, pp. 99–115.

The Man in the Grey Flannel Suit. 1956. Produced by Darryl F. Zanuck, Directed by Nunnally Johnson, Written by Nunnally Johnson and Sloan Wilson. Los Angeles, CA: 20th Century Films.

Master of Fundraising Management. 2014. Columbia University. ce.columbia.edu/fundraising-management (accessed April 10, 2014).

McCallum, J. January–February 2007. "In War and Business, It's The Terrain That Matters." *Ivey Business Journal*. http://iveybusinessjournal.com/topics/strategy/in-war-and-business-its-the-terrain-that-matters#.U5EC7HJdWSo (accessed June 4, 2014).

Mirivs, P., D. DeJong, B. Googins, L. Quinn, and Van Velsor. 2010. "Responsible Leadership Emerging." http://www.grli.org (accessed March 2011).

Modern Times. 1936. Produced Directed and Written by Charles Chaplin. Los Angeles, CA: United Artists.

Moore, K., and D. Lewis. 1999. *Birth of the Multinational: 2000 Years of Ancient Business History—from Ashur to Augustus*. Copenhagen, Denmark: Copenhagen Business School Press.

Morrison, A. 2003. *International Management*. 5th ed. New York: McGraw-Hill/Irwin.

Nash, B., and A. Zullo, eds. 1995. *Lawyer's Wit and Wisdom*. Philadelphia, PA: Running Press.

Nash, G. 1977. "Teach Your Children." On *Déjà Vu* album, Producers: Crosby, Stills, Nash & Young. New York: Atlantic Records.

National Philanthropic Trust. n.d. "Charitable Giving Statistics" http://www. nptrust.org/philanthropic-resources/charitable-giving-statistics/(accessed June 1, 2014).

Nickols, F. 2000. Strategy: Definitions and Meaning, Distance Consulting LLC. http://home.att.net/~nickols/strategy_defnition.htm (accessed September 9, 2009).

Nike v. Kasky. (2002). For Non-legal Practitioners. http://www.firtamend mentcenter.org/facilbrary/case.aspx?case=Nike_v_Nasky (accessed September 2006)

Nocera, J. 2014. "Sympathy for the Devil: Those Bogus Claims Against BP." *New York Times.* http://www.nytimes.com/2014/08/02/opinion/joe-nocera-sympathy-for-the-devil.html?emc=edit_th_20140802&ni =todaysheadlines&nlid=46276944&_r=o (accessed August 1, 2014).

Nunnold, W. 2012. "Blog: Business Ethics Taught by a White Collar Criminal?" globalEDGE (blog), June 28. http://globaledge.msu.edu?Blog/Post/1311/ Business-Ethics-Taught-by-a-White-Collar-Cr-... (accessed June 14, 2012).

Paine, L.S. 2003. *Value Shift: Why Companies Must Merge Social and Financial Imperatives to Achieve Superior Performance.* New York: McGraw-Hill/Irwin.

Perlmutter, H.W. 1969. "The Tortuous Evolution of the Multinational Corporation." *Columbia Journal of World Business* 3, no. 1, pp. 9–18.

Phatak, A.V., R.S. Bhagat, and R.J. Kashlak. 2005. *International Management.* New York: McGraw-Hill/Irwin.

Place, R.M. 2000. Leonardo's Vitruvian Man. http://thealchemicalegg.com/ VitruvisN.html (accessed June 7, 2003).

Porter, E. 2014. "Motivating Corporations to Do Good." *New York Times*, July 16. http://www.nytimes.com/2014/07/16/business/the-do-good-corporation. html?emc=edit_th_20140716&nl=todaysheadlines&nlid=46276944&_r=0

Porter, M. 1980. *Competitive Strategy.* New York: Free Press.

Porter, M. 1990. *The Competitive Advantage of Nations.* New York: Free Press.

Price, T. 2005. *Understanding Ethical Failures in Leadership.* New York: Cambridge University Press.

Reed, C., and C. Beed. Spring 2005. "Applying Judeo-Christian Principles to Contemporary Economic Issues." *Journal of Markets & Morality* 8, no. 1, pp. 53–79.

Roger & Me. 1989. Produced, directed, and written by Michael Moore. Los Angeles, CA: Warner Bros.

Saloner, G., A. Shepard, and J. Podolny. 2001. *Strategic Management.* New York: John Wiley & Sons.

Santa Clara County v. Southern Pacific Railroad Co., 118 U.S. 394 (1886).

Schmida, S. January 13, 2005. A Russian Twist on Responsibility. *Moscow Times.* http://www.themoscowtimes.com/stories/2005/01/13/005.html   (accessed February 1, 2005).

Schreckinger, B. 2012. "Virtue Inc." *Boston Globe*, November 25. http://www. bostonglobe.com/ideas/2012/11/25virtue-inc/sMNhJRcOlgZ0rqjpLTALrN/ story.html (accessed December 2012).

Sethi, S. 1975. "Dimensions of Corporate Social Performance: An Analytical Framework." *California Management Review* 17, no. 3, pp. 58–64.

Seymour-Smith, M. 1998. *The 100 Most Influential Books Ever Written.* New York: Barnes and Noble Books.

Shakespeare, W. 1881. *Henry VI.* In Vol. 8 of *The Complete Works of William Shakespeare*, ed. H. Hudson, 217. Boston, MA: Ginn, Heath, and Co.

Sisodia, R., J. Sheth, and D. Wolfe. 2014. *Firms of Endearment: How World-Class Companies Profit from Passion and Purpose.* 2nd ed. Saddle River, NJ: Pearson FT Press.

Starbucks. 2013. *Global Responsibility Report, Goals & Progress 2013.* http://www. starbucks.com/responsibility/global-report

Steiner, G. 1979. *Strategic Planning.* New York: Free Press.

Tarr, P. Summer 2004. "Seven Steps to Protecting Reputation Abroad." *Business Ethics*, 2. http://www.business-ethics.com/seven_steps_to_protecting_ reputation_abroad 1.htm (accessed October 27, 2007).

Tong, M., and G. Hu. 2005. Gong Zhu He Xie She HUI: Gou Zhu Ruo Shi Qun Ti De Bao Zhang Fang Xian [Building a Harmonious Society: Protecting the Underprivileged Groups]. *People's Daily.* http://www.people.com.en/ CB/14576/14840/3274975.html (accessed September 1, 2005)

Traylor, M. 2012. "Business Ethics—An Industry in Decline?" *Globalethics,* April 16. http://www.globalethics.org/newsline/2012/04/16/business-ethics -41/comment-page-1/ (accessed April 18, 2012).

Trompenaars, F., and C. Hampden-Turner. 1998. *Riding the Waves of Culture.* 2nd ed. New York: McGraw Hill.

Verschoor, C. Winter 1999. "Corporate Performance is Closely Linked to A Strong Ethical Commitment." *Business and Society Review* 104, no. 4, pp. 407–15.

Vickey, T. April 2002. "Social Accountability in Central America." *World Trade*, 48, 50, 53.

Wall Street. 1987. Produced by Edward R. Weiser, directed by Oliver Stone, written by Oliver Stone and Stanley Weiser. Los Angeles, CA: 20th Century Fox Film Corporation.

Weber, H. 2010. "Time To Scrap BP Brand? Gas-Station Owners Divided." *Associated Press* (wire service), December 19. (accessed 30 July 2010).

Webley, S., and E. More. 2003. *Does Business Ethics Pay? Ethics and Financial Performance.* London: Institute of Business Ethics. www.ibe.org.uk (accessed April 15, 2007).

Wecker, M. 2011. "Business Schools Increasingly Require Students to Study Ethics." http://www.usnews.com/education/best-gaduate-schools/top-buisness-schools/articles/2011/09/20/business-schools-increasingly-require-students-to-study-ethics (accessed October 10, 2011).

Welch, B.S. October 28, 2009. "Workers Want Ethical, Socially Responsible Companies, Kelly Services Survey Finds." *Crain's Detroit Business.* http://www.craindetraoit.com/article/20091028/FREE/910289983 (accessed November 3, 2009).

Westen, J. 2012. "282 Corporations Have Stopped Funding Planned Parenthood." https://www.lifesitenews.com/news/bob-evans-restaurants-gq-glamour-wyndham-hotels-on-new-list-of-planned-pare (accessed on April 1, 2012).

Wild, J., K. Wild, and J. Han. 2003. *International Business.* 2nd ed. Upper Saddle River, NJ: Prentice Hall.

Wild, J., K. Wild, and J. Han. 2006. *International Business.* 3rd ed. Upper Saddle River, NJ: Prentice Hall.

Wolf of Wall Street. 2013. Produced by Martin Scorsese, directed by Martin Scorsese, and written by Terence Winter based on the book by Jordan Belfort. West Hollywood, CA: Red Granite Pictures.

Yardley, J. 2012. "Horrific Fire Revealed a Gap in Safety for Global Brands." *The New York Times*, December 6. http://www.nytimes.com/2012/12/07/world/asia/bangladesh-fire-exposes-safety-gap-in-sup... (accessed December 7, 2012).

Young, S., and M. Makhija. 2014. "Firm's Corporate Social Responsibility Behaviors: An Integration of Institutional and Profit Maximization Approaches." *Journal of International Business Studies* 45, pp. 670–98.

Index

OTHER TITLES IN THE INTERNATIONAL BUSINESS COLLECTION

Tamer Cavusgil, Georgia State; Michael Czinkota, Georgetown; and Gary Knight, Willamette University, Editors

- *Tracing the Roots of Globalization and Business Principles* by Lawrence A. Beer
- *Trade Promotion Strategies: Best Practices* by Claude Cellich and Michel Borgeon
- *As I Was Saying... Observations on International Business and Trade Policy, Exports, Education, and the Future* by Michael Czinkota
- *China: Doing Business in the Middle Kingdom* by Stuart Strother
- *Essential Concepts of Cross-Cultural Management: Building on What We All Share* by Lawrence A. Beer
- *As the World Turns...: Observations on International Business and Policy, Going International and Transitions* by Michael Czinkota
- *Assessing and Mitigating Business Risks in India* by Balbir Bhasin
- *The Emerging Markets of the Middle East: Strategies for Entry and Growth* by Tim Rogmans
- *Doing Business in China: Getting Ready for the Asian Century* by Jane Menzies, Mona Chung, and Stuart Orr
- *Transfer Pricing in International Business: A Management Tool for Adding Value* by Geoff Turner
- *Management in Islamic Countries: Principles and Practice* by UmmeSalma Mujtaba Husein
- *Burma: Business and Investment Opportunities in Emerging Myanmar* by Balbir Bhasin
- *Global Business and Corporate Governance: Environment, Structure, and Challenges* by John Thanopoulos
- *The Intelligent International Negotiator* by Eliane Karsaklian

Announcing the Business Expert Press Digital Library

Concise e-books business students need for classroom and research

This book can also be purchased in an e-book collection by your library as

- a one-time purchase,
- that is owned forever,
- allows for simultaneous readers,
- has no restrictions on printing, and
- can be downloaded as PDFs from within the library community.

Our digital library collections are a great solution to beat the rising cost of textbooks. E-books can be loaded into their course management systems or onto student's e-book readers.
The **Business Expert Press** digital libraries are very affordable, with no obligation to buy in future years. For more information, please visit **www.businessexpertpress.com/librarians**. To set up a trial in the United States, please email **sales@businessexpertpress.com**.

www.ingramcontent.com/pod-product-compliance
Lightning Source LLC
Chambersburg PA
CBHW060323200326
41519CB00011BA/1812